Arthur Schopenhauer

Arthur
SCHOPENHAUER

*The Life and Thought of
Philosophy's Greatest Pessimist*

DAVID BATHER WOODS

The University of Chicago Press
Chicago and London

The University of Chicago Press, Chicago 60637
The University of Chicago Press, Ltd., London
© 2025 by David Bather Woods
All rights reserved. No part of this book may be used or reproduced in any manner whatsoever without written permission, except in the case of brief quotations in critical articles and reviews. For more information, contact the University of Chicago Press, 1427 E. 60th St., Chicago, IL 60637.
Published 2025
Printed in the United States of America

34 33 32 31 30 29 28 27 26 25   1 2 3 4 5

ISBN-13: 978-0-226-82976-0 (cloth)
ISBN-13: 978-0-226-84441-1 (ebook)
DOI: https://doi.org/10.7208/chicago/9780226844411.001.0001

Library of Congress Cataloging-in-Publication Data

Names: Bather Woods, David, author.
Title: Arthur Schopenhauer : the life and thought of philosophy's greatest pessimist / David Bather Woods.
Description: Chicago : The University of Chicago Press, 2025. | Includes bibliographical references and index.
Identifiers: LCCN 2025010525 | ISBN 9780226829760 (cloth) | ISBN 9780226844411 (ebook)
Subjects: LCSH: Schopenhauer, Arthur, 1788–1860. | Philosophy, German. | Pessimism.
Classification: LCC B3148 .B38 2025 | DDC 193 [B]—dc23/eng/20250403
LC record available at https://lccn.loc.gov/2025010525

♾ This paper meets the requirements of ANSI/NISO Z39.48-1992 (Permanence of Paper).

*In loving memory of Philip Woods,
the best of all possible dads*

One can't say that in order to live well it is best not to live. That would be pure nonsense.

Jean Améry

Contents

Preface: Live, Laugh, Love ix

Introduction: It's a Wonderful Life 1

1 Living with Schopenhauer: How Schopenhauer Embraced Solitude 13

2 A Sure Compass: How Schopenhauer Accepted Punishment 35

3 My Dear Son, Adieu: How Schopenhauer Destigmatized Suicide 58

4 A Philosopher in the Asylum: How Schopenhauer Humanized Madness 73

5 Live First, Then Philosophize: How Schopenhauer Left Academia 96

6 Love Stories Without Love: How Schopenhauer Never Married 118

7 The Second Sex: How Schopenhauer Underestimated Women 140

8 Metaphysics into Action: How Schopenhauer Expanded Ethics 159

9   Portrait of the Philosopher as an Old Man: How Schopenhauer Found Fame   185

10   You Are Not Nothing: How Schopenhauer Survived Death   214

Postscript: Silhouettes   230

Acknowledgments   237
Chronology   239
Notes   245
Bibliography   269
Index   277

PREFACE

Live, Laugh, Love

There is a popular style of philosophical biography that presents the philosopher's life as a model for how to live well.[1] Introducing Schopenhauer to this genre faces a major obstacle, and not just because of his many personal flaws. For Schopenhauer, for the most part, there can be no question of living a good life. The very idea is a contradiction in terms. To live is to suffer, and to suffer is no good; it is therefore simply unwise to live.

But this won't do. We are already here; we already live, and we don't have much of a say in the matter. So, to put the question a touch more positively: how can we live with life, such as it is? Perhaps we should laugh. As the Irish playwright Samuel Beckett once confessed to a friend, "I am reading Schopenhauer. Everyone laughs at that."[2] As a Schopenhauer scholar, I can well relate. If I quote one of Schopenhauer's gloomier sayings to an audience of students or the public—claims such as "life is a business that does not cover its costs" or "life swings like a pendulum back and forth between pain and boredom"—it often produces a murmur of laughter. Not gales, by any means, but unmistakable signs of amusement. I have come to anticipate it, and I am even a little bit disappointed if there isn't at least a chuckle from someone, somewhere.

What exactly is the source of this laughter, I have sometimes wondered? As it happens, Schopenhauer had his own theory about the origins of laughter. According to him, laughter expresses the sudden perception of an incongruity between a concept and its intended object.[3] Take the following joke, for example:

"My dog has no nose."
"How does he smell?'
"Awful!"

Here the humor exploits an ambiguity in the word "smell" that puts the two speakers on different trains of thought. The concept of smell in the inquirer's question refers to the dog's sensory faculty, whereas the dog owner interprets it as referring to the dog's odor, which, it turns out, is unpleasant. The answer is therefore incongruous with the object in question. Schopenhauer divides humor into two further categories: wit and foolishness. Wit is when the incongruity between thought and thing is deliberate, whereas foolishness is by mistake. As the teller of the joke, technically I am being witty—although with this old joke, still not very witty—whereas the dog owner in the joke, who misunderstands what they are being asked, is simply foolish. Unless, of course, they are wittily playing the fool.

When Schopenhauer's gloominess amuses people, what incongruity could they be spotting? Perhaps that his gloomy claims do not match up with their own experience of life. There is a grain of truth to them, of course, for who could deny that life is often a drudge. But his way of putting things will seem, to some, comically overblown. Our experience of life may be better, or at least more mixed, than Schopenhauer allows. On dark days, the business of living feels as though it is making losses everywhere; on sunnier days, however, it feels like one enormous gain. Perhaps, indeed, life is nothing like a business in the first place; if it's about gains at all, perhaps it is more like a gift than a transaction, something you are simply grateful for—or not, as the case may be. Naturally, Schopenhauer objects to the gift analogy: "it is clear as day that anyone who could have first seen and looked the gift over would have said 'no thank you very much.'"[4] Nevertheless, the incongruity between Schopenhauer's relentless pessimism, on the one hand, and our more varied experience of life and the world, on the other, may partly explain what all the laughter is about.

Still, this can't be the whole of the story. Schopenhauer's theory notwithstanding, humor is often about more than mere incongruity between thought and world. Sometimes, in fact, it's about the exact opposite: accuracy, recognition, realization. Observational comedy works in precisely this way: "Yes," our laughter seems to declare, "life really is just like that!" It's funny, in other words, because it's true.

Of course, merely reporting facts is not sufficient for humor. A platform announcement is rarely funny even when it is perfectly true. What makes a fact feel funny is sometimes a hidden incongruity between how things are and how they *should* be. If, for example, an observational comic performs a routine about the British queuing system—a convoluted etiquette of passive aggression communicated exclusively in the form of tuts and eye rolls—it reminds us what strange creatures we are compared to our image of how any truly rational being really ought to behave. So, when we are amused by Schopenhauer's misery-guts persona, we may not be detecting anything obviously faulty in his views. By recognizing the accuracy of what he is saying, in fact, our laughter might even begin to acknowledge faults within ourselves.

But why should this be funny? In most other contexts, it's unpleasant to spot a flaw, especially one in ourselves. Other theorists of humor (Freud, for example) add yet another social and psychological layer to our experience of facts as humorous. Acknowledgment of an incongruity between how life is, on the one hand, and how it should be, on the other, is funniest when it safely relieves the tension of suppressing this very incongruity. We all correctly hate queuing, but when we find ourselves in an actual queue, unless we are in a mood to start a minor revolution, we must suppress our sense of its manifest absurdity. By contrast, when a stand-up regales us with their queuing-related ordeals, it's as if all that pressure finally finds the release valve. "Yes, life is like that, but really it shouldn't be—and *finally* someone is saying it!" This realization, lightning fast, is pleasant in the least, but often it goes beyond mere pleasure into audible eruptions of irrepressible glee.

I suspect that the audiences who find Schopenhauer amusing are mixed. Some find his pessimistic claims plainly incongruous with their own experience of the world, while others are relieved to have their worldview reflected back to them with such crisp precision. But there is one more source of tension to be acknowledged if we are truly to understand why Schopenhauer is sometimes quite funny. When I hear people laugh at—with?—Schopenhauer, I detect not only recognition but also some uneasiness, perhaps a hint of what is often called nervous laughter. As I said, it certainly isn't gales of laughter that I hear; there is clearly some restraint. Here's what could be going on: it is mildly amusing to acknowledge the deficiencies of our lives in the form of witty epigrams, but at the heart of these witticisms there is a reminder that, in the end, the joke is on us. Eventually we must get back to the troublesome business of living, and here the laughter stops.

So much for laughter, then. Rather than admit defeat, perhaps we can take things up a notch. If laughing at life is a short-lived response, can we respond with love instead? Now, this is a suggestion that Schopenhauer can get on board with, albeit in his own Schopenhauerian way. After many years of studying Schopenhauer's philosophy—and regularly being asked, "But don't you find it all too depressing?"—at a certain point I realized what it is that stops me from throwing out all his books in despair. Schopenhauer's picture of life is bleak because he severely doubts that we will ever come close to the happiness that we so crave; but it would be far bleaker, intolerably bleak, if in the midst of it all we couldn't still love one another. Fortunately for us, Schopenhauer doesn't doubt love.

Admittedly, he only really believes in one basic form of love: "All genuine *love* is compassion," he once wrote in his notebook.[5] But Schopenhauer went on to say many profound things about this, the only form of love, including that it is an essential quality of human nature. Human beings, that is, are not *accidentally* capable of compassion: rather, being compassionate is part of what it means to be human. For this reason, as Schopenhauer astutely points out, the words "compassion" and "humanity" are often used interchangeably: if we see someone acting callously, we may ask them to show a little of either one.[6]

To be clear, this does not mean that Schopenhauer found the world loveable—or even most actual people, for that matter: "We ought to love men and women. A difficult task!" reads another notebook remark.[7] The love with which we may respond to the world is not, in Schopenhauer's view, to be directed *at* the world. Instead, we should direct it at each other. We are, after all, all in the same boat. And this sentiment of universal solidarity gives Schopenhauer's (somewhat abstract) love for humanity an admirably cosmopolitan flavor:

> the conviction that the world and therefore also mankind is something that actually should not be, is designed to fill us with forbearance towards one another, for what can be expected of beings in such a predicament? Indeed, from this point of view one could arrive at the notion that the really proper mode of address between human beings, instead of *Monsieur, Sir*, etc. would be *Leidensgefährte, Socî malorum, compagnon de misères, my fellow-sufferer*.[8]

Here Schopenhauer isn't just showing off his language skills. Just as compassion emanates from all humanity, it embraces all humanity. And potentially beyond: if you are seeking something endearing about Schopenhauer, I submit the fact that he was ahead of his time, at least as far as European philosophers are concerned, in recognizing the moral status of nonhuman animals. He was, more specifically, a dog lover; and one wonders—or I do at least—whether his all-encompassing compassion also extended to affectionately addressing his many French poodles as his *compagnons de misères*.

In every chapter of the following book, the reader should be able to find at least one instance, or sometimes several instances, of such love. The love in question may not be obvious at first, and it is rarely romantic. But there are examples to be found, nonetheless, of one human being caring deeply for another (and for the occasional nonhuman being). Sometimes it will be mixed into a complex of negative and conflicted emotions, as in the case of

Schopenhauer's relationships with his family members and theirs with him. Often it is abstracted, at a distance, or between strangers, concerned not with any particular human being but rather the universal human condition. As some biographers have already argued, Schopenhauer's philosophy itself emerges from a sincere concern with all the suffering that forms the subject matter of his signature pessimism.[9] Whatever shape it takes, whether it be concrete or abstract, personal or philosophical, the love is there.

Moments ago, I said we are all in the same boat. I didn't pick this cliché blindly. By opening this book, you have committed to spending quite a bit of time in the company of Arthur Schopenhauer, who, by his own admission, composed his philosophy in a minor key. There are also several unflattering stories from his life. In this preface I have aimed to give you something to keep your spirits afloat. At the same time, I wanted to avoid taking all the gravity out of Schopenhauer's picture of the world. And so, as metaphors for floating go, a vessel caught adrift at sea is better than, say, the weightlessness of a helium balloon. Far from being weightless, it is love, and love alone, that holds up the immense weight of our lives. We all may climb aboard this hope, even Schopenhauer.

INTRODUCTION

It's a Wonderful Life

When I have mentioned to people that I am writing a book, a few have generously asked, "What is it about?" An obvious answer starts with the basic facts. Arthur Schopenhauer was a German philosopher born in Danzig (now Gdańsk, Poland) on February 22, 1788. He died in Frankfurt-am-Main on September 21, 1860. According to the deeply pessimistic philosophy for which he is best known, his existence—and yours and mine—was a big mistake. This book explores how the events of his life, philosophical or otherwise, can be read in the light of his thinking, and vice versa. In doing so, it raises the question of whether Schopenhauer's pessimism is a livable philosophy. Topics include life and death, crime and punishment, solitude and society, love and sex, gender, fame, madness, and revolution.

If, however, I were limited to introducing Schopenhauer with a single fact, then I would probably pick a different one. When Schopenhauer was seventeen years old, his father died in a suspected suicide. Why would I start here? Not because I propose a biographical reading of Schopenhauer's philosophy—or a philosophical reading of his biography—based on this fact alone, tempting though it might be to attribute his sorrowful outlook on life to such a tragic early loss. Rather, I propose that if his father hadn't died, then we never would have heard of Arthur Schopenhauer.

Arthur and his father, Heinrich Floris, were descended from generations of Hanseatic shipping merchants. A few months before his untimely death, Heinrich Floris arranged an apprenticeship for Arthur in Hamburg, where the Schopenhauer family now lived. They had relocated in 1793, fleeing the Prussian annexation of Danzig. (London, where Heinrich Floris had lived for several years in the 1770s and acquired a strong Anglophilia that Arthur later inherited, had been explored more than once as an alternative option—a fork in the road that offers the image of Schopenhauer growing up an English gent.) In all likelihood, had his father not died, Arthur would have accepted his mercantile destiny and dutifully completed his apprenticeship, perhaps even taking over the family business one day. If he had, then it's highly unlikely that we would still be talking about Schopenhauer today: as a rule, humdrum Hamburgian businessmen rarely go down in history.

That's assuming, of course, that Schopenhauer would indeed

Figure 1. Heinrich Floris Schopenhauer.

have accepted his fate. He might, on the contrary, have rejected it in violent fashion. Probably, Schopenhauer would have at least tried to follow further along in his father's footsteps; he did, in fact, carry on with his apprenticeship for a good while even after Heinrich Floris's death. But going too far down this road is unlikely to have led to a happy ending for Schopenhauer. It is hard to imagine him satisfied with any life other than the philosophical one that he went on to live. As he later wrote from the vantage point of 1831, had this life not been possible, then "I would be useless to mankind and would perhaps have the most wretched existence a man of my nature had ever had."[1] For someone who thought that every man in his own way lives a wretched existence, the world's most wretched man would be a remarkable title to claim. Had Heinrich Floris not prematurely ended his own life, in other words, then it isn't out of the question that, at some later point, Arthur would have done so himself.

There are complications for this counterfactual thesis. After all, had Heinrich Floris not died, certain other details of Arthur's life might also have been vitally different. Perhaps, for a start, Arthur wouldn't have found life and the world so generally intolerable had he not lost his father at such a formative age. Much of his persistent misery might have been rooted in this loss. Or, if not—if, that is, his misery was just a fact of his existence—then turning to his revered father, rather than to philosophy, might have been a sufficient source of consolation. Perhaps, moreover, the philosophical life that Heinrich Floris's death made possible was itself the primary source of Arthur's misery. Without such boundless opportunities to dwell on it, life might simply have satisfied him more.

But this is not how Schopenhauer saw the source of his melancholy temperament, nor its relation to his chosen vocation. Always an anxious and sensitive child, he was already prone to solitary rumination long before Heinrich Floris's death. "From early youth," he once reminisced, "my dreams of happiness were always based on scenes of seclusion, peace, quiet, solitude and the enjoyment of my own company." On these grounds, he deemed himself unsuited to "the natural way of life"—that is, embarking on a salaried profession, marrying, settling down, and starting his own family.[2]

The free and independent lifestyle of a philosopher, by contrast, stood him a much better chance of making these lonely dreams of happiness come true. Such a life was therefore always Schopenhauer's stronger destiny, which, if denied, could have had the most dire consequences.

In any case, the mere possibility that he did not become the great philosopher he was but rather the latest in a long line of merchants—or worse, dead—offers us the thought of a world without Schopenhauer as we know him. How would things be if Arthur Schopenhauer had never existed?

:::

A strong case can be made that the world would be culturally poorer for Schopenhauer's nonexistence. An incomplete list of Schopenhauer's many literary admirers alone includes Leo Tolstoy, Ivan Turgenev, Émile Zola, Guy de Maupassant, André Gide, Marcel Proust, Thomas Hardy, Joseph Conrad, D. H. Lawrence, Franz Kafka, Hermann Hesse, Thomas Mann, Samuel Beckett, Jorge Luis Borges, and more.[3] These writers would not disappear altogether from a world without Schopenhauer, of course, although certain passages of their works that mention Schopenhauer by name—from Borges's lapidary short stories to Proust's everlasting novel—would certainly be erased. (It can be no coincidence that when Konstantin Dmitrievich Levin in Tolstoy's *Anna Karenina* is contemplating suicide, he has recently been reading Schopenhauer.) Despite their wide variety of styles and subject matter, all of these writers were magnetically drawn to Schopenhauer; he had something, or rather many things, that called forth and emboldened the manifold qualities in their own temperaments that attracted them to him. In some cases, it was his own writerly sensibility that was so attractive: Thomas Mann, for one, called Schopenhauer "an artist of thought."[4] For others, it was his grand world-building aspirations and his ability to speak to and from the deepest depths of humanity's metaphysical need. Artists were surely also flattered that Schopenhauer gave their craft such an elevated position in his philosophy of value. Beauty and the sublime, according to Schopenhauer, were one step closer to salvation from this worst of all possible worlds. When André Gide discovered Schopenhauer in his final year of school, and specifically Schopenhauer's high regard for poetry, it sealed his resolve to become a writer. "It is a poet I want to be!" Gide exclaimed. "It is a poet that I am!"[5]

To the above list of writers who were in some way indebted to Schopenhauer, which is noticeably masculine, can be added the literary and philosophical works of Iris Murdoch and even Simone de Beauvoir. (I say "even" because it might come as a surprise to learn that the regrettably sexist Schopenhauer—a matter for later discussion—influenced one of the foremost feminist philosophers of the twentieth century. Some argue that the title of Beauvoir's philosophical masterpiece *The Second Sex* is taken from Schopenhauer's troubling essay "On Women." Know your enemy, I suppose. But the reception wasn't all negative either: Beauvoir said of Schopenhauer's work that it contained "the most beautiful pages that I have ever read" and that its "problems are posed in such a direct and human way!")[6] Murdoch had a novel way of characterizing Schopenhauer, who is usually presented as unremittingly gloomy: "He is a self-proclaimed pessimist," she wrote, "but he is also merry."[7] Far from the arch and abstract style of other German philosophers from his generation, and anything but austerely analytical like later generations, Schopenhauer wrote with "an insatiable omnivorous muddled cheerful often casual volubility." "Schopenhauer's relation to his reader," Murdoch continues, "is relaxed, amicable, confiding, that of a kindly teacher or fellow seeker. He tells stories and makes jokes."[8] How, one might ask, are all these winning qualities compatible with the darkly pessimistic philosophy that Schopenhauer nevertheless defended? One answer is that the world, though it drove him to despair, was an endlessly fascinating object of study for Schopenhauer. He relished the opportunity to interpret and articulate it, honestly, unflinchingly, and without obfuscation, to a sympathetic audience of fellow sufferers.

Schopenhauer's influence on other well-known philosophers is not quite as extensive as it is among creative writers. But, where there is influence, it is often all the more intense. Perhaps the best examples are Friedrich Nietzsche and Ludwig Wittgenstein, both of whom, like Schopenhauer, had strong philosophical personalities (sometimes seemingly multiple ones), as well as a lifelong adversarial relationship with academic philosophy. Some version of Nietzsche was no doubt destined to emerge with or without Schopenhauer's help—one chapter of his sarcastically unhumble intellectual autobiography, *Ecce Homo*, is titled "Why I am a Destiny"—but it is hard to imagine what this Nietzsche would be like. Though they never met, Nietzsche counted Schopenhauer among his greatest teachers. Schopenhauer set the terms for the question that Nietzsche's philosophy attempted to address in increasingly creative and sometimes feverish ways: Is life a thing to be rejected or affirmed? Nietzsche, in contrast to Schopenhauer, thought affirmed, and so his next challenge was, How?

Nietzsche developed a simple yet vivid thought experiment for telling whether someone is disposed to affirm or deny life. A demon visits you to announce that, in fact, your life repeats itself over and over, forever, down to the last and tiniest detail. There is no heaven, nor hell exactly, but there isn't nothingness either: there is this, and only this, again and again. Some—the deniers of life—will react poorly at the mere thought and collapse in despair. They would prefer total annihilation or a proper afterlife, anything but more of the same. Others, however—the affirmers—will celebrate and declare the demon a god: life, this life, and more of it, is precisely what they crave. Whichever camp you would fall into, the thought should weigh heavily upon your next moves, knowing that the future you make for yourself now is the future of all your lives, including your past lives. Note, however, that Nietzsche's demon doesn't offer us even so much as a choice between eternal recurrence, with its perverse immortality, or true death. The situation is imposed upon us; our options are sink or swim. Indifference is not on the table.

Nietzsche put this thought into print in his 1882 book *The Gay Science*. Beforehand, however, a version of it made a fleeting appearance in Schopenhauer's 1818 masterpiece *The World as Will and Representation*. Schopenhauer proposed yet another kind of immortality, one that he thinks may be a source of consolation for death: since our true essence lies not in our individual existence, but rather the lifeforce of which we are a manifestation, he argues, the essential aspect of ourselves can never perish.[9] He continues:

> Someone who has thoroughly integrated the truths stated so far into his way of thinking, without at the same time having any personal experience or far-reaching insight into the continuous suffering that is essential to all life; *someone, rather, who is perfectly happy and content with life and who, after calm reflection, could wish that his life as he has experienced it so far would be of endless duration, or of perpetually new recurrence*, and whose thirst for life is so great that he would gladly and willingly take on all the pain and hardships that life is subject to in return for its pleasures; such a person would . . . have nothing to fear.[10]

For Schopenhauer too, then, willingness eternally to repeat one's life is the sign of a life-affirming attitude. There are, however, some key differences between Schopenhauer's eternal returner and Nietzsche's. Aside from knowing that their true essence is untouched by death, Schopenhauer's returner is fortunate—very fortunate!—to have lived a happy life overall. Their personal experience of suffering has not been very deep, he says, and in any case it is offset by a quantity of pleasure, at least in their own accounting book. Why must Schopenhauer's eternal returner be this way? Because if they had really seen too much suffering, they would surely never want to come back for more.

Nietzsche's eternal returner diverges from Schopenhauer's in directly opposing ways and is all the more challenging for it. For a start, Nietzsche doesn't specify that his eternal returner has enjoyed a relatively happy life. They may, on the contrary, have had deep personal experience of life's essential sufferings and little to no pleasure for compensation. Also, for Nietzsche, one must not affirm life's pains merely for the sake of its pleasures, but rather somehow affirm the pains of living themselves. Nietzsche's warts-and-all philosophy is *premised* on, as Schopenhauer puts it, "far-reaching insight into the continuous suffering that is essential to all life," rather than its absence. Elsewhere Nietzsche cast doubt on the sincerity of Schopenhauer's pessimism on the curious grounds that in his spare time he was a keen flutist: "Schopenhauer, pessimism notwithstanding, *actually*—played the flute . . . every day, after dinner. You can read it in his biography . . . is this really—a pessimist?"[11] Nietzsche's question, once again, is, How? How is such affirmation possible?

The eternal return is a thought that travels. It comes in for examination at the start of Milan Kundera's 1984 novel *The Unbearable Lightness of Being*, for example. The core idea that the challenge of life has an infinitely cyclical structure, always moving but never going anywhere, rather than linear and progressive, also finds its way into the central motif of Albert Camus's 1942 essay, and foundational text of French existentialism, *The Myth of Sisyphus*. Camus retells the story of Sisyphus, a man condemned by the gods eternally to push a boulder up a hill only for it to roll back down again. Judging whether life under conditions like these is even worth living, Camus claimed, is the one true philosophical problem. The decision to commit suicide or not, he added, is this judgment put into action.

Schopenhauer clearly had a hand in setting the pessimistic challenge that generations of thinkers attempted to overcome in nineteenth- and twentieth-century Europe. Camus even cites him as such, although not in the most flattering light: "Schopenhauer is often cited, as a fit subject for laughter, because he praised suicide while seated at a well-set table."[12] This, as it happens, was neither charitable nor accurate of Camus: Schopenhauer's views on suicide were complex and sensitive in ways that it truly is hard not to read at least a little biographically.[13] According to Schopenhauer suicide is not immoral, as some philosophers held, but it is also not to be recommended or encouraged either, so long as other and better forms of escape from misery are still possible—a fitting view for someone who mourns the loss of a loved one, but also wishes to withhold moral judgment.

Camus was not the only critic to place our image of Schopenhauer at the dinner table. "Schopenhauer's system," wrote the Hungarian Marxist György Lukács, well laid out and architecturally ingenious in form, rises up like a modern luxury hotel on the brink of the abyss, nothingness and futility. And the daily sight of the abyss, between the leisurely enjoyment of meals or works of art, can only enhance one's pleasure in this elegant comfort.[14]

Considerations of class, wealth, and status clearly guided Lukács's selection of imagery. Schopenhauer (Lukács suggests) was prone to dwell on the darker and despairing aspects of life, and yet he demonstrated no real commitment to addressing these concerns as resolvable social problems, but instead took refuge in bourgeois pursuits, not least the perverse pleasures to be had in entertaining philosophical pessimism itself. And in fairness to Lukács, apart from the fantastical yawning abyss, the scene that he describes is not far off what Schopenhauer's life was actually like. One famous anecdote combines both his habitual fine dining and his dumbstruck reverence for the arts. In late August 1856, Schopenhauer discovered that his favorite musician, the Italian composer Gioachino Rossini, was staying at his favorite place to dine, the Englischer Hof in Frankfurt. On the advice of the hotelier who had tipped him off, Schopenhauer reserved a five o'clock table for himself and a friend, the French painter Jules Lunteschütz, right next to his musical hero.[15] Rather than go over and make Rossini's acquaintance, however, Schopenhauer left him in peace, possibly too intimidated. It was not the first time that Schopenhauer backed out of meeting one of his artistic idols either: in early 1819, he was in Venice at the same time as Lord Bryon. He spotted the Romantic poet riding around on horseback and was even, according to some accounts, in possession a letter of introduction written by the German literary icon Johann Wolfgang von Goethe, suggesting that the encounter with Byron, as with Rossini, had been carefully premeditated. But again Schopenhauer failed to seize the opportunity. This time, with Byron's reputation as a womanizer in mind, he attributed it to the fact that he was traveling with a female companion. "I was afraid of being cuckolded," he later explained. "I still regret this."[16]

Lukács was so pleased with his vividly drawn repudiation of Schopenhauer that he couldn't help reusing it against an opposing group of Marxist theorists, who, like Schopenhauer, also came from bourgeois stock and saw salvific potential in the arts, but in a radically different way. In the 1962 preface to his earlier book *The Theory of the Novel*, Lukács wrote: "A considerable part of the leading German intelligentsia, including Adorno, have taken up residence in the 'Grand Hotel Abyss.'"[17] The mention of Frankfurt-born cultural critic Theodor W. Adorno was a reference to the school of critical theory that was spearheaded by the city's famous Institute for Social Research. Adorno in fact had an even tighter geographical connection to Schopenhauer: they had both lived on the same riverside street in Frankfurt, Schöne Aussicht, albeit in different centuries. Adorno was also receptive to Schopenhauer's ideas, but not uncritically so. Like Schopenhauer, Adorno took the age-old philosophical problem of how to live and converted it from a question of living well into one of living at all; but he also sharpened its point. As a Jewish refugee from Germany in the 1930s, the events of the Holocaust haunted Adorno's later thought, especially reports of the atrocities committed at Auschwitz, which were being prosecuted in Frankfurt in the early 1960s. After Auschwitz, Schopenhauer's binary options of either affirming life or denying it seemed inappropriate to Adorno: "Spellbound," he cautioned in 1966, "the living have a choice between involuntary ataraxy—an esthetic life due to weakness—and the bestiality of the involved. Both are wrong ways of living."[18] Neither wholeheartedly embracing life nor resigning from it altogether could be the right way to register this unprecedented catastrophe. Samuel Beckett, one of the few contemporary writers to satisfy Adorno's exacting critical standards—and a noted Schopenhauer admirer too—penned the impossibility and necessity of postwar living: "I can't go on, I'll go on," utters the anonymous-eponymous narrator of Beckett's novel *The Unnamable*. Of all the descending branches in Schopenhauer's philosophical family tree, these are among the deepest and darkest.

Other thinkers whose lives, like Adorno's, were shaped by the Holocaust, took different messages away from Schopenhauer. According to the Austrian writer Jean Améry, who survived both torture at the hands of the Gestapo and captivity at Auschwitz, Schopenhauer's lesson is not that we must figure out how to go on living, but that the life force dwelling within us will always push such existential questions to the margins:

> I know that what Schopenhauer called the *will* (and he was no fool in using this term, even if it is conceptually strained to the point of exhaustion) and the instinct to preserve the ego and the species that makes us all live and endure, even to struggle to the end in a most unequal battle, already lost from the start, is so powerful that, though it cannot offset the absurdity of human existence, it probably can suppress it.[19]

By contrast, the social theorist Max Horkheimer, a founding member and celebrated director of the Institute for Social Research to which Adorno belonged, was struck by Schopenhauer's uncanny ability apparently to predict the future of the coming century: "Anyone who would have dared, in Schopenhauer's day or even at the turn of the century, to predict the course of history up to the present moment would certainly have been decried as a blind pessimist. Schopenhauer was a clairvoyant pessimist."[20] Horkheimer spoke from the vantage point of 1961, but Schopenhauer's pessimistic prophecy continues to unfold in our own present day. And yet, surprisingly, Horkheimer found a way to put the hope back into Schopenhauer. The relentless negativity of Schopenhauer's philosophy doubles up, in Horkheimer's view, as a critique of all false forms of consolation, including the same political absolutism that conjured the disasters of the twentieth century. These creeds all too easily fill a void that Schopenhauer insists on keeping open. Our solidarity in facing the void together, not in a common dogma that denies it, is the foundation for genuine hope: "There are few ideas that the world today needs more than Schopenhauer's," says Horkheimer, "ideas which in the face of utter hopelessness, because they confront it, know more than any others of hope."[21]

:::

Perhaps the most charming tribute to Schopenhauer comes in the form of an anecdote about Jorge Luis Borges, the Argentinian writer of poems and short stories on such philosophical themes as infinity, identity, and order in the cosmos. It is told by the public philosopher and self-proclaimed Schopenhauer enthusiast Bryan Magee:

> When I met Borges some time ago and remarked that I was about to embark on writing a book about Schopenhauer he became excited and started talking volubly about how much Schopenhauer had meant to him . . . and when people asked him, as they often did, why he with his love of intricate structure had never attempted a systematic exposition of the world-view which underlay his writings, his reply was that he did not do it because it had already been done, by Schopenhauer.[22]

If we are to take Borges at his word, then in a world without Schopenhauer, he would have been left to craft his philosophical system for himself. A missed opportunity, Borges fans might well think, but an enormous compliment to Schopenhauer all the same. As Voltaire once said of God: If he did not exist, it would be necessary to invent him.

Fortunately—at least in some sense of that word—Schopenhauer did exist. We shall now see how he came to be. In the first chapter, we will meet Schopenhauer in the grip of both a midlife crisis and a global health crisis, and we will briefly touch on the beginning, middle, and end of his story. The structure of the remaining chapters is linear and looping.[23] There is a chronological thread of life events running through the book, from birth and teenage years to adulthood and old age, each of which illustrates the thematic topic of the chapter. But in every case we shall also take note of how these events echoed in, and occasionally a little after, the rest Schopenhauer's life and thought.

CHAPTER 1

Living with Schopenhauer
How Schopenhauer Embraced Solitude

In early 1832, a pandemic was ripping westward through Europe. It was the second global outbreak of a newly recognized disease: cholera, which had first emerged from the banks of the River Ganges in 1817. Within three months it was all over Bengal and emanating into China and the Middle East, soon reaching Russia and the Baltics. A ship from Riga to Danzig carried it over to Prussia, and in August 1831, it arrived in Berlin. On November 14, rumors began to circulate that cholera had claimed the life of the city's best-known philosopher, Georg Wilhelm Friedrich Hegel.[1] A much lesser-known philosopher, Arthur Schopenhauer, having no professional or family commitments to tie him down, had already fled Berlin at the first sight of the pandemic, and was safely ensconced in new rooms in Frankfurt-am-Main by August 28. But he was hardly unscathed: tired of the world and everyone in it, Schopenhauer locked himself away in complete solitude for the first two months of 1832. His beard grew out and his hair turned gray.

Living with Schopenhauer was never easy, even for him, and he often found himself alone. His own mother, Johanna, kept him at arm's length for almost all of his adult life. On November 6, 1807, when he was nineteen years old, she wrote him a letter to explain why:

> You are not an evil human; you are not without intellect and education; you have everything that could make you a credit to human society. Moreover, I am acquainted with your heart and know that few are better, but you are nevertheless irritating and unbearable, and I consider it most difficult to live with you. All of your good qualities become obscured by your super-cleverness and are made useless to the world merely because of your rage at wanting to know everything better than others; of wanting to improve and master what you cannot command. With this you embitter the people around you, since no one wants to be improved or enlightened in such a forceful way, least of all by such an insignificant individual as you still are; no one can tolerate being reproved by you, who also still show so many weaknesses yourself, least of all in your adverse manner, which in oracular tones, proclaims this is so and so, without ever supposing an objection. If you were less like you, you would only be ridiculous, but thus as you are, you are highly annoying.[2]

He was, in a word, unlikeable. This was long before he was tired and gray. In his youth, curly locks of ash-blond hair fell over Schopenhauer's forehead, as was fashionable at the time. He briefly sported a mustache on his upper lip, rather than an unkempt beard, and his mouth was full and beautiful, rather than wide and thin as it became after he lost his teeth. His height was always below average, but his figure was slim, compact, and strong, with broad shoulders and a wide chest that gave him a booming voice. His eyes were large, bulging even, and set a little far apart—a family trait. They blazed with a brilliant blue.[3]

Johanna hadn't written her scorching letter of 1807 just to be hurtful. Not for the first time, she was concerned about the impression Arthur gave off to others. Although she could not bear his company, she still wished her son a happy life: "It is necessary for my happiness to know that you are happy," she wrote, "but not to be a witness to it." She could see that he had some redeeming qualities: he was obviously intelligent and—less obviously—kindhearted, but he was nowhere near socially adept and still far from esteemed. He had never bothered to endear himself to others and thereby earned

Figure 2. Schopenhauer in 1815 by Ludwig Sigismund Ruhl.

the right to put his talents on display. It was off-putting, in Johanna's opinion, and the lonely road to a miserable life.

Matters were if anything worse by 1832, including the strained dynamic between mother and son. We know that Arthur spent the first months of that year in self-isolation only because Johanna brings it up in another letter that she wrote to him, worried once again for his welfare.[4] The correspondence ended a twelve-year period of silence between them—she learned of her son's latest depressive stint from her alarmed daughter, Adele, who was on slightly better terms with her brother—and although he must have sent replies, we cannot be sure what he said because Johanna was

Figure 3. Schopenhauer in 1845 by Jacob Seib. Courtesy of Schopenhauer-Archiv der Stadt- und Universitätsbibliothek Frankfurt am Main.

long in the habit of destroying his letters immediately after reading. In the intervening time, while Arthur had spent all of the 1820s and early 1830s struggling to emerge from under Hegel's shadow in Berlin, Johanna had just brought out a twenty-four-volume collected edition of her own published works.[5]

Many of the qualities that Arthur lacked, and some that he possessed, Johanna had in abundance. After her husband's death on April 20, 1805, without too much delay, she had set about fulfilling her stifled childhood ambition of becoming an artist. She liquidated the family business before the end of the following year, giving her the funds to start a new life with Adele in fashionable Weimar. There she found success as an author, specializing in travelogues and novels. Her salon, which required the social skills that Arthur never quite mastered, was attended by the none other than Johann Wolfgang von Goethe, the Frankfurt-born lodestar of Weimar's cultural scene since his move there in 1775 on the wishes of his patron Duke Karl August of Saxe-Weimar. Goethe's conduct set a high standard for public intellectuals that, judging by Johanna's letter, her aspirant young son was sorely failing to meet. His sheer congeniality made him capable of fruitful intellectual friendships, the most famous being with the poet and playwright Friedrich Schiller. More to the point, he had earned the respect and esteem of his public: being improved and enlightened by Goethe, even if it were in a forceful way, was nothing short of a privilege. Goethe also knew when, and when not, to get clever with others. In her letter, Johanna reminded Arthur of one of his own favorite lines from Goethe's poetry: "Act the fool with fools, as is befitting."[6] On Arthur's reading (according to Johanna) this meant treat fools with the mocking contempt that they deserve. On hers, however, it meant politely humor them.

Johanna sent her critical letter of 1807 after receiving the news that Arthur, having finally quit his miserable merchant's apprenticeship in Hamburg, was considering moving to Weimar too. On this occasion, therefore, her concern was partly for herself. If reconstructing Arthur for his own sake was too much to expect—perhaps even in his youth, it was too already too late for him—then she could at least wall off the new life that she had created for herself out of her own talents. Until he could change, he must stay away.

And stay away he did. By 1850, Arthur was the sole surviving member of his immediate family: Johanna died on April 17, 1838, and Adele on August 25, 1849. He attended neither of their funerals. For all his mother and sister knew when they went to their graves, Arthur would carry on being too clever for his own good. But in this, the final decade of his life, his fortunes reversed. He began to be read and reviewed internationally; his talents were noticed, appreciated, even celebrated. People from all over the world were eager to meet this wizened sage of Frankfurt. Judging by his

Figure 4. Johanna and Adele Schopenhauer.

writings from around the time, however, Schopenhauer's attitude toward others had softened little in all those lonely years.

: : :

It was a two-volume work titled *Parerga and Paralipomena* (Greek roughly for "offshoots and offcuts") that began to earn Schopenhauer a respectable readership. After six years of writing and composing, including harvesting materials from decades-old notebooks, the book appeared in print in the fall of 1851. It was a project of finishing off thoughts, tying up loose ends, and filling in the details of the ambitious philosophical system that he had been elaborating since 1818's youthful work *The World as Will and Representation*. By choice, it would be his last new publication: "I want to prevent myself from bringing into the world weak children of old age who accuse their father and vilify his reputation," he wrote in a proposal to his previous publishers F. A. Brockhaus, who passed on it.[7]

Once it saw the light of day, *Parerga and Paralipomena* had such mass appeal partly because of a short series of chapters that contained detailed practical guidance for living a happy life. Unriddling the secret of earthly happiness was an age-old branch of philosophical study—Schopenhauer called it "eudaemonology" after the Greek term for living well that was central to Aristotle's ethics—but for him it was a one-off experiment under controlled conditions. In his official view, eudaemonology was a nonstarter because it rests on a fundamental error: the error, namely, of assuming that a so-called happy life is even possible. By this time, Schopenhauer was already convinced that happiness, if it even exists, is nothing like what we think. But, for argument's sake, he suspended these conclusions and proceeded on the assumption that it was indeed possible to live well.

He titled this section "Aphorisms on the Wisdom of Life." To this day, it effectively functions as a standalone work. As its epigraph, he adopted a maxim from the French aphorist, and fellow pessimist, Nicolas Chamfort: "Happiness is no easy matter; it is very difficult to find in ourselves and impossible to find elsewhere."[8] The motto conveniently set out two running themes of Schopenhauer's dabbling in eudaemonology: first, even once it is (erroneously) accepted that a truly happy life is possible, the problem still remains that it is a challenge to achieve. Second, if we do find happiness, we will not find it anywhere other than within ourselves alone. Among the problems that Schopenhauer was still trying to settle, in other words, were his final thoughts on a solitary existence like his own.

He often presented his solitariness as a choice: "Were I a King," he once said, "my prime command would be—Leave me alone."[9] It was, moreover, a virtuous choice in his view. He found ample precedents in the classics, including Aristotle ("Happiness belongs to those who suffice themselves") and Cicero ("Whoever is completely on his own and relies on himself, cannot but be perfectly happy"), studiously ignoring that neither thinker can have meant total isolation, since both also advocated participation in social and political life.[10] (Aristotle especially, like the French essayist Michel de Montaigne after him, had as much time for friendship as he did for solitude.) More recently, debates around the value of solitariness had been revived by the elite Swiss-German physician Johann Georg Zimmermann in his 1784 book *On Solitude*. Zimmermann was personally known to the Schopenhauer family: he gave Heinrich Floris Schopenhauer a consultation about his hearing in 1787 and prescribed a stay at the spa in Bad Pyrmont, Lower Saxony, where he then paid them frequent visits. While staying there, Johanna read Zimmermann's book, possibly in the very edition that ended up in Arthur's own hands, and which, judging by his student notebooks, he consulted during his university days.[11] The mature Schopenhauer duly cited Zimmermann's monumental work on solitude in his own *Aphorisms*, correctly surmising that a chief source for Zimmermann was another one of his own favorite writers: Petrarch, "who loved solitude so strongly and consistently," as was evident from his decades of work on *The Life of Solitude*, started around 1346.[12]

Despite his Petrarchan credentials, however, Zimmermann's views on solitude were not in fact allied with Schopenhauer's own. According to Zimmermann, the solitary life signaled a sickness and malaise that went against the grain of a healthy human disposition toward sociability: "Affectionate intercourse," Zimmermann wrote, "is an inexhaustible fund of delight and happiness . . . for which the solitary hermit, and even the surly misanthrope, continually sighs." Rather than a principled outsider stance, at bottom solitude was a lamentable, and hopefully temporary, flight from society by those unfit to thrive within it.[13] The title of the first English translation of Zimmermann's book made this unmistakably clear: *Solitude Considered with Respect to Its Dangerous Influence upon the Mind and the Heart*. It came out in 1796, the year after Zimmermann died—with sad irony, as it happens, having spent his declining years in his own depressive solitude.[14]

It is a wonder, then, why Zimmermann's first English translators did not opt for "Loneliness" in the title instead of "Solitude" in order further to signal its dangers. Or rather it would be, were it not for the fact that the English edition was a retranslation from J. B. Mercier's earlier French edition, *La solitude: Considérée relativement à l'espirit et au coeur* (1792). The German word for solitariness used in Zimmermann's original title, *Einsamkeit*, leaves more room for interpretation. In today's English, it can be translated with obviously different connotations as either solitude or loneliness.[15] Which of the two distinct states Schopenhauer had in mind when he discussed these matters in his *Aphorisms* can only be told from context. For example,

> Genuine, profound peace of heart and perfect peace of mind, these highest earthly goods after health, are to be found in solitude [*Einsamkeit*] alone, and, as a permanent disposition, only in the deepest seclusion. And if our own self is great and rich, we enjoy the happiest state that can be found on this miserable earth.

And,

> Loneliness [*Einsamkeit*] is the lot of all eminent minds, which at times they will bemoan, but always choose as the lesser of two evils.[16]

The first form of solitariness, Schopenhauer presents as a state of peace and tranquility, and therefore as worth seeking on its own merits. In this case, then, it is solitude. In its purest form, Schopenhauer suggests, solitude requires rich inner resources as well as some physical distance from others. The second form of solitariness, however, is more of a burden than a choice, in which case it is loneliness. There is no peace here, but rather an evil to bemoan. The still greater evil, to Schopenhauer's mind, even worse than loneliness, is society. It is unclear, though, whether Schopenhauer means to say that great minds must reject society or rather—and crucially different—must accept being rejected by society.

Schopenhauer ended *Parerga and Paralipomena* with a short chapter of allegories, parables, and Aesopian fables. Solitude must still have lingered in his thoughts, as many of the tales meditate on the relationship between the individual and society. By far his most memorable story, and most charming, is the fable of the porcupines:

> On a cold winter's day a community of porcupines huddled very close together to protect themselves from freezing through their mutual warmth. However, they soon felt one another's quills, which then forced them apart. Now when the need for warmth brought them closer together again, that second drawback repeated itself so that they were tossed back and forth between both kinds of suffering until they discovered a moderate distance from one another, at which they could best endure the situation.—This is how the need for society, arising from the emptiness and monotony of our own inner selves, drives people together; but their numerous repulsive qualities and unbearable flaws push them apart once again. The middle distance they finally discover and at which a coexistence is possible is courtesy and good manners. In England, anyone who does not stay at this distance is told: "Keep your distance!"—Of course by means of this the need for mutual warmth is only partially satisfied, but in exchange the prick of the quills is not felt.—Yet whoever has a lot of his own inner warmth prefers to stay away from society in order neither to cause trouble nor to receive it.[17]

Rather than let his readers come to their own conclusions, Schopenhauer draws his intended lesson in the final sentence. On his reading, his fable is about the importance of self-reliance: those with well-stocked inner resources—such as, we are given to assume, he himself—can readily afford to withdraw from society altogether. These solitary individuals will thereby avoid getting pricked by the quills of others, but also, less selfishly, will avoid pricking them back. (An alternative ending seems to have eluded Schopenhauer: a porcupine of such superabundant endogenous heat might well have allowed others to gather round and warm themselves at a safe distance.) Noticeably, however, Schopenhauer appears to have misinterpreted the thrust of his own fable. Minus the gloss of the final sentence, the image of the oscillating porcupines perfectly captures the necessity of mutual social dependence, and not just as a dangerous dilemma but also as an unavoidable fact of human life. As often happens with such fables, Schopenhauer's prickly presentation of the problem turned out to be more compelling than its neat resolution.

Another story of social dependence with an ambiguous meaning can be found in an anecdote from Schopenhauer's own life. When dining at the Englischer Hof in his later Frankfurt years, he would often lay out a piece of gold on his table. "That piece of gold," he explained, "is to go to the poor, whenever I hear the officers discuss anything more serious than women, dogs, and horses."[18] On the one hand, the gold represented a boundary, marking the distinction between himself and the other patrons with their inane and uncouth conversations. On the other, however, it was also an invitation: an incentive for his unchosen company, however substandard, to connect with him. At the end of every meal, he returned the gold piece back into his pocket. The ambiguity of the whole routine makes it hard to tell whether his expectations of humanity were left satisfied or disappointed.

In any case, Schopenhauer armed himself with reasons for rejecting society before it could reject him—or because it had rejected him, as the case may be. First, he argued, casual sociability with a diverse group of people requires a tiresome form of intellectual leveling: "every society requires mutual accommodation and a mutually agreed temper; hence the larger it is, the duller," he wrote. "The so-called good society accepts all kinds of merits, except intellectual ones; these, in fact, are contraband." Great minds must hide when in company. They must hold their tongues, tolerate nonsense, almost apologize for existing: "It obligates us to show infinite patience with every folly, stupidity, perversity, and dullness. In contrast, personal merits are supposed to beg for forgiveness or disguise themselves; for intellectual superiority offends by its mere existence."[19] Thinking back to Johanna's eviscerating letter of 1807, this is evidently not an obligation that Arthur always managed to obey. He never quite disguised his cleverness, assuming he even tried. Second, social ranking is often in inverse order of other more important rankings: "whereas nature has established the greatest moral and intellectual diversity between human beings, society... sets up artificial differences and degrees of class and rank instead, which are often diametrically opposed to the ranking list of nature."[20] Whom we have the opportunity to speak with, in other words, is not determined by who is worth speaking to. Mixing with society's upper echelons is therefore no guarantee of finding decent, intelligent people with abundant natural talent, who can more often be found on the lower rungs of the social ladder. Given Schopenhauer's own bourgeois background, this is his least self-flattering reason for social withdrawal. Third and finally, given people's general inability to change their minds, most social engagement is futile anyway: "just as the body assimilates what is homogeneous to it, everyone *retains* what *interests* him, i.e., whatever fits into his system of thoughts or suits his purpose."[21] This cuts both ways: Schopenhauer would not expect to enlighten his company, just as he would not expect to be enlightened by them in return.

In sum, in Schopenhauer's experience, society came with too many costs and too few rewards. It rarely did anything for him other than disturb, demand, and deny: "being frequently surrounded by heterogeneous beings has a disturbing, even adverse effect on [a man], robs him of his self and has nothing to offer as compensation."[22]

Observant readers will have noticed that none of Schopenhauer's reasons are good grounds for rejecting society in all its forms. Not one of them is a necessary and universal truth of socializing. At most, they are true of a certain specifically tedious form of society, albeit the form to which Schopenhauer had easiest access: namely, so-called polite society. They therefore do not immediately apply to other forms of society: if it is really true, for example, that naturally talented people are in shorter supply among the upper classes, then this, in itself, is no reason for those among the lower classes to withdraw from their peers—except, perhaps, for the fact that the wealth and resources that can help to develop those talents tend to accumulate at the top. Plus, if it is also true that the social order is an artificial convention, not a natural fact, then it follows that it might be revoked. Schopenhauer's observation that social rankings do not correspond to the distribution of natural talents might therefore be used equally well, or perhaps even better, as an argument for overthrowing those very rankings. He need not have abandoned all hope of companionship, then, at least not on these grounds. What he really needed was better company.

He also made a few exceptions. Children, Schopenhauer noticed, tend to be more gregarious than adults, which, he surmised, must be for a good reason: "The younger people are, the more they have to learn in every respect; nature has referred them to the mutual instruction that we all receive when associating with our peers."[23] He was therefore in favor of an essential social component in early education. He also realized that another adverse effect of excessive solitude is a painfully heightened social sensitivity when compelled to stand in the company of others. Those who are well accustomed to socializing, by contrast, seem to develop thicker, more protective skins: "our mind becomes so sensitive due to its constant seclusion and loneliness that we feel worried or insulted or hurt by the most insignificant incidents, word, or even mere facial expressions, whereas those who are constantly in the thick of the fray do not even notice such things."[24]

Given these exceptions, Schopenhauer had a few words of wisdom for any young person who like him is solitary by disposition but, by force of circumstance, must reluctantly be sociable. Like much of the above advice, it seems to come straight from the heart of personal experience:

> Someone who, particularly during his early years, is unable to endure for any length of time the barrenness of solitude, as often as the justified dislike of people may have driven him into it, this person I advise to become accustomed to carry a part of his loneliness with him in society, hence to learn even in society to be alone to a certain degree and not to tell others immediately what he is thinking and, on the other hand, not to take too literally what they are saying. . . . Then he will not quite be in their company, although he is in their midst.[25]

One can readily imagine the Schopenhauer of *Parerga and Paralipomena*, older and wiser as he entered his sixties, using these words to counsel his nineteen-year-old self, still raw from his mother's epistolary upbraiding. Admittedly, it sounds like an unhappy compromise. In fact, it sounds like a heartbreakingly lonely way to live: those qualities of yours that people are bound to find unlikeable, try in future just to keep them to yourself. But a positive spin might be put on the idea of carrying your solitude around inside you. In essence, Schopenhauer's advice was to be among others, and hide your true self if you must, so long as you keep the best part of yourself in reserve. Above all, do not lose your grip on who you really are, and what you really think, just for the sake of social appeasement.

∴

Besides the occasional necessity—or rather unavoidability—of society, other things appeared to conflict with Schopenhauer's yearning for solitude. It was hard to be totally solitary while simultaneously practicing another one of his closely held values: worldliness. Like sociability, according to Schopenhauer, worldly experience ought to be at the center of education. "The main point of education," he wrote, "would be that an acquaintance with the world . . . should begin from the proper end."[26]

To an extent, Schopenhauer was brought up in just such a worldly fashion: between May 1803 and August 1804, he was taken by his cosmopolitan parents on a long grand tour of several European nations (a privilege not extended to his younger sister). The tour covered France, the Netherlands, Switzerland, Austria, and other parts of Germany, plus a miserable twelve-week stay at a boarding school in Wimbledon, England, while Heinrich Floris and Johanna went sightseeing around other parts of Britain. As an adult, however, apart from a couple of sojourns in Italy, he was never the model of a globetrotting inquirer. For comparison, in the same January of 1832 that Schopenhauer spent holed up in his new Frankfurt apartment, Charles Darwin was setting sail on his famous *Voyage of the Beagle*. "On the 6th of January we reached Teneriffe," Darwin writes, "but were prevented landing, by fears of our bringing the cholera: the next morning we saw the sun rise behind the rugged outline of the Grand Canary island. . . . On the 16th of January, 1832, we anchored at Porto Praya, in St. Jago, the chief island of the Cape de Verd archipelago."[27] By these standards, Schopenhauer could hardly make a claim to rugged worldliness.

While travel no doubt broadens the mind, however, it was not strictly essential to Schopenhauer's understanding of a worldly education. More specifically, he had in mind a "natural education" as distinct from an "artificial" one. When the mind is artificially educated, Schopenhauer argued, it is "stuffed with concepts by means of telling, teaching and reading."[28] Natural education, by contrast, involves forming one's concepts out of extended engagement with the world itself. But this didn't mean all observing and no thinking: "Pure empiricism," Schopenhauer wrote, "relates to thinking as eating to digestion and assimilation. When experience boasts that it alone has promoted human knowledge through its discoveries, it is as if the mouth were bragging that the existence of the body is its work alone."[29] Experience may provide the necessary raw ingredients, but it can hardly account for the entire body of knowledge, which also requires a good amount of cognitive digestion. Plus, the naturally educated person will never get very far without at least an initial amount of telling, teaching, and reading—that is, engagement with the thoughts of others—which, like it or not, are sources of the very concepts that allow us to make our own first provisional observations of the world. But whatever concepts we do use for our thinking must pass the test of experience if and when the time comes. Otherwise, rather than help us to make contact with the world, these false concepts will simply get in the way.

The conflict between solitariness and worldliness, then, is surface deep. Further down, for Schopenhauer, they are rooted in a common virtue: thinking for yourself. This was Schopenhauer's master virtue, as far as intellectual activity was concerned, from which all others derived. There is even a single German word for it, *Selbstdenken*, which Schopenhauer used as the title for one of the essays in *Parerga and Paralipomena*. Thinking for yourself produces the best-quality knowledge, Schopenhauer argued, because true wisdom is not simply a matter of possessing all the correct facts. It is as much about the acquisition and composition of the body of knowledge. For example, full intellectual ownership can only be guaranteed by thinking for yourself: "Truth that is merely learned sticks to us like an artificial limb, a false tooth, a wax nose," Schopenhauer wrote, "but what is acquired through one's own thinking resembles the natural limb, and it alone truly belongs to us."[30] There is no knowledge that we have not in some way made our own. The knowledge generated and developed by thinking for yourself, because it has come from you, will also be better organized and more deeply integrated than it would be if it were to have come from someone else:

> Even if occasionally we could have conveniently found ready made in a book the same truth or insight that we produced only with great effort and slowly by means of our own thinking and combining, still it is worth a hundred times more when it has been obtained through our own thinking. For only then does it enter into the whole system of our thoughts as an integrated part, as a living member, connected with it completely and firmly . . . it is lodged firmly and cannot disappear again.[31]

"One can only think through what one knows," Schopenhauer added, "which is why we should learn something; but one also knows only what has been thought through."[32]

For Schopenhauer there was, therefore, a tight connection between solitariness, on the one hand, and independence, on the other. As he wrote in a notebook started just after his flight from the Berlin cholera outbreak: "The man who does not like *loneliness* also does not really like *freedom*; for when a man is not alone (and has no peace and quiet), he is not free."[33] Seen in this light, Schopenhauer's advice to lonely youths such as he once was makes even more sense. Anyone who would sacrifice his inner solitude sacrifices not only himself, but also the very intellectual virtue in which all genuine knowledge is rooted.

:::

It's ironic that Schopenhauer finally earned his readership with advice like this, advice that is, at times, explicitly anti-reading. To read is to think with someone else's mind, he warned, and while arguably this is precisely why we do it, it can all too easily come to replace the act of thinking for yourself. Excessive reading—meaning not enough thinking—was, in his view, the surest sign of an artificial education. "The book philosopher," he wrote, rather than owning an authentic, organically integrated body of knowledge, "resembles an automaton put together from foreign materials, while the thinker resembles a living, begotten human being."[34]

He does not appear to have led by example: almost every page of Schopenhauer's works and notebooks is peppered, and sometimes completely covered, with quotations from texts both ancient and modern, Western and Eastern, displaying his own immense erudition and strong bookworm tendencies. Since he knew several languages besides German, including English, Spanish, Italian, Latin, and Greek, he often left these quotations in the original, indicating not only the sort of audience he expected but also that he had accessed these sources unmediated by a translator's interpretations. Such firsthand knowledge was a crucial point of difference between himself and other book learners:

> Books are written about this or that great mind of antiquity, and the public reads them, but not the thinkers themselves, because it wants to read only what is freshly printed, because "like is attracted to like," and the shallow, tasteless gossip of a contemporary pinhead is more agreeable and convenient to them than the thoughts of great minds.[35]

(In light of these remarks, it's troubling to imagine what Schopenhauer would make of a book like the one currently in your hands, and its author.)

It was no accident that Schopenhauer could always back up his own conclusions with a consensus of opinions from past thinkers—and not, he would have us believe, simply because he gathered, curated, and presented them very selectively. Because their views, too, were rooted in worldly experience, it followed that they could not fail ultimately to agree with one another. Schopenhauer therefore took from his sources not the content of his own views, or their justification, but rather the courage to air them in public:

"Often I was pleasantly surprised," he wrote, "to find formulations in ancient works by great men of propositions that I had hesitated to bring before the public because of their paradoxical nature."[36] His favorite authors were also a source of encouragement when it came to developing his style. Though reading could never directly impart good style, it could at least awaken a budding writer's nascent talents:

> There is no literary quality, as for instance power of persuasion, wealth of imagery, gift of comparison, boldness, or bitterness, or brevity, or grace, or ease of expression, nor wit, surprising contrasts, laconism, naïveté and so on, that we can acquire by reading writers who have them. But by reading we could indeed summon such qualities in us if we already have them as an inclination, hence potentially, and we could become aware of them, could see all the things we could do with them, could be strengthened in our tendency, even in our courage to apply them, and we could evaluate the effect of their use by example and thus learn to use them properly, only after which, of course, we would possess these qualities actually.[37]

It's clear, then, that while reading was no substitute for thinking for yourself, it was a fitting substitute for something else, something of which Schopenhauer was personally in short supply: suitable company, at least of an intellectual kind. And in this way, perhaps, it was often superior to the real thing. A written work, Schopenhauer thought, or a good one at any rate, is the distilled essence of the mind who created it. It is free from the haphazard digressions, errors, and infelicities with which a living, breathing person might formulate their thoughts on the spot, as well as any off-putting personality traits or irritating social mannerisms. "*Works*," Schopenhauer wrote,

> are the *quintessence* of a mind; they will therefore be incomparably richer in content than his company, and will also essentially replace this—indeed, far exceed and leave it behind.... Therefore we can read books by people whose company would afford us no pleasure, and this is why elevated spiritual culture eventu-

ally brings us to the point where we find entertainment almost only in books, and no longer in other people.[38]

This effect has its advantages for readers and writers alike. For readers, the distance suits those who generally find real flesh-and-blood people hard to tolerate at close quarters. For writers, on the other hand, it benefits those who are equally judged by others to be insufferable in person. Someone, that is, precisely like Schopenhauer on both counts.

The advantages as a writer to Schopenhauer in particular were manifold. Transposed into his works, his potentially repellent personality traits, as memorably listed by Johanna in her biting letter of 1807, were free to become compelling literary and intellectual qualities, so long as they found the right audience. His "super-cleverness," his "rage at wanting to know everything better than others," were simply his unquenchable thirst for ever-increasing knowledge. His desire "to improve and master what you cannot command," his "adverse manner, which in oracular tones, proclaims this is so and so," the fact that "no one wants to be improved or enlightened in such a forceful way"—these were not problems when presented in book form. If Schopenhauer were to have held forth uninvited on philosophical matters among the officers in the Englischer Hof, no doubt it would have come across as irritating arrogance. But since his readers, once he had any, first had to come to him, there was no such imposition: they would expect his proclamations on what is thus and so—this being the pact between reader and writer after all—and if they did begin to find him tiresome, unlike in person they could always put him down and pick him back up again whenever they pleased.

His problem, therefore, was not that his flaws got in the way of his virtues. Rather, his flaws were his virtues showing up in the wrong place. If he was bad company, he could at least be a good read.

∴

Once Schopenhauer finally did find his audience, he was clearly very grateful. His gratitude can be charted through the development of the prefaces that he wrote for the three editions of his main work, *The World as Will and Representation*.

The first edition was released in December 1818, evidently at least a month sooner than his publishers anticipated, as it erroneously bore the publication date of 1819. Though young, Schopenhauer was wise enough to realize that he had not written a book for every audience. It didn't help that his preface, written in Dresden in August 1818, began by recommending some of his earlier work, including the hardly tantalizingly titled *On the Fourfold Root of the Principle of Sufficient Reason*, which was his first published work from 1813, as well as his 1814 work in optical science, *On Vision and Colours*, developed in close collaboration with Goethe (leaving Germany's greatest poet with misgivings about Schopenhauer consistent with his mother's). In addition, Schopenhauer recommended that, before continuing, the reader should ideally become acquainted with the three main sources of philosophical influence on his thought: Immanuel Kant, Plato, and—probably more surprising to his contemporary readership—the Upanishads. Taken together these were not small preparatory tasks.

The one thing that undercut the danger of Schopenhauer coming off, once more, as a know-it-all, was a modicum of self-awareness: "How, the indignant reader might ask, will there ever be an end to it if we have to do so much work for a single book," Schopenhauer inquired on his reader's behalf. "Who wants to put up with all this? So my advice is simply to put down the book."[39] He realized that this would not quite get him off the hook, for his reader had already paid good money for a copy, and so he added a disarming set of tips for things to do with an unread book:

> The reader who has come as far as the preface only to be rebuffed by it has paid good money for the book, and wants to know how he can be compensated.—My last resort now is to remind him that he knows other things to do with a book besides reading it. It can fill a space in his library as well as any other book, and it will look quite good there with its fresh, clean binding. Or he can leave it in the dressing room or on the tea table of his educated lady friend. Or finally, by far the best option of

all and one that I would particularly advise, is for him to write a review of it.⁴⁰

All joking aside, Schopenhauer could scarcely conceal the defensive tone of his first preface. For a man so supposedly self-confident in all intellectual matters, he was clearly braced for an unimpressed response, or even no response at all, and consoling himself with the thought that everything will come in time:

> I am calmly resigned to the fact that [this book] will fully share the fate that truth has met with in every branch of knowledge, and most of all where the knowledge is most important, that of being granted only a short victory celebration between the two long periods of time when it is condemned as paradoxical or disparaged as trivial.⁴¹

Judging by his preface to the second edition, written in Frankfurt in February 1844, this form of consolation for obscurity had proved ineffective over the years. Twice as long as the first, the new preface consisted almost entirely of a tirade against the German philosophical orthodoxy, especially the collusion that Schopenhauer perceived between the universities, the church, and the state, embodied in the numerous imitators of his former Berlin bête noire, Hegel. If the tone of the first preface was preemptively defensive, the second was bitterly paranoid about the "silent treatment" that his work had received, as though it were a shady conspiracy hatched by a cabal of elite philosophy professors: "An entirely new age would have to dawn before my philosophy could ever be taught from the teacher's lectern.—That would be a fine thing, for a philosophy like this, which cannot be lived by, to come out into the open air and even win general admiration! That is why it had to be prevented, and had to be opposed to a man."⁴² Still, Schopenhauer had not abandoned all hope that one day—one day!—the lasting value of his work would be vindicated:

> Genuine works will always have an entirely distinctive, quiet, slow and powerful effect, and in the end they can be seen rising

above the turmoil as if by a miracle, like a balloon that flies up above this planet's thick atmosphere into purer regions, and having arrived there, stays put, and no one can pull it back down again.[43]

By the time of his third and final preface, a few years after the surprisingly successful reception of *Parerga and Paralipomena*, Schopenhauer could drop all his defenses. Also written in Frankfurt, his adoptive home city for almost three decades, in September 1859, precisely one year before he died, he kept it short and sweet: just a few paragraphs long. The only disappointment for which he still needed consoling, he wrote, was that it had taken him his entire life to get this far. "I find consolation for this in Petrarch's words: 'If someone who has been running all day arrives in the evening, it is enough.'" He continued:

> I too have finally arrived and have the satisfaction of seeing the beginnings of my influence at the end of my career, with the hope that this influence, according to an old rule, will last all the longer, since it was so late starting out.[44]

Aside from a few acolytes that he had gained along the way, he was still alone in the world, with no close family to speak of. But the 1850s brought a few signs of gradual recognition: some German universities offered lecture courses on his work; one even set an essay competition. After a lifetime of self-isolation in some form or another, he finally emerged.

CHAPTER 2

A Sure Compass

How Schopenhauer Accepted Punishment

On April 22, 1796, a group of convicts at the Bicêtre asylum, Paris, were bound together in chains. Decades later, a guard vividly recalled one of the men. Between his heavy sobs and the hammer blows that riveted an iron collar around his neck, the prisoner could barely utter an audible word. His crime: stealing a loaf of bread to feed his widowed sister's seven starving children. When the chain gang was complete, they were dispatched to the infamous Bagne of Toulon, a slave labor prison, condemned to work on France's fleet of galley ships. The journey south by cart took twenty-seven days. On arrival, each man was re-attired in a red smock and given a number by which henceforth to be known. His was 24601. Entering Toulon in 1796, after four failed escapes, he wasn't formally released until 1815.

The young Arthur Schopenhauer, aged sixteen, visited the Bagne on April 8, 1804. He therefore might have seen prisoner 24601 at work—were this prisoner not fictional. The wretched man condemned for stealing bread was, of course, Jean Valjean, the protagonist of Victor Hugo's 1862 novel *Les Misérables*. But, to apply one of Schopenhauer's own principles—"the creations of authentic genius . . . are just as true as real people"[1]—Hugo's documentarian portrayal may as well have been the truth. Arthur, too, saw men in chains. Some were quite literally chained to their fate. Instead of being joined to other convicts, those deemed to have committed the worst crimes were permanently shackled to their benches, where they would not only work, eat, and sleep, but eventually die. Naturally, this scene of human misery unsettled the teenager, who asked himself in his travel diary, "Can one think of a more terrible feeling than that of one of these unfortunates as he is chained to the bench in the dark galley and from which nothing but death can separate him?"[2] He worried just as much about the fate of those who were fortunate enough to avoid perishing in the Bagne. To him it was inconceivable that after such treatment any man could ever find a welcome place in society again. "He must become a criminal for a second time and end up on the gallows"[3]—a roughly accurate prediction (except for the ending) in the case of Jean Valjean, who was recaptured on July 25, 1823, and sent back to Toulon as prisoner 9430. Later in life, Schopenhauer would compare this period of his youth to the story of the Buddha's awakening, when, as the young Nepalese prince Siddhartha Gautama, he first ventured out into the world only to be confronted everywhere by sickness, pain, and death.[4]

Even before he encountered the galley slaves of Toulon, however, Arthur was not a total stranger to the horror and brutality that human beings wreak upon one another in the name—supposedly—of justice. On the morning of Wednesday, June 8, 1803, for example, he witnessed a hanging. Three, in fact. He watched from the window of a pub named the Magpie and Stump, opposite the doors of Newgate Prison in London. Though he was shocked and saddened by the spectacle, in that day's diary entry he took solace in the fact that death by this method appeared to be swift. It lasted no more than thirty seconds, caused not by strangulation, he surmised, but a broken neck. The English style of execution was unceremonious even, albeit still public, with no prolonged journey to the scaffold, no death knells ringing out to call in the crowds. It was almost routine; the audience was quite small, as hangings happened around every six weeks. Later that day, Arthur cheerfully attended a performance by Monsieur Fitz-James, the famous French ventriloquist, to which he dedicated an equal amount of space in his travel diary.⁵ By letters the next month, he compared notes with a schoolfriend back in Hamburg, who on his own trip to England had seen the decaying corpse of the notorious Wimbledon highwayman Louis Jeremiah Abershawe, hanging in chains.⁶

From his balanced account of these hangings, as if he were conducting a comparative study, it is clear that Arthur could already think of gristlier, even more humiliating, possible ways to be killed. The one moment that seems to have made a more profound impression on him was right before the drop, when out of fear the condemned men began to pray. "One of them," he reported, "who moved his hands up and down as he prayed, made the same movement a couple more times after he had fallen."⁷ Late into his adulthood, Schopenhauer would collect newspaper transcripts of gallows sermons, the profound religious epiphanies that doomed men and women mystically proclaimed as they contemplated certain death. "I am convinced that unless *the natural heart be broken and renewed by divine Grace, however noble and amiable it might appear to the world, it can never think of eternity without shuddering inwardly*," declared Henry Hocker in a report for *The Times* of April 29, 1845, the day before he was hanged at the very same spot that the philosopher had visited as a child four decades ago.⁸

How, at such a tender age, had Arthur already become a connoisseur of the most dreadful spectacles? It was all thanks to the grand tour of Europe that he took with his parents, which they had arranged for him not as a generous gift, but a cunning bribe.

: : :

In a way, it was the trio's *second* tour. The first began on June 24, 1787, when Heinrich Floris, already fearing a Prussian invasion of Danzig, was investigating the prospect of moving his business to England. Johanna came too, unknowingly pregnant. It was at the start of this trip that they met with the physician and solitude expert Johann Georg von Zimmermann. After following his advice to take the spa waters of Lower Saxony, the couple traveled around and out of Germany to Belgium and then France, spending four weeks in Paris in the dying years of the ancien régime. Upon realizing that Johanna was pregnant, just after reaching London, they abruptly headed back to Danzig in November. They did so with a heavy heart; British citizenship for their child would have satisfied their shared Anglophilia and given him, assuming it was a boy, a career advantage as an international merchant like his father. To compensate, and on much the same cosmopolitan grounds, they named him Arthur.[9]

Another tour was in order at some point in the future, therefore. As before, the motives for the sequel were a mixture of business and pleasure.

From the age of eleven, Arthur attended a school in Hamburg run by Dr. Johann Heinrich Christian Runge. In its cohort and curriculum, Dr. Runge's school aimed to train the next generation of shipping merchants, with lessons on languages (mostly modern with a little Latin for show), geography, topography, and basic arithmetic.[10] At age fifteen, however, when Arthur's higher intellectual gifts were already evident, Dr. Runge made a personal appeal to Heinrich Floris to consider a less vocational and more academic institution for educating his son. After giving it some thought, Heinrich Floris decided instead to engineer a dilemma that would put Arthur's seriousness about scholarship to the test. There were two options. Option one, Arthur could accompany his father and mother on their upcoming tour of Europe, with all its natural splendors, cultural jewels, and social spectacles. Option two, he could stay behind and work seriously on his Latin. If he picked the first option, then he had to agree to go into the family business afterward. If the second, then he was free to follow his true vocation. Arthur went with immediate gratification and signed on for the tour, and by extension for the life of a merchant like his father.[11]

Heinrich Floris had Arthur's best interests at heart, at least as he understood them; income was the bottom line, as far as he was concerned. Unless Arthur's devotion to the life of the mind was utterly unshakable—which at this point, clearly, it wasn't—then he should not be allowed to jeopardize his future. Still, it later seemed to Arthur like a cruel trick, to tempt a talented young person off a potentially promising path in life. When after Heinrich Floris's death there was the chance to resume this path, Arthur complained about the temporary detour in a rueful letter to his mother. On reflection Johanna disapproved of Heinrich Floris's tactics too, but at the time she felt powerless to stand in his way. In a long letter of April 28— one of many such letters in 1807, as together they thrashed out the terms of his escape from his Hamburg apprenticeship—she wrote, "Oh, dear, dear Arthur, why did my voice count for so little then? What you wish now was once my warmest wish." For all their differences, stifled ambition was one thing they had in common, and she knew all too well "what it means to live a life that goes against our heart's desire."[12]

It was a fairly safe bet that Arthur, before he knew any better, would swallow the bribe. His father had already instilled in him a taste for travel. Not long after the birth of Louise Adelaide Lavinia Schopenhauer, better known as Adele, on June 12, 1797, Heinrich Floris dropped off Arthur, aged nine, for a two-year stay with one of his business associates in Le Havre, France. André Charles Grégoire de Blésimaire had a son, Jean Anthime, who was around the same age as Arthur and likewise destined for a merchant's life. Seemingly, Heinrich Floris never made a decision about any aspect of his son's development without first considering the business angle. Luckily for Arthur, his stay in Le Havre enriched his life in ways far beyond his father's strictly professional hopes. Arthur and Anthime bonded quickly and deeply, not only because they had similar upbringings and family pressures, but also because they had matching moody temperaments that tended toward the morose. The Grégoires, like the Schopenhauers, were also highly cultured. It's no wonder that Arthur already excelled in French at Dr. Runge's, what with all the frequent readings aloud of Voltaire in the household at Le Havre. Those days, destined to be lost to the past, were by his own estimation the happiest of Arthur Schopenhauer's entire existence.[13]

The promised grand tour, by contrast, turned out not to be such a happy time. The chief source of Arthur's misery was not even the hangings he witnessed, or prisons he visited, but rather the twelve weeks he spent at the Reverend Thomas Lancaster's academy in Wimbledon, England, from June 30 to September 20, 1803.

Up until that point, the trip had been going rather well. Having cut short their visit the previous time, London was high on the Schopenhauers' itinerary. As before, they sailed from Calais to Dover—Arthur, seasick, spent the whole time on deck gasping for air—and arrived at around one o'clock on Tuesday, May 24. After a short stopover in Canterbury, they were in the City of London the next afternoon. Arthur was immediately impressed:

> We walked through some of the liveliest streets of the city today. I found that London surpassed my expectations; I really had not imagined it to be *like this*, and was astonished to see the magnificent houses, the wide streets and the rich shops which one finds in front of every house in every street in all their colourful variety.[14]

He spent many hours, often alone, wandering London's streets and marveling at its sights: the Tower of London, Westminster Abbey, Hampton Court, Kew Gardens, and more. In the week prior to seeing the three hangings at Newgate, he went to visit the Monument, a giant Doric column built to commemorate the Great Fire of London. The week after, he went back to climb its internal spiral staircase—erroneously counting its steps to 345—for a view above the inner city's smog-shrouded spires. Walking back from a private viewing of George Seddon's furniture warehouse at 150 Aldersgate Street, on a fine summer's day on Friday, June 24, the Schopenhauers passed by the infamous Bedlam asylum. "It is no longer shown to the public, because it is considered cruel to make the misery of lunatics into a spectacle to satisfy people's idle curiosity," Arthur noted in his diary. Instead of entering, then, the Schopenhauers gazed at the two recumbent figures, sculpted by the Danish artist Caius Gabriel Cibber in 1680, draped over the asylum's arched entryway. Titled *Raving Madness* and *Melancholic Madness*, the pair of sculptures depicted two seminude men, one bound in chains and contorted by torrents of inner turmoil, the other unrestrained but immobilized nevertheless by a deep-seated apathy. Two days later, the family paid a visit to the German-born astronomer William Herschel at his home in Slough, where he had constructed his extraordinary telescopes.[15]

Besides these and other stops on the London leg of the tour, Arthur spent most of his time at the theater or the opera, especially in Covent Garden, observantly reviewing each performance in his daily diary. That and, of course, being brought along to social calls on Heinrich Floris's various business associates. They frequently dined at the Sydenham home of the banker Samuel Percival, with his wife, Mary, and their son George, who was less than a year younger than Arthur. Arthur occasionally passed the time with George—watching a boat race from Westminster Bridge, sneaking into the Quaker Meeting House on St. Martin's Lane and being baffled by the service—but never became as friendly with him, or indeed anyone, as with Anthime. On Monday, June 27, 1803, the Schopenhauers and the Percivals took Arthur to meet and dine with Mr. Lancaster at his Wimbledon school. Three days later it was to be Arthur's home for the next several weeks. Naively, he might even have welcomed a break from the city, as some of its sights were already growing a little stale. Of a return visit to the famous Vauxhall Pleasure Gardens, he wrote in his diary, "It was exactly the same as last time."[16]

:::

With Arthur deposited in Wimbledon, Heinrich Floris and Johanna were free to explore the rest of Britain. It was a treat for them both, but for Johanna it was a dream come true.

A shared appreciation of British culture played a major part in bringing Heinrich Floris and Johanna together in the first place. While both were born and bred in Danzig, they were, nevertheless, of different generations: when they married on May 16, 1785, Heinrich Floris was almost thirty-eight while Johanna was only eighteen. By then, Heinrich Floris had already spent much of the 1770s in London—doing what exactly is unknown—and almost stayed there for good. Johanna's exposure to Britain, by contrast, had largely been mediated by a kindly next-door neighbor. On November 26,

1764, a couple of years before Johanna's birth, a Scottish Episcopalian minister by the name of Dr. Richard Jameson took the job of chaplain at the English Chapel in Danzig, which happened to stand next to the home of Johanna's parents Christian Heinrich and Elisabeth Trosiener. For reasons relating to trade, Danzig had a sizable congregation of English and Scottish families, but the chapel also ministered to the native Danzigers; Heinrich Floris even donated to its Anglo-Scottish Fund for the Poor. Judging by her own account of her youth, Johanna was captivated by the gentle and erudite chaplain next door, along with his two pets, a large black cat named Tamerlane and a small white dog named Frei.

Jameson was not the first to notice and nurture Johanna's keen mind. Her enlightened father, a fishing merchant and city councillor, insisted on a liberal education for his daughter with a special emphasis on languages.[17] She was even briefly placed in a local school run by the painter and engraver Daniel Niklaus Chodowiecki. But, for all their enlightenment, her family drew the line at her wish to become an artist herself.[18] Jameson soon became her tutor and mentor instead. He introduced her to classical and modern poetry, including Shakespeare, Milton, Pope, and what would one day become her son's favorite novel, *The Life and Opinions of Tristram Shandy, Gentleman* by Laurence Sterne. Jameson had been schooled at the cutting edge of the Scottish Enlightenment. His time as a divinity student at the University of Edinburgh had coincided with a series of public lectures by Adam Smith, which contained the seeds of thoughts later developed in Smith's 1759 masterpiece in moral philosophy, *The Theory of Moral Sentiments*.[19]

It cannot be overstated just how much this sort of education made Johanna stand out, not just to a discerning man of the world like Heinrich Floris Schopenhauer, but also against her peers. The mere fact that she knew English was a striking novelty, by which, except for Jameson's encouragement, she was almost made to feel ashamed. "A girl learn English!" she later wrote,

> what good in the world could that do her? This question was put again and again by friends and relations, for it was a thing unheard of in Danzig. At last I grew almost ashamed of my knowl-

edge of English, and some years later resolutely refused to learn Greek, though I longed to do so in my heart, and Jameson kindly urged me to begin."[20]

On July 19, 1789, the year after Arthur was born, Jameson returned to Britain and settled in Newcastle, England, where he became involved in its Literary and Philosophical Society. When he died on Tuesday, January 26, 1796, the society's annual report remarked that "his conversation was always animated and judicious, and his manners were distinguished by a liberality and simplicity which will be long recollected by his friends with a pleasing regret."[21] Little wonder that Johanna was eager to know her mentor's homeland better.

The trip was nothing if not thorough. On their way up north they stopped at the spa towns of Bristol and Bath, and then on to the bustling industrial centers of Birmingham and Manchester. They visited Newcastle, Jameson's final resting place, although Johanna was overpowered by the pervasive look and smell of coal everywhere, its main industrial product. Once they reached Scotland, the aesthetic clash of Edinburgh's Old Town—its stacks of tumbledown houses lodged into the rockface like swallows' nests, and its famously narrow, crooked, and winding alleyways—with the New Town's spacious, well-paved squares, fine buildings, and pretty gardens, gave Johanna a mixed impression: "at one and the same time a most beautiful and a most ugly place."[22] Journeying toward the highlands, they sampled salmon freshly caught from Loch Tay in wilderness surroundings that put Johanna in mind of the scenery described by the legendary Gaelic poet Ossian (as fabricated, it later turned out, by the contemporary Scottish forger James Macpherson).

On their way back down, after a trip to the Lake District, they visited Liverpool, which they found not as scenic as Edinburgh but much more hospitable than anywhere else in Britain. They were touched by what they saw at its charitable school for the blind, where the members were tutored in music and handicrafts. "On the whole," Johanna wrote, "these blind people, like almost all their fellow sufferers, are always bright, cheerful and talkative."[23] After viewing the imposing ancient exterior, but disappointingly redecorated interior, of Warwick Castle, and before heading back to London, they made a pilgrimage to Shakespeare's birthplace in Stratford-upon-Avon. Under the watchful eye of the cottage's current occupant—"a butcher, who appears very poor but watches over this sacred place, knowing that the visits of strangers provide a very welcome support to his meagre income"—Johanna marveled at the old wooden chair next to the fireplace, where she imagined Shakespeare's father once sat "worrying about his son's youthful pranks."[24] She was no stranger to such perennial parental worries.

:::

All the while, they wrote to Arthur. It is fortunate that they did, because for his entire stay in Wimbledon he left his travel diary completely blank. It falls eloquently silent on June 30 and resumes without further explanation on September 20. Nobody seems to have kept the letters that Arthur must have sent in reply, including those to his sister and his school friends back home, so we can only piece together his experience from the things that other people say about it. By all accounts, it was a thoroughly dismal period.

In her own diary, Johanna compared the English and German schooling styles as she saw them: English pupils "were taught the Classical languages, geography, history, writing, arithmetic, and French. . . . Other subject worth knowing, such as we teach our children in Germany, were completely ignored."[25] Mr. Lancaster's mostly pragmatic curriculum was therefore not all that far from Dr. Runge's, especially compared to the academic curriculum of a German gymnasium where Arthur truly belonged. (It was equally far from the syllabus that Johanna had enjoyed with Jameson.) As a penalty for any infringement of the school rules, the boys were required to memorize a page of Latin or Greek; and if that didn't do the trick, then they were sent to the reverend for a personal thrashing—"with no regard for whether the boy was six or sixteen," Johanna adds, "and in a most disgraceful manner."[26] She was appalled by the rife injustice at the school, where seemingly the merest accusation of misbehavior was sufficient for punishment. She affected, disingenuously, to suspend her personal judgment on the lasting effects of growing up under such an oppressive educational regime: "We refrain from making comments on such a system of education. Everyone may draw his own conclusion as to what can be expected to be the eventual outcome of such treatment at an early ages, and reflect on the advantages we have over these proud islanders."[27]

Worst of all were the Sundays: "All games or amusing diversions were frowned upon and sternly punished."[28] Instead, the reverend would start the day by practicing his weekly sermon on the boys before he gave it for real at his parish in the nearby town of Merton. The boys spent the remainder of the day listening to yet more sermons in church as well as an additional evening service in the schoolroom. The Schopenhauers were roundly stunned by the utter tedium of English Sundays. In their German experience, the day of rest, though religious, still meant leisure and relaxation, including music, dancing, and theater, not litanies, supplications, and endless preaching. For Arthur, forever after, Sunday became the symbol of soul-crushing boredom: "Just as need is the constant scourge of the people," he was later to write in *The World as Will and Representation*, "boredom is the scourge of the respectable world. In middle-class life it is represented by Sunday, just as want is represented by the other six days of the week."[29] He took Anglicanism itself as the symbol of self-conceited hypocrisy, as though weekday misdeeds scarcely mattered so long as one was suitably pious on Sunday morning. England's backward church put it in such intellectual peril that, decades later in *Parerga and Paralipomena*, Schopenhauer still spoke of it as a country that required urgent aid from enlightened continental missionaries:

> there is no nation which it is so painful to see methodically made stupid by the most degrading blind faith than the English, which in intelligence surpasses all the others. The root of evil is the lack of a ministry for public education in England, which has therefore remained entirely in the hands of the clergy, who have made sure that two thirds of the nation cannot read or write and who even, on occasion, have the audacity, with the most ludicrous presumption, to grumble against the natural sciences. It is

therefore a human duty to smuggle into England, through every conceivable channel, light, enlightenment and science in order to finally put out of business those most well-fed of all priests.[30]

In their letters to Arthur, his parents hardly helped to relieve his misery. Though they presented a united front that Arthur should try his hardest, where he could, to spend his time in Wimbledon profitably, they adopted contrasting styles of approach. Johanna composed long letters listing her complaints, including the length of time Arthur last took to reply, his untidy handwriting, his reversion back to reading German authors instead of practicing his English, and, as ever, his frank manner of expression. (Freely expressing, no doubt, his newfound distain for the Anglican church: "Expressions," Johanna warned, "which civilized, well-educated people should not allow to slip out even in the heat of the moment in conversation, expressions like 'infamous' bigotry.")[31] Heinrich Floris, by contrast, dashed off terse missives with words mostly to the effect of please do as your mother asks. His parents were at least of the same mind that, by the time they got back, he should have broken his habit of constantly slouching. "Your mother expects, as I do, that you will not need reminding again to walk straight, like other properly brought-up people, and sends her love," his father wrote from Liverpool on August 10, 1803. In the same letter, Heinrich Floris dangled the bribe that they would rescue Arthur from Lancaster's school just as soon as his handwriting improved, "for a would-be merchant simply must be able to write well and fluently."[32] If Arthur felt cheated, he wouldn't be wrong. His father's wishes—to which, admittedly, with a little added incentive, he had freely assented—were already invading what was supposed to be his reward.

Once they had mercifully collected Arthur from Wimbledon, it was on with the tour. After exhausting London, the Schopenhauers headed back to mainland Europe. This time they set sail first to the Netherlands then rode through Belgium and into France, which gave Arthur a precious opportunity to reunite with Anthime in Le Havre for a week in December 1803.[33] After a couple of months in Paris, which Arthur didn't think compared to London, the Schopenhauers went south to the Mediterranean coast. It was there that in April 1804, he witnessed the galley slaves of Toulon. On the same trip, Arthur visited the island fortress of Château d'If, which—legend had it—once held France's infamous inmate, the Man in the Iron Mask. By then, he was already used to troubling landmarks like these: in Paris on December 2, 1803, he had stood at the ruined site of the Bastille, where Louis XIV's most mysterious political prisoner really had once been confined.

: : :

Aside from some shuttling around Germany in the middle third of his life, Schopenhauer traveled relatively little after his teenage grand tour, and went abroad only on a couple more occasions. Nevertheless, he evidently kept abreast of news from overseas. He never sailed to America, for example, but in his later work he invoked the recent—and disastrous—radical reforms to its penal system. He did so in connection with his theory of boredom.

"Boredom," Schopenhauer wrote in *The World as Will and Representation*,

> is certainly not an evil to be taken lightly: it will ultimately etch lines of true despair onto a face. It makes beings with as little love for each other as humans nonetheless seek each other with such intensity, and in this way it becomes the source of sociability. For reasons of political prudence, public precautions are always taken against it, as against other universal calamities.[34]

Boredom, in Schopenhauer's view, is a fatally underestimated form of suffering. It is the retiring twin of its showier sibling, pain: "life swings back and forth like a pendulum between pain and boredom."[35] The oscillation between pain and boredom is explained by the fact that we are either in a state of frustrated desire, in which case we experience the painful lack of what we want, or else we are satisfied, in which case we feel a different sort of lack. Without the distraction of our usual yearnings, we discover a void at the center of our being. Our very existence becomes a burden to us; we literally do not know what to do with ourselves—until, of course, we discover new needs and become inflamed by desire once again. (Notably, for Schopenhauer, the constant need for stimulation can have both a bonding and a divisive effect, as it pushes people to socialize as well as to revolt.) Both of these forms of suffering reveal our essentially restless nature, but from two different ends: pain, on the one hand, is our restlessness in motion, whereas boredom, on the other, is the internal pressure that builds up when we are slowed down to a halt. Only pain, however, is outwardly obvious, precisely because it is the movement of our desires. Boredom, by contrast, though it may be just as intolerable, is a deeply inward, and therefore often hidden, form of suffering. Except perhaps for a vacant look or a wince of desperation, if the above passage is any guide, boredom's signs are subtle, almost invisible, and one might well fail to spot, or to care, how badly someone else is suffering from it.

To underline the unseen seriousness of boredom, Schopenhauer added a line to the 1844 second edition of *The World as Will and Representation*: "Philadelphia's strict penitentiary system makes boredom into an instrument of punishment, through loneliness and inactivity: and it is so horrible that it has already driven convicts to suicide."[36] (At the same time he also added the line about tedious Sundays.) On its face, it may seem like a throwaway reference to prisons in general, as boredom is surely a fact of most if not all forms of incarceration. In fact, Schopenhauer had something highly specific in mind.

A remarkable new prison had opened up in Philadelphia on October 25, 1829. The Eastern State Penitentiary, as it was called, was the logical conclusion of what had come to be known as the Pennsylvania system of prison discipline. The system had been partially implemented at other Pennsylvanian prisons, but Eastern State was purpose built to take it to the extreme. What distinguished the Pennsylvania system from its competitors was its universal enforcement of round-the-clock solitary confinement. In theory, every prisoner was to be kept away from all the others, day and night, in the absolute solitude of their individual cells. It contrasted with the Auburn system, named after New York's Auburn Prison, which in penological terms was a silent system rather than a solitary one. Under the Auburn system inmates were housed in solitary confinement overnight, but by day they labored in groups, albeit silently. In addition to the penal labor itself, the Auburn system was overtly brutal: the warden of Auburn Prison, Elam Lynds, who also presided over New York's notorious Sing Sing Prison, was a zealous advocate of severe corporal punishment. As his successor at Sing Sing, Robert Wiltse, once put it, "The best prison is the one prisoners consider the worst."[37] Inhumanity was part of the point.

Initially, Eastern State Penitentiary had been lauded as a humane triumph. First, it was simply better equipped than other prisons. According to the designs of its British-born architect John Haviland, each prisoner was to have a centrally heated private cell, complete with a small adjoining yard, a skylight, and a flushing toilet at a time when even the White House lacked running water.[38] (How well these designs were implemented, however, was another matter.) More importantly, its overall orderliness made brutally physical forms of discipline less necessary. Instead, the prolonged time spent away from others was supposed to encourage extended reflection and, ideally, some penitence (hence "penitentiary"). Where the Auburn system favored force over reform, the Pennsylvania system still held out hope for reconstructing criminal characters and safely releasing them back into society.

By the time that Schopenhauer came to revise *World as Will and Representation* for its second edition in 1844, however, the abject failure of the Pennsylvania system was evident to all. Given his daily routine of reading *The Times* of London (another anglophile habit carried over from his father), he might well have caught on to the trajectory of the following reports. On Monday, August 24, 1818, "a respectable Correspondent" praised the Pennsylvanian system's positive effect on crime reduction. An article on October 5 of the same year reported similar effects on moral reform—but that was well before Eastern State. On Thursday, April 23, 1835, William Crawford, secretary of the London Society for Improvement of Prison Discipline, was reported to have submitted a glowing review of recently constructed Eastern State Penitentiary—although he did, admittedly, encounter four "insane persons" and one "idiot." On Friday, June 21, 1839, the House of Commons debated emerging reports of shortcomings in Philadelphia's penitentiaries, including their high labor intensity, extreme costliness, and general inefficiency. By Saturday, January 27, 1844, *The Times* openly preferred New York's Auburn system, partly on the grounds of Eastern State's startlingly high mortality rate, which, due to its high standards of hygiene, could not easily be explained by any physical illness. Contrary to its previous reports, on Saturday, April 6, 1844, *The Times* claimed that Eastern State's methods had actually proven ineffective at its chief aim of moral reform. Monday, November 25, 1844, brought news of the successful escape of a double-murderer. On Thursday, January 28, 1847, the increasingly alarming mortality rate at Eastern State was compared unfavorably with that of standard British prisons. And finally, on Friday, April 18, 1851, a meeting of magistrates in Middlesex noted the sky high incidences of complete insanity.

While Eastern State had improved physical prison conditions, in other words, it had also inadvertently proven the ravaging mental effects of unbroken solitude. Along with several other European nations, Britain watched the experiment from afar—hence all the discussion in the Commons—as the recommendations of the Crawford report were intended to feed into the construction of London's new Pentonville Prison.[39] Incredibly, at the First International Prison Congress held in Frankfurt, Schopenhauer's then city of residence, the Pennsylvania system was almost unanimously endorsed by international delegates.[40] Across the United States, however, the Auburn system was favored in practice and had ultimately triumphed: Eastern State Penitentiary officially abolished its separate system in 1913, but evidently it had been unofficially abandoned for quite some time, as by 1870 there were already 671 inmates to only 560 cells.[41]

With this in mind, it is worth recalling Schopenhauer's remark that "Philadelphia's strict penitentiary system makes boredom into an instrument of punishment, through loneliness and inactivity: and it is so horrible that it has already driven convicts to suicide." It is certainly one way to explain Eastern State's morbidly puzzling mortality rates: prisoners were literally dying of boredom, albeit by their own hand.

Schopenhauer was not the first notable intellectual to be dismayed by the Pennsylvania system—he wasn't all that notable at the time, for a start. Better-known thinkers were already using their public platforms to draw attention to its horrors. Earlier in the 1840s, Charles Dickens had inspected Eastern State Penitentiary during his tour of the United States. In his *American Notes*, he describes the plight of the prisoners as "a depth of terrible endurance . . . which none but the sufferers themselves can fathom . . . a secret punishment which slumbering humanity is not roused up to stay."[42] Dickens's criticisms, too, were reported in *The Times*.[43] Like Schopenhauer, he was specifically concerned about the hiddenness of the harm, to which everyone—except of course those subjected to it—seemed blind. The German poet and journalist Heinrich Heine, in a similar mood, aptly branded the prisons of the Pennsylvanian system "small silent American hells."[44]

Still, Schopenhauer's interpretations were very much his own, and in a way they had to be. Prisons like Eastern State were founded on an ideal of human self-sufficiency; the Philadelphian physician and Founding Father Benjamin Rush, for example, thought of individuals as social atoms, which, after breaking away from the unifying force of British monarchical rule, required civic intuitions as a way to keep them held together in peace. (Rush was such a zealot for therapeutic solitude, in fact, that he attempted to cure his son John's clinical depression with solitary confinement at Pennsylvania Hospital. John Rush remained there, uncured, until his death twenty-seven years later.)[45] The failed experiments in Pennsylvania exploded the myth of the self-reliant individual. Or that would seem to be the natural conclusion for anyone to draw, except that Schopenhauer was just as prone as the architects and theorists of the Pennsylvania system to endorse the benefits of solitude.

Instead, then, Schopenhauer offered up his alternative analysis in terms of boredom. Sociability was a cure for boredom—often in fact the best cure—but it did not follow, to his mind at least, that a lack of sociability was its root cause. We all have our social needs and bonds, but in Schopenhauer's view these derive from an even more basic need for stimulation of any sort. If this represents a blind spot on his part to the intrinsic and independent value of social relations, then it at least forced him to think even further about the sort of good that those held in the solitary confinement seem to lack. First, evidently, some people volunteer to withdraw from society altogether; Schopenhauer, for one, had an intermittent form of this tendency, and in sustained forms it can be observed in hermits, monastics, and recluses. These groups seem not to need company in the same way that others do, but they still need something, if not someone, to preoccupy them. Second, and relatedly, even those who are involuntarily solitary, like the prisoners under the Pennsylvania system, can find at least partial relief in nonsocial forms of activity, or solitary-social forms such as reading and writing. Often, indeed, their sanity desperately depends on such activity. These facts suggest that general stimulation is just as fundamental a human need as social contact.

Additionally, solitary confinement broke one of Schopenhauer's cardinal rules of punishment. In his view, the sole justifying aim of punishment was deterrence.[46] To him, inflicting pain even on the guilty was never intrinsically good, nor was it the point of the justice system to dish out harms that people supposedly deserved, nor was it even the case that criminals could be deeply reformed by punishment. Rather, the point to him was disincentivizing citizens from causing even more harm to one another in the future. From this he derived the rule that "the apparent suffering a punishment involves should, where possible, exceed its actual suffering."[47] It's a remarkably consistent application of the deterrence theory of punishment: where possible, punishments should always *look* worse than they *are*. For if you can maximize deterrence while minimizing harm, then you must, because there is no further justification for causing any more harm than the deterrent strictly requires. "Solitary confinement," however, "does the opposite. There are no witnesses to the enormous suffering it involves, and those who have not experienced it do not anticipate it, so it is not a deterrent. It threatens those tempted into crime by deprivation and need with the opposite pole of human misery, boredom." It is worse than it looks—much, much worse.

Solitary confinement is thus as ineffective as it is injurious, and therefore unjust. By adopting this position, Schopenhauer pitted himself against two apparently opposite views. There were the well-meaning reformers behind the Pennsylvania system, on the one hand, who proposed solitary confinement as a humane alternative to corporal punishment, public humiliation, and hard labor. And there were those, on the other, such as the pitiless wardens of the Auburn system, who still clung on to the barbaric old ways. Both sides are premised on the common but fatal misconception that solitary confinement is the softer option. In reality, Schopenhauer argued, it is anything but.

What next, then, for the penitentiary system? Schopenhauer did not go so far as to propose an alternative, and perhaps that is for the best. Had he expressed a preference, then he (like Dickens) might have favored the overtly punishing Auburn system over the quietly devastating Pennsylvania system, on the grounds that the former at least stood a better chance of establishing an effective deterrent. The fact that he did not express any preference, however, may signal that although Schopenhauer was confident that solitary confinement was a wrong turn, he was still undecided about the right way forward. The supermax prison of today's America, indefinitely in lockdown for twenty-three hours per day, is surely not it.[48]

: : :

The theme of punishment recurred throughout Schopenhauer's written work, not always in forms as specific and literal as his references to the American penitentiary system. Myths and metaphors of punishment were always on hand in Schopenhauer's imagination when he attempted to articulate his darkly pessimistic worldview.

For example, there was no better repository of images than the terrifyingly creative penalties handed down by the gods of ancient Greek mythology:

> concern for the constant demands of the will, whatever form they take, continuously fills consciousness and keeps it in motion: but without peace, there can be no true well-being. So the subject of willing remains on the revolving wheel of Ixion, keeps drawing water from the sieve of the Danaids, is the eternally yearning Tantalus . . .
>
> . . . then suddenly the peace that we always sought on the

first path of willing but that always eluded us comes of its own accord, and all is well with us ... for that moment we are freed from the terrible pressure of the will, we celebrate the Sabbath of the penal servitude of willing, the wheel of Ixion stands still.⁴⁹

Each of these three myths adds something to the picture. Ixion's flaming wheel, to which he is bound after attempting to seduce Zeus's wife Hera, is quite literally infinitely cyclical. The Danaids, who murdered their husbands at the behest of their father Danaus, are set the incompletable task of filling up a vessel punctured with holes at the bottom. And Tantalus, from whose story we get the word "tantalize," is dropped into a pool of water beneath the hanging branches of fruit trees, only to find that both recede from his reach whenever he attempts to either drink or eat. Taken together, we arrive at the composite image of a task that goes on forever because the desire that sets its end can never really be satisfied: and that is precisely how Schopenhauer viewed life—for the most part. Even Ixion's wheel is said occasionally to stand still, although it does not stop turning when we (impossibly) find permanent satisfaction. Rather, it only ever ceases when we, somehow, have stepped off the cycle of desire altogether, and even then only momentarily.

Optimists are bound to object that this is a one-sided worldview, and maybe so. But still, the optimist must account for all that it calls to our attention. The following Dantesque tour of hell on earth, Schopenhauer suggests, should be enough to defeat them:

> if you led the most unrepentant optimist through the hospitals, military wards, and surgical theatres, through the prisons, torture chambers and slave stalls, through battlefields and places of judgement, and then open for him all the dark dwellings of misery that hide from cold curiosity, and finally let him peer into Ugolino's starvation chamber, then he too would surely come to see the nature of this best of all possible worlds. Where else did *Dante* get the material for his hell if not from this actual world of ours? And a proper hell it became too.⁵⁰

Schopenhauer's comparison of the world to hell, the ultimate place of punishment, was not entirely metaphorical. As he points out, historically real episodes of punishment were the inspiration for many of the scenes in Dante's *Inferno,* including the imprisonment of Ugolino della Gherardesca and his sons, who were left to starve to death by Ruggieri degli Ubaldini, archbishop of Pisa. (While both are banished to the lowest circle of hell, Dante lets Ugolino get his own back on Ruggieri as the former, with an appetite for revenge, eternally devours the skull of the latter.) In cases like these, even the greatest artists can do little better than to record and amplify the horrors of real life.

Moreover, thinking of the world as something like hell gives it a kind of intelligibility that it would otherwise lack. After all, it certainly doesn't resemble heaven. If reward and bliss are the goal, then the world is very poorly designed. But if, on the other hand, the purpose of the world is to test and punish us, then its design seems much more fitting, albeit less comforting. Schopenhauer therefore interpreted the diabolical aspects of life as heavy hints that, contrary to what the optimist says, all is not well in the world: "because it would be better for our situation not to exist, everything around us bears the trace of this—just as everything in hell reeks of sulphur."[51] He was fully aware that, to many, this interpretation of the meaning of our existence was the most off-putting feature of his philosophy: "People have complained loudly that my philosophy is melancholy and comfortless: but this is only due to the fact that instead of making up a future hell as the equivalent of sin, I proved that there is already something hellish where the guilt lies, in the world."[52]

On the whole, then, Schopenhauer encouraged us to navigate life as though it were one of the many sites of punishment he had witnessed as a teenager:

> In order to have a sure compass always in hand for finding our bearings in life, and in order to view life always in the proper light without ever going astray, nothing is more useful than to accustom oneself to regarding this world as a place of penance, hence as a prison, a penal colony as it were, a labour camp.[53]

It is a difficult pill to swallow, but at least one of its therapeutic benefits is obvious. Even a cursory glance at the world—never mind the chilling up-close and personal view that Schopenhauer got on his grand tour—should lead us to abandon the naive assumption that pleasure in life is guaranteed. Too many of us are utterly deprived of pleasure for that to be true, and so it can only make us more outraged, resentful, and confused by life.

What kind of therapy is this, one might well ask? It seems not to make us feel any better. If anything, it might seem like a double dose of misery, rather than a cure. After all, the implication is not only that we must suffer in life but that, in some sense, the blame lies with us. To pain, this only adds guilt.[54] It is possible, however, to pull Schopenhauer back a little from this stance: he may not *literally* believe that punishment is our true purpose. It's not always clear, in fact, that he believes life has any actual purpose at all. Often when he raises the possibility of such a purpose, he does so hypothetically: "*If* suffering is not the closest and most immediate goal of our life, then our existence is the most inexpedient thing in the world."[55] The view that Schopenhauer recommends, therefore, is not quite that we should add the moral pain of guilt to our physical and psychological pains. Rather, these latter pains should simply come as no surprise to us given what sort of creatures we are. Like it or not, we are propelled through life by a cycle of desire best captured by the Greek myths of endlessly tantalizing tasks. The error of thinking otherwise is soon punished.

∴

These melancholy realizations evidently occurred to Schopenhauer fairly early in his life. In the unusually self-searching notebook that he started after fleeing the Berlin cholera epidemic, he writes:

> In my seventeenth year, without any proper schooling, I was affected by the *misery and wretchedness of life*, as was the Buddha when in his youth he caught sight of sickness, old age, pain and death. . . . Certainly the *destiny of suffering* is written all over human existence; it is deeply immersed in suffering, never escapes this and its continuation and termination are always tragic; here a certain deliberateness is unmistakable. . . . For this reason,

the world appeared to that wholly one-sided view of my youth to be the work of a devil, but as far as it could see such a view was right.[56]

The reference to his age suggests that this diabolical worldview was prompted by the scenes of the grand tour. Yet, even after the tour was over, Schopenhauer's education in the misery of life was incomplete. Something else was still to come, something much closer to home.

CHAPTER 3

My Dear Son, Adieu

How Schopenhauer Destigmatized Suicide

On April 20, 1805, Schopenhauer's father was found dead in the canal behind the family home in Hamburg. Like everything in Heinrich Floris Schopenhauer's world, the house at Neuer Wandrahm 92 mixed life with business. At the front, there were the living quarters, including a gallery, a library, and even a moderately sized ballroom. At the back, there were various storerooms and a counting house.[1] Publicly, the death was presented as accidental. For the notice in a local newspaper, Johanna wrote: "I hereby do my sad duty to announce to my relatives and friends the death of my husband, Mr. Heinrich Floris Schopenhauer, which was caused by an unfortunate accident. Expressions of condolences are not requested; they would only increase my grief."[2] He was presumed to have fallen from the attic window of the warehouse, several stories high above the water. To some, this was plausible enough, as Heinrich Floris habitually inspected everything at the business end of the compound, even including its upper reaches. Anything else was a nasty rumor.[3] To others, however, the story didn't add up. In the winter of 1804, not long after returning from the grand tour, Heinrich Floris had become physically unwell; and mentally, he was anxious, erratic, and exhausted. In his current unfit state, he was unlikely to be presiding over his affairs as normal and therefore had no official reason to be carrying out inspections of the warehouse loft.[4] Privately, the family suspected suicide. It seems rarely to have been openly discussed, except on at least one occasion. When the surviving Schopenhauers were facing financial difficulties in 1819, putting such immense strain on their relationships that it ended in a rupture lasting for years, Arthur wrote Adele a letter insinuating that their mother's profligate behavior had contributed to Heinrich Floris's untimely downfall. Certainly, Arthur came to believe that Johanna had neglected her husband in his enfeebled state; as he reportedly told a friend later in life, "My Frau mother gave parties while he was wasting away in solitude."[5] When Johanna found Arthur's unforgivable letter, "a horrible scene followed," according to Adele's diary. "She then talked of my father; I learned the dreadfulness that I had suspected."[6]

:::

Shame and blame: all of Schopenhauer's future thinking about suicide was bound to reckon with these two. Philosophically, the battle lines were already drawn. On one side, there was Schopenhauer's compatriot philosopher from a previous generation, Immanuel Kant. Schopenhauer venerated Kant above any other modern philosopher, but that didn't stop him from subjecting Kant's philosophy to rigorous criticism. He was critical, especially, of almost every aspect of Kant's ethics, and the Kantian view of suicide was a case in point.[7] On a standard interpretation, Kant was opposed to suicide in virtually all its forms.[8] He was opposed on the grounds that, although human beings are self-legislating creatures—we are free, that is, to live by rules given to ourselves—our self-legislation still does not permit voluntary self-destruction. A pillar of Kant's ethics was the principle that we should self-legislate as if we were deciding how the whole of humanity naturally behaves. Suicide, in Kant's view, does not pass this test: it is irrationally inconsistent to wish for living beings such as ourselves to be governed by the rule that we end our lives as soon as they become too difficult, or else we would soon cancel ourselves out entirely.

Kant's point was not that suicide is imprudent. If anything, it is perfectly prudent to end things at the point when carrying on will only prolong our pain and suffering. His point, rather, was that it is immoral to think so prudently about these matters. Perhaps the best way to appreciate what makes it immoral, in Kant's view, is to focus on the way it mistreats the value of human life. As self-legislating creatures, Kant thought, we have a special status in relation to our deliberations over what we should do. Specifically, we, the legislators, should not factor our own existence into our deliberations. Although in some circumstance it might be prudent to ends one's life, it is wrong to treat the value of any life as if it were a mere matter of prudence in the first place. That kind of thinking, generally applied, would lead us down a shady street, where human lives are sized up like assets to be traded, balanced, and offset, rather than, as he firmly believed, having their own priceless dignity.

On Kant's view, then, there would be moral grounds to blame Heinrich Floris for his dereliction of the duty to value himself in the appropriate way. Ranged on the other side of the debate, however, was another heavyweight thinker of the previous century, the Scottish philosopher David Hume. In a 1755 essay titled "Of Suicide," Hume effectively asked: Whose life is it anyway? Some, Hume noted, would argue that our lives are not ours to throw away—that they belong, instead, to God, to nature, or at least in part to our neighbors in the society to which we ourselves belong. But if that were true, then how do we tell apart the things we are and aren't permitted to do with our lives? In Hume's view, when it came to deciding what was in accordance with God's will or the natural order, and what went against it, people tended to make arbitrary discriminations. We are apparently free to put our lives at the disposal of some things—and not only the things that promote and enhance life, but also the things that might involve taking lives—but not others. The solution, to Hume, was to avoid making decisions about what to do with our lives on the assumption that they don't belong to us. Instead, he thought, we can be trusted with weighing things up for ourselves, and we are free to think prudently about it, including what is in our own best interest and the interests of those around us. If someone does decide that suicide is their best option, then we have reason to respect their judgment. As the most famous line in Hume's essay put it, "I believe that no man ever threw away life, while it was worth keeping."⁹

For the most part, Schopenhauer sided with Hume. He agreed that on self-concerning matters such as suicide, our lives are more or less at our own disposal. In fact, on this front, he thought the matter was fairly simple. For something to be wrong, Schopenhauer thought, it must actually or potentially injure *someone else*. The reason why it has to be someone else is because the type of injury that Schopenhauer had in mind was not simply a physical or mental harm, but also a moral one: in other words, a true injury consists partly of an injustice. An injustice in turn, for Schopenhauer, consists in acting against someone's else will, and from this it follows that, unless they are significantly misinformed, a person cannot deliberately perpetrate an injustice upon themselves. In sum: if someone does something to themselves, then they will it; if they will it, then there is no injustice done to them; if there is no injustice, then there is no injury; and without any injury, there is no wrong. The right to suicide, Schopenhauer thought, was a paradigm case of this logic.[10]

Of course, the logic here seems to assume from the start that the act of suicide harms no one other than the person who performs it. But this is patently false: for example, despite his family's vagueness and hush around Heinrich Floris's suspected suicide, there is evidence that Arthur confided the deep pain that he felt over his father's death to his French pen pal and closest companion, Anthime. A few months after the event, Anthime wrote to console Arthur, who in his view had suffered enough by now: "It is my wish that your grief might have moderated, now that you have paid nature its due of the mourning that every good son owes to the memory of a venerable father, and that you might have begun to face your grief more philosophically."[11] (Anthime was a fellow sufferer in a more immediate sense: his own father died the same year.) Undoubtedly, then, suicide is almost never a purely self-concerning act. It often has enormous effects on others too.

On Schopenhauer's view, however, even this consideration does not always override the right to suicide. In most cases, it would amount to the demand that a person should stay alive just for the sake of someone else's interests: "That the one who no longer wants to live for himself should now continue to live merely as a machine for the use of others is an extravagant demand."[12] If there is any wrongdoing in the matter of suicide, therefore, then it is usually on the part of those who apply excessive moral pressure against it. There was one possible exception for Schopenhauer, it would seem, but a painfully relevant one:

> Only *one* obligation is known to me that is *not* assumed by means of an agreement but rather immediately through a mere action, because the one to whom one has it was not yet there when one assumed it: that is the obligation of parents to their children. Whoever puts a child into the world has the *duty* to maintain it until it is capable of maintaining itself: and should this time *never* arrive, as with a blind person, cripple, cretin and the like, then the duty too never ceases.[13]

Schopenhauer never explicitly weighed a parent's special duty of care for their dependent child against the right to suicide, but the two would certainly seem to clash. When his father died, Arthur the seventeen-year-old apprentice was admittedly on the cusp on personal independence, largely due to Heinrich Floris himself. Seven-year-old Adele, however, was certainly not. Was it therefore a condemnable dereliction of his parental duty? It depends on whether such a duty, or any duty, extends to an unconditional claim on another person's very existence, even when that person has no use for it themselves.

A greater part of Schopenhauer's admiration for Hume's stance was due to the Scotsman's demolition of the stigma, taboo, and superstitions around suicide. Both noted that the (philosophically groundless) prohibition against suicide was often reinforced by social attitudes and that established religion especially was to blame for the arbitrariness with which people were granted or denied dominion over their own lives and bodies. In Hume's case, the power of the church even led him to self-censor his essay on suicide. After initially sending the manuscript to his publisher in 1755 for inclusion in his *Five Dissertations*, he was later persuaded by his friends to withdraw it due to the controversy that it was bound to cause. Apparently, though, the essay's existence was something of an open secret, with even a pirated French translation circulating from 1770.[14] In accordance with his wishes, the original essay was properly published the year after Hume died—albeit anonymously, as though the church might still catch him in the afterlife. For Schopenhauer, Hume's publishing debacle was another prime opportunity to bash the Anglican church:

> it redounds to the great disgrace of the English nation that a purely philosophical essay, using cold reason to refute the current objections to suicide and stemming from one of the leading thinkers and writers of England had to be secretly smuggled from there, like a churlish ruse, until it found refuge abroad. At the same time it shows what kind of conscience the Church has in this point.[15]

Notably, according to Schopenhauer, Anglicanism was not only a travesty of the English mind; it was a travesty of Christianity too. "Neither in the Old nor the New Testament can we find any kind of prohibition or even disapproval of [suicide]."[16] Only an optimistic (ergo erroneous) interpretation of Christianity could condemn suicide, he thought, and even then it would be on the grounds of the act's implicit denunciation of optimism itself:

> Could it not be this, that the voluntary giving up of life is a poor compliment to the one who said "everything was very good"? Then once again it would be the obligatory optimism of these religions which denounces the killing of oneself in order not to be denounced by it.[17]

Schopenhauer's objections to the church's stance on suicide were not purely intellectual either; there were practical considerations too. Aside from the fact that "those many human beings whom we honored and loved" were labeled sinners and criminals, which is painful enough for their surviving families, those labels also came with barriers to religious rites and legal rights, respectively. The clergy could "deny an honest burial to those who depart this world voluntarily," with consequences that can only fall to those left behind. "Who has not had acquaintances, friends, relatives who have voluntarily departed this world?" Schopenhauer asked, speaking from personal experience. "And everyone is supposed to think of them with revulsion, as criminals? I say no and no again!"[18] Back in Danzig where the Schopenhauers hailed from, if a person committed suicide at home, it was forbidden to remove them by the front door. Instead the body was lowered by pulleys from the window. The window frame, tainted by association, was then ritually burned.[19]

Much as we might admire Schopenhauer for his anti-superstitious, nonjudgmental attitude toward suicide, we might still urge him to apply the emergency brakes. To some, the mixture of Humean liberty, on the one hand, and Schopenhauerian pessimism, on the other, will seem like a deadly cocktail. We are granted an almost unrestricted right to take our own lives, which, given the conditions of our existence as Schopenhauer has so far described them, we appear also to have a strong motive to exercise.

Luckily, and perhaps surprisingly, Schopenhauer opposed this line of thought. "Suicide," he firmly wrote, "is not a solution."[20] Moreover, he criticized other schools of thought for their failure to stanch it. For instance, to its discredit, the ancient Greco-Roman school of Stoicism was logically committed to recommending suicide, he argued. Like all eudaemonistic schools, Stoicism sought to work out the constituents of a good life, and it came to the conclusion that such a life involved cultivating the virtues that can help us to manage adversity and reduce our own sufferings. However, since on Schopenhauer's view suffering is essential to life—and the Stoics would not entirely disagree—the only way completely to eliminate suffering is, of course, to eliminate life itself. "It is completely contradictory to want to live without suffering," Schopenhauer explained. "The Stoics are forced to include in their guide for a blessed life . . . a recommendation for suicide in the case of excessive and incurable bodily suffering incapable of being philosophized away with principles and inferences, just as oriental despots include a fine vial of poison among their splendid jewels and utensils."[21] If Schopenhauer wanted to avert the same conclusion, he would have to adopt a different stance from the one that he attributed to the Stoics.

His initial attempt was on psychological grounds. Although Schopenhauer stood by his pessimistic picture of the world, he was under no illusion that a philosophical argument, however convincing, is likely to affect people's basic will to live. The fear of death is almost entirely unshakable in most people: "the horrors of death . . . [are] nevertheless considerable; they stand so to speak as guards before the exit gate."[22] Even if someone intellectually accepted an argument for suicide on the grounds of philosophical pessimism, therefore, in practice it was unlikely that they would follow it through to the bitter end.[23]

In his second attempt to caution against suicide, Schopenhauer departed from Hume. While both were unconvinced by the standard moral arguments, Schopenhauer nevertheless proposed other ethical grounds for discouraging suicide. In his briefest formulation of these grounds, he said: "It lies in the fact that suicide is counter to achieving the highest moral goal insofar as it substitutes a merely illusory redemption from this world of misery for the real one."[24] When a person contemplates suicide, according to Schopenhauer, what they really seek is not an end to life as such, but rather an end to living miserably. This subtle difference may not even be clear to the person themselves; if only there were an obvious way to end misery in life, then they wouldn't leap to consider ending life altogether. Schopenhauer proposed that misery could always be ended by stepping off the cycle of desire in which it is rooted. In fact, he thought, this very uprooting of the source of our misery may be prompted by the same suffering that leads a person to consider suicide in the first place. In their intolerable misery, a suicidal person is on the verge of a profound insight into life—namely, that it is plagued by pain and suffering—except suicide, in Schopenhauer's view, is the wrong way to follow this insight through. They are, he says, "like a sick person who, having started undergoing a painful operation that could cure him completely, does not allow it to be completed and would rather stay sick."[25] For this reason, there was only one form of suicide that Schopenhauer could possibly bring himself to admire on ethical grounds: "It is the death by voluntary starvation that emerges at the highest levels of asceticism."[26] In this case, suicide is the logical outcome of having stepped off the cycle of desire for good. But even with an ethical form of suicide in view, Schopenhauer still maintained an unjudgmental attitude toward suicide in general. Suicide on any grounds other than asceticism is closer to a tragic mistake than an offence, unwise rather than immoral, and it was therefore "a long way from this error to a crime, which is what the Christian clergy want to make it out to be."[27]

How well Schopenhauer applied the emergency brakes to his views on suicide is of course debatable, and he knew it.[28] More than most, he understood that the causes of suicide are various, deeply personal, and often tragically unpreventable. He did not underestimate the influence of severe mental anguish, and how a mood of excessive despair, even if fleeting, can vanquish every other opposing consideration, including the fear of death itself. "This becomes especially noticeable in those who are driven to suicide by purely pathological and deep depression," he wrote. "It costs them no self-overcoming at all, they do not need to make a run at it, but instead as soon as their appointed sentry leaves them alone for two minutes, they quickly make an end of their life."[29]

Understandably, Schopenhauer returned to the motives, metaphysics, and morals of suicide throughout his life. He gathered his final thoughts in *Parerga and Paralipomena* with an essay titled, like Hume's, "On Suicide." But he began to develop the core of his views much earlier, including several notebook entries from the years even before *The World and Will and Representation* was first published.[30] These decades of reflection were not wasted; the result was something of a memorial to his father's sad demise. Schopenhauer discovered a philosophical position on suicide that was neither judgmental nor encouraging, striking the right balance between compassion and commiseration. Should we end it all? No, he answered. But if we did, should we be shamed and blamed for it? Equally, no.

:::

The tragic loss of a loved one appears elsewhere in Schopenhauer's philosophy. Almost as a companion to his theory of laughter,

Schopenhauer proposed a novel theory of weeping. To illustrate his theory, he picked the following poignant example: "Even if age and illness had made life a misery to the father, and his helplessness had made him a heavy burden to the son, the son will nonetheless weep bitterly over the death of his father."[31] Whether or not this detail was consciously autobiographical, it sheds yet another light by which to read Schopenhauer's response to the death of his father.

Though they are opposites, laughing and crying are in fact related, according to Schopenhauer. First, they both appear to be distinctively human.[32] We may see nonhuman animals in states of joy and delight, or pain and misery, but rarely, if ever, do we see them laughing or crying. Second, although they are spontaneous and involuntary reactions, at least when they are genuine, laughing and crying are still not quite the same as purely physical reflexes such as flinching from bodily pain.[33] They are in some way mediated by the mind. It is natural to connect these two points: there is something unique to human minds that enables a special class of spontaneous responses.

In fact, on Schopenhauer's theory, it is *two* essential human capacities that combine to make weeping possible: compassion and imagination. "*Weeping*," says Schopenhauer in his briefest formulation, "is *compassion for ourselves*."[34] When we cry, we are imagining our pain from the outside, and we take pity on ourselves. We are not immediately reacting to the pain and misery that we are crying about, as if we were merely flinching; we are reacting to the *idea* of our pain. Rather than being reflexive, weeping is reflective.

This would explain a few things. It explains, for a start, the two previous observations about weeping, namely, that only humans, with their advanced powers of reflection, are capable of weeping, and that it is different from an immediate physical reaction. It would also explain why an immensely painful event might not make us cry, at least not at first, while a much less painful event can still reduce us to tears. It depends, crucially, on whether we have an opportunity to reflect on the matter. There are some events so overwhelming or so quick that, at the time, there just isn't even the right moment to reflect on them.

Another instance of delayed crying is the way that children sometimes cry. "Children in pain," Schopenhauer wrote, "usually only weep when someone pities them, which is to say not because of the pain but rather because of their idea of the pain."[35] It's a common sight: a child falls and shows all the right physical reflexes—bracing before they hit the ground, wincing shortly afterward—but whether they cry or not seems to be optional. If no one around them reacts, they might simply pick themselves up and carry on, depending on how hurt they are. If, however, an adult comes over to comfort them, suddenly they may start to see their fall through the eyes of someone who cares, and only then come the waterworks. To Schopenhauer, this sort of delayed crying in children is not a cunning ploy for more attention, as it might uncharitably be interpreted, but rather an early exercise in imaginative self-love. It is not even exclusive to children, as shown by the following news story that Schopenhauer included in the second volume of *The World as Will and Representation*: "I might include an anecdote from the English paper, the *Herald*, of 16 July, 1836, that supports my explanation. A client, upon hearing his lawyer present his case to the court, burst into tears and cried out: 'I did not know I suffered half so much until I heard it here today!'"[36]

Weeping therefore requires two of humanity's finest qualities, reflection and compassion, albeit turned inward. For this reason, the sight of somebody weeping is likely to encourage fellow feelings of sympathy and mercy among human beings: "it can disarm anger because we feel that anyone who can still weep must also necessarily be capable of love, i.e. of compassion for other people."[37] When we weep, we are at our most human, and we thereby transmit our humanity, almost irresistibly, to those around us.

There is, however, a less appealing way to present Schopenhauer's theory of weeping: Is it not just self-pity? A test for this would be how Schopenhauer deals with cases of weeping for others. Does Schopenhauer maintain that even when we appear to weep for others, really we weep for ourselves? At first, it doesn't look promising:

> When we are moved to weep by someone else's suffering rather than our own, it is because we either vividly imagine ourselves in the place of the person who is suffering, or we see in the person's

fate the lot of all humanity, and thus primarily our own, which means that in a very roundabout way we are still really only weeping for ourselves.[38]

On this analysis, it sounds as though we make someone else's misfortune about ourselves: we take what has happened to them, imagine it happening to us, and only then do we get upset about it. But, seen from another perspective, even this procedure is a little nobler than pure self-pity. It at least involves imaginative participation in someone else's suffering. It is not pity for oneself specifically, but rather for the tragic fate that we all share with the rest of humanity: "He is mainly overcome with compassion for the lot of all humanity . . . for the fact that every life, however ambitious and productive, must be extinguished and come to nothing."[39] Weeping over our common fate is less self-centered than, for instance, weeping over the impact that their misfortune has had on our life. As Schopenhauer says, "It is not his loss that causes the mourner to weep: he would be ashamed of such egoistic tears."

It is precisely this observation about weeping for the fate of humanity, in fact, that brings Schopenhauer to the example of the tears shed by a beleaguered son over the loss of his enfeebled father: "Above all, he sees his own lot in that of all humanity, and the more so the closer he was to the one who died, and thus most of all if it was his father. Even if age and illness had made life a misery to the father, and his helplessness had made him a heavy burden to the son, the son will nonetheless weep bitterly over the death of his father."[40] There is therefore a lot in these remarks to unpack. First, Schopenhauer assumes that a son is closest to his father, which is both unsubstantiated and ambiguous—it could mean anything from tender intimacy to mere similarity. Second, this particular father has become a burden to himself and his son alike, such that, for both, death could be seen as a source of relief. Third, even though death relieves the father's suffering, the son still cries bitterly, and rightly so. (It is left unsaid by Schopenhauer whether the father in question dies of the illness that plagues him or something else.) Taken together, Schopenhauer's theory of weeping makes it possible, on the one hand, to view Heinrich Floris's death as being in his own interest—albeit not in his ultimate interest, if Schopenhauer's argument against suicide from a higher perspective is correct—and yet, on the other, to experience it as every bit the tragedy that it was.

∷

If this is the manner in which Schopenhauer mourned his father, then it may seem to us like a rather abstract lament. Instead of weeping over the tragic fate of all humankind, why not weep for Heinrich Floris, the man, directly and specifically? There can be no doubt that Schopenhauer venerated his father in death: in 1828, he considered dedicating a second edition of *The World as Will and Representation* to Heinrich Floris, and even drafted a preface filled with fulsome praise, before he opted instead for the scathing attack on Hegel and his ilk.[41] In life, however, it clearly wasn't always easy to be his father's son.

From September to December 1804, in the months before his father's death, Arthur worked as an apprentice to another one of Heinrich Floris's associates, Jakob Kabrun, who was based back in Danzig.[42] Kabrun, like the Schopenhauers, was a Danzig institution; like Heinrich Floris, he was a donor to the English chapel at which Richard Jameson had formerly ministered, and even had a closer connection to Jameson due to his Scottish roots, "Kabrun" being a Germanification of Cockburn. Arthur evidently liked Kabrun: later, he sent him an inscribed copy of his first published work.[43] Johanna joined Arthur in Danzig to reconnect with family and friends, and brought Adele along with her, leaving Heinrich Floris all alone in Hamburg. (It is possible that this is what Arthur referred to with his later remark that she "gave parties while he was wasting away.") After the Schopenhauers were fully reunited again in Hamburg, Arthur started his second apprenticeship, under the local businessman and senator Martin Johann Jenisch. Training for the family business was, after all, Arthur's end of the bargain when he accepted the terms of the grand tour, which he even honored for two years after Heinrich Floris's death.

There are two extant letters from Heinrich Floris to Arthur during the latter's Danzig apprenticeship. Both reveal the kind of pressure that Heinrich Floris never failed to apply. The first is dated October 23, 1804. "My dear son," it begins, "now that you have given me your written word to learn to write well and fluently, and to calculate perfectly, I will rely on you to do so, with one further request: that you will also manage to bring yourself to walk straight, as other people do, in order that you will not get round shoulders, which look horrible."[44] Just as he had done in his letters a year ago, when his son languished miserably in Wimbledon, Heinrich Floris continued to obsess over his son's handwriting and posture. In the same letter, he declined to send Arthur his new flute and suggested that he make do with his old one, albeit only for impressing his Danziger hosts, rather than—the thought never occurred to Heinrich Floris—spending any time recreationally. He encouraged Arthur to continue working on his language skills (French, English, and German—modern, then, not classical), for "I should prefer you not to return to Mr. Jenisch's office here in the capacity of a learner, and now God be with you."[45]

The other letter is dated November 20, 1804. Posture was once again high on Heinrich Floris's agenda, and this time he had a slightly sinister, if jocular, suggestion: "And as for walking and sitting straight, I advise you to ask anyone who associates with you to strike you a blow when you are found to have neglected this important matter. This is how princely children are treated, and they do not shy away from the pain for long, lest they appear as louts all their lives."[46] He also advised Arthur to hold back on dancing and horse-riding lessons until his handwriting was perfected; his lettering was still far too large and loopy, almost as if German wasn't his first language—partly Heinrich Floris's own fault for educating his son abroad so much. While in Danzig, Arthur was confirmed at Saint Mary's Church, where he had been baptized; but even so, Heinrich Floris added at the end of his letter, once he was back in Hamburg he would still attend the theology lectures at Dr. Runge's school and "always behave modestly, morally, and diligently. Adieu."[47]

Thus, Arthur continued to endure all the pressures of being the first and only son. Heinrich Floris fully intended to follow through with their agreement, however Arthur might have felt about it.

But this is not quite the impression of Schopenhauer's father that one might have got from the fragments of his unpublished book dedication:

> You were mindful of the case [i.e., Arthur] that it might not be suitable for tilling the soil or for otherwise using its power through a mechanical vocation to ensure its subsistence. And, proud republican, you appear to have foreseen that your son could not have the talent . . . to grovel and cringe before ministers and councillors in order to beg sordidly for a morsel of bread that is to be paid for by hard labour. . . .
>
> . . . That I was able to develop and apply the powers, given to me by nature, to that for which they were destined; that I was able to follow my inborn impulse and to think and work for innumerable people, whereas no one did anything for me; for all this I thank you, my father, I thank your activity, your good sense, your thrift and thoughtfulness for the future. . . . And so let my gratitude do the only thing it can do for you who has finished; let it carry your name as far as my name is able to carry it.[48]

Unless read carefully and in context, this dedication could give the impression that Heinrich Floris had actively encouraged Arthur to pursue his real vocation in life. Clearly, that was never so. It's true that he didn't raise Arthur to live by the sweat of his brow, but Heinrich Floris nevertheless expected his son to earn a living; and certainly he meant to impart all the necessary skills for garnering the good graces of the rich and powerful. Schopenhauer's independent spirit *might* have come from his father's parenting style, but the effects of Heinrich Floris's death, rather than any efforts he made in life, would make a far greater material contribution. In truth, Heinrich Floris had raised a free thinker by accident—by feeding, then starving, his son's curiosity about the world before he exited it. Evidently, if the final line is anything to go by, Schopenhauer's drive to become renowned as a philosopher was partly fueled by the obligation he felt to keep his family name alive by other means.

CHAPTER 4

A Philosopher in the Asylum

How Schopenhauer Humanized Madness

Some of Schopenhauer's long-standing fears intensified toward the end of his life. Death itself didn't scare him, on philosophical grounds, but he did fear how it might happen. If he somehow managed to avoid dying in obscurity, a strong possibility for most of his career, then he feared his legacy would only be mangled and misappropriated by lesser minds. He was afraid of an agonizing, drawn-out, undignified death; he was gravely afraid of being buried alive. None of these things were to happen—though, just to be sure about the latter, he did make arrangements for an unusually long stay in the mortuary.[1]

Above all, he was terrified of losing his mind, which was not an unreasonable fear in his case. His philosophical hero, Immanuel Kant, had ended his days in a state of senile dementia, not even a shadow of the great mind he had once been. The poor mental health that (suspectedly) drove his father to suicide did not help matters either: he was convinced he had inherited the same disposition. Fortunately, aside from his acute bouts of depression and paranoia—for he wasn't completely wrong about his family inheritance—Schopenhauer's moments of madness were not only temporary but even mildly charming. Once, he was spotted by the keeper of the conservatory at the Dresden Zwinger pacing around and posing questions to himself about the mysterious inner being of plant life. When the keeper approached this peculiar gentleman to ask who he was, Schopenhauer replied: "Yes, if you could tell me who I am, I should be greatly indebted."[2]

The keeper was not making a philosophical point, presumably, but he happened to strike upon the right question. Schopenhauer's own theory of madness was all about the integrity of one's sense of self. The seeds for this view went as far back as his university days, and his regular trips to the local asylum.

: : :

Schopenhauer started university in October 1809. It was a pivotal year for other reasons too. Having turned twenty-one in February, he received his share of the estate that his father had left behind. The other two-thirds were allocated to Johanna and Adele, who had already moved, without Arthur, from Hamburg to Weimar three years before. The inheritance did not make the family rich, as Johanna was prone to point out, but it did make them comfortable.[3] More importantly, it allowed them to pursue entirely different paths in life from the ones they were on while Heinrich Floris still lived: the obedient wife in Johanna's case and the merchant's apprentice in Arthur's. Since they no longer needed to live *by* their talents, they could now afford to live *for* them. Johanna would fulfill her lifelong ambition of becoming an author, while Adele, receiving her education exclusively in the form of her mother's literary salons, through which she befriended Ottilie von Goethe, daughter-in-law of Johann Wolfgang, would go on later in life to publish volumes of poetry, short stories, a novel, and beautiful cut-out silhouettes.

Arthur disapproved. He regarded his female family's newfound vocations as frivolous. Johanna in particular was not playing the part of the grieving widow to his satisfaction, even though he was just as liberated by their shared tragedy. Through her connections and encouragement, he would leave his Hamburg apprenticeship in May 1807. Doing so enabled him to embark on the more serious business of contemplating life itself, which, he thought, was a nobler pursuit than Johanna's and Adele's artistic trifles. "Life is an unpleasant business; I have resolved to spend it reflecting upon it," he would soon write to the revered poet Christoph Martin Wieland (another close friend of his mother's).[4]

If Arthur's attitude toward Johanna and Adele should seem hypocritically sexist, that is because it was. He was, presumably, embittered by the fact that his mother and sister had seemed to put the past behind them so swiftly while he lagged behind. But also at the root of his hypocrisy were deeply mixed feelings, of gratitude and guilt, about his own portion of the inheritance. Without it, and by extension without his father's death, he could never have sustained himself as an independent philosopher; it was, he later reflected, his "consecrated treasure."[5] It came with the responsibility to be used wisely and not frittered away: "I would therefore regard it as the most ungrateful and unworthy misuse of so rare a fate, if I were to spend possibly half my income on tailors, milliners, and dealers in fancy goods in the expectation, so often disappointed, of living a life that is more than enjoyable."[6] He allowed himself to feel, almost mystically, that he had a vocation in life that went beyond his personal existence and even, it seems, his personal happiness. To him it was as if this blessed inheritance was divinely ordained to bankroll his higher purpose.

An insight into his state of mind while he still wasted his talents on his apprenticeship is captured in a fragment from one of the few extant letters he sent to Johanna during this period, given her lifelong practice of quickly destroying them. It was prompted in response to a protracted letter from her on October 19, 1806, detailing the occupation of Weimar by Napoleon's troops after their triumph at the Battle of Jena. Arthur's tone in his reply was bleakly brooding to say the least (he was still a teenager at the time, after all):

> Everything is annulled by the passage of time. The minutes, the countless atoms of small details into which every action decays are the worms that consume everything great and bold. The monster, ordinary life, pushes down everything that strives upwards. There is nothing serious in life, because the dust is not worth the trouble.[7]

Naturally, missives such as these alarmed Johanna. Arthur was not the only one who worried about, as she put it, "the melancholy brooding that you received as the inheritance from your father."[8] At first, she hoped he might simply cheer up over time or at least not get any worse than usual, until another alarming (now nonextant) letter from him on March 28, 1807, clearly warranted an intervention. After a period of reflection, she wrote back with her own reawakened doubts about both of their recent life choices:

> You are undecided by nature, I perhaps only too quick, too resolute, too inclined, perhaps, to choose the apparently most wonderful of two paths, as I did when determining my whereabouts, by instead of going to my hometown to friends and relatives, as almost any woman would have done in my position, choosing the almost completely foreign Weimar.[9]

Johanna and Arthur had faced totally different dilemmas in the first place. Johanna's choice was between an old life she knew all too well versus an exciting new one that she had once envisaged as a child but until now never dreamed she could actually achieve. Arthur, by contrast, was still deliberating about what sort of start to make in life.

Always preferring to look ahead, Johanna did not ruminate on the past for too long. She turned to her friend Karl Ludwig Fernow, an arts critic and professor at the University of Jena, for help with a plan of action. Fernow's journey, she thought, could be something of an inspiration to Arthur, as Fernow too had abandoned a professional apprenticeship for a life of the mind, and not without some difficulty. Johanna was right; when Arthur received and read a letter of encouragement from Fernow, he burst into tears.[10] Henceforth, the offer was always there: if Arthur really wanted out, he only needed to ask.

While offering this lifeline, however, Johanna felt it necessary to remind Arthur about the arduous, unglamourous, impecunious life of a scholar, thereby channeling his father's spirit one last time. Additionally, there were still some foundations first to be laid: until that point, Arthur had followed Heinrich Floris's curriculum for a would-be merchant, but if he wanted to attend university, then he would need to study the academic syllabus of a German gymnasium. He failed his first attempt: on December 23, 1807, he was effectively expelled from Gotha gymnasium for the grave offense of writing a biting satirical poem about one of its teachers. For his next attempt, he decided it was best to study in Weimar, which prompted Johanna immediately to set some ground rules. While she had been willing to use her connections to help him escape his misery in Hamburg, the two of them were still not getting along. His manners were not enough like hers, and his temperament too much like his father's, for cohabitation ever to work. He was wisely lodged with one of his tutors, the classicist Franz Passow, under the artful cover that it would fast-track his Latin and Greek.

Eventually, Arthur matriculated at the University of Göttingen on October 9, 1809. He was nominally a medical student, though he studied widely in science and history during his short time there. His notebooks reveal that the courses he took profoundly reoriented the future direction of his thinking. Arnold Heeren's lectures on ethnography introduced him to southeast Asian cultures and religions, where he was especially intrigued by traditions deriving from classical Indian thought, Buddhism in particular. Johann Friedrich Blumenbach, in his lectures on physiology, spoke somberly about the horror and cruelty of vivisection, leaving a permanent impression on Schopenhauer's sympathies toward nonhuman animals.[11] Nevertheless, he did not stay at Göttingen for long either, due to the influence of yet another impressive teacher: Gottlob Ernst Schulze. Noting his student's aptitude for metaphysics, Schulze advised Schopenhauer to study works by Plato and Kant, thus nudging him closer to the trinity of influences on his mature philosophy. As he would write in 1816: "I do not believe my doctrine could have come about before the Upanishads, Plato and Kant could cast their rays simultaneously into the mind of one man."[12]

These first few semesters, then, decisively changed Schopenhauer's trajectory. In April 1811, while on vacation from Göttingen, he was back in Weimar and engaging in the correspondence with

Wieland that culminated with his declaration that he should devote himself to reflecting on the unpleasant business that is life. "Young man, I now understand your nature," Wieland wrote back: "Stick to philosophy."[13] Acting as a mediator between Arthur and Johanna—who, despite their financially comfortable position, still thought it wiser for her son to take a more lucrative course of study—Wieland gave his commanding blessing that the young man was to become a philosopher. But to do so, first it was necessary to move to Berlin.

:::

Berlin was Johann Gottlieb Fichte's city. A founding faculty member of its new university, which had opened less than a year before Schopenhauer's arrival, Fichte was its top-ranking philosophy professor. His journey to the top, however, had not been straightforward.

Like Schopenhauer later, the young Fichte had been willing to travel to progress his philosophical career. In 1791, under a cloud of acrimony, Fichte resigned from a private tutoring job in Leipzig and journeyed eventually to Königsberg, specifically to meet with Immanuel Kant.[14] For his trouble, Fichte only managed to have one personal consultation with his philosophical idol, on July 4, who was not immediately impressed. He nevertheless remained in Königsberg for the next six weeks or so, intensively working on a manuscript, *Attempt at a Critique of All Revelation*. Its title clearly, if cautiously, aped those of Kant's recent groundbreaking trilogy of works: *Critique of Pure Reason* (1781/1787), *Critique of Practical Reason* (1788), and *Critique of Judgement* (1790). Despite what it might seem to imply, Fichte's first major opus did not make a critical case against all religious revelation, but rather a conditional argument for its very possibility; in true Kantian style, to "critique" here meant to confine a phenomenon within its appropriate boundaries. By the time the manuscript was complete, however, Fichte had run out of money, and so he asked Kant for a loan to cover the costs of his return journey to Saxony. Instead, Kant shrewdly advised Fichte to generate the funds for himself by selling his manuscript to Kant's own publisher, Hartung, and he even helped to secure another tutoring job for Fichte in Kraków. In

1792, Fichte's book was published with Hartung anonymously—for reasons unclear—and so it was only natural for the public to assume that the book was the latest installment of Kant's own critical writings, rather than the work of some unknown pretender.

As it happened, in the last decade of his sane life, Kant really had embarked on a series of writings applying his critical method to religious matters, gathered in his ambitious 1793 collection *Religion Within the Boundaries of Mere Reason*. Public semi-awareness of Kant's work on these topics further encouraged the misattribution of Fichte's anonymous book to him. (To Schopenhauer's later condemnation, Kant's late works on religion were suppressed by the state under Frederick William II on October 4, 1794, on the trumped up charges of "distorting and disparaging several principal and fundamental doctrines of Holy Scripture and of Christianity."[15] The censorious zeal of the Prussian authorities was perhaps one genuine reason for Fichte to have chosen to publish anonymously.) After a positive review that attributed Fichte's work to Kant, Kant was forced publicly to deny authorship in a letter to the editors: "I have neither in writing nor in conversation . . . taken the smallest part in the work of this gifted man, and thus see it as my duty that the honour due to it should be left undiminished to him to whom it is owed."[16] To have been mistaken for the master was one thing; to be complimented by him on one's gifts was quite another. Fichte couldn't have asked for a better publicity stunt.

It set him off on a starry academic trajectory, including a professorship at Jena, later the awarding university of Schopenhauer's doctoral degree and fast becoming the training ground for a new generation of post-Kantian thinkers, with F. W. J. Schelling joining in 1798 and G. W. F. Hegel in 1801. But Fichte's career almost ended as suddenly as it had begun when in April 1799 he was dismissed from his post on the grounds of encouraging atheism. This time, Kant would not come to the rescue. If anything, he only made matters worse with yet another public letter, now denouncing Fichte for presuming that he had completed Kant's philosophical system, which Kant never considered incomplete in the first place.[17] (This would not stop other post-Kantians, Schopenhauer included, from laying claim to being, in some way or other, Kant's one true heir.)

At the turn of the century Fichte was forced to move once again, and so he reestablished himself in Berlin.

:::

Despite his ups and downs, or perhaps because of them, Fichte was the main draw to Berlin for any young philosopher. Schopenhauer arrived with high hopes, but a later reflection on this period sums up the reality: "In 1811 I moved to Berlin in the expectation that in Fichte I should become acquainted with a genuine philosopher and great mind. But this *a priori* veneration was soon changed into disdain and derision."[18]

Schopenhauer was, at least, an attentive student: his notes on Fichte's lecture course through the winter of 1811–12 ("On the Facts of Consciousness, and on the Doctrine of Sciences") run for hundreds of pages, forming the bulk of his carefully preserved student notebooks. As was usual for the time, Schopenhauer's style of note-taking mainly consisted of transcribing the lecturer's words. Fichte's lecturing, by contrast, was unusual, pioneering even, in that he didn't dictate from a preprepared script, meaning that there was no undisputed master text for his students to refer to. Though small in stature, he was by all accounts a charismatic lecturer, with a ruddy complexion, bristling hair, and piercing eyes. Schopenhauer quickly became irritated by Fichte's sagacious-sounding but, in his view, ultimately empty phrases. He registered his disapproval in private interjections in his notes, marked with the word "Ego." Schopenhauer's insertions of "Ego" only became more frequent—and exasperated, and derogatory—as Fichte's course went on. When one of his classmates, Johann Baptist Reinert (who became a close friend of Fichte's family and even tutored his son Immanuel), loaned Schopenhauer some notes from Fichte's 1812 lecture course on jurisprudence, he copied and annotated them as follows:

> Morality therefore is concerned with the certainty of something in the future and with certainty that everything is developed only for the future.—
> [Schop.] *Ego. We are only manure for future melons.*

The world has as its plan the education of man for morality. It is a world of preparation and formation:
[Schop.] *Manure!*
it exists only for the sake of its purpose
[Schop.] *Manure!* . . .
The moral will in this life always has as its aim morality outside itself: this
[Schop.] *namely a smell of manure*
is the sure criterion.[19]

The style may have been profane, but the substance was philosophical. With his repeated cries of "manure," Schopenhauer was not referring to Fichte or his philosophy. He objected, rather, to Fichte's claim that the world exists for some lofty higher purpose, namely, the moral education of humanity. On the contrary, Schopenhauer insisted, all humanity is but fertilizer for future fruit: *we* are the manure.

At one point, Schopenhauer is said to have been sufficiently provoked by Fichte to engage him in a "lengthy argument" in the middle of a lecture. For the most part, however, he aired his grievances safely within the confines of his notebook.[20] One of his earliest, longest, and most animated annotations concerns a passing remark by Fichte on the topic of madness. According to Schopenhauer's notes, it occurred within the first two hours of Fichte's introduction to his lectures in the autumn of 1811.[21]

Fichte started at the very beginning: with an attempt to define philosophy itself. For this, he needed first to make a series of distinctions. Since philosophy is, or ought to be, a kind of knowledge, he distinguished between two kinds of knowledge: scientific and historical. Scientific knowledge derives from reason and delivers the laws that govern the world and our experience of it. Fichte's eventual point would be that philosophy is this kind of knowledge, indeed that it is the science of all sciences. Historical knowledge, by contrast, is transmitted by communication, and is thus secondhand. It is itself subdivided into two further kinds: historical knowledge that cannot be confirmed by our own perceptions (e.g., we cannot now witness Julius Caesar's assassination) and the kind that can (e.g., we can repeat Aristotle's dissections of cuttlefish to see if he was correct about their physiology). There are then two different kinds of perception too: outer perceptions, which correspond to objective, external matters, and inner perceptions, such as dreams, visions, and the effects of madness, which are purely subjective. Inner perceptions shouldn't really be counted as knowledge at all, according to (Schopenhauer's) Fichte, because they can never be repeated and verified by others. It seemed to Fichte, furthermore, that when subjects have such perceptions, they are not even proper subjects at all, for proper subjects "must be capable of experiencing the same modifications" as one another.[22] They need to be, at bottom, the same sort of subject. Visionaries and madmen are eccentric subjects, and so on this basis they are to be excluded from the community of genuine knowers.

At this point in the lecture Schopenhauer had already begun to lose his patience. "This is obscure," he noted to himself:

> and not adequately explained, yet it may be that I failed to catch a few remarks, for *Fichte's* delivery is indeed clear and he speaks slowly. However, for me he often dwells too long on things that are easy to understand and repeats them in different words so that one's attention wearies at having to listen at greater length to something already understood, and in this way one is distracted.[23]

Fichte paused to anticipate a response to the claims he had just made. Aren't geniuses, like madmen, eccentric subjects too? And yet, we don't see this as a reason to disregard geniuses as unreliable. If anything, we credit them with authority in the same breath that we prize them for their rarity. It would follow, then, that experiencing the same things as everyone else is not a necessary condition of being taken seriously as a knower after all, since the capacity to have unique experiences is precisely what interests us about geniuses. The objection was merely a pretense, however; Fichte already had a counterargument. Even geniuses are, like the rest of us, human beings first: "A rational and ethical man; let everyone first become this, and then we will speak of genius."[24] Geniuses may well be specially modified subjects, but they are specially modified *human* subjects. To supplement his point, Fichte stressed that geniuses are exceedingly rare anyway, and much that passes for genius is, in fact, sheer madness. While geniuses are human, if also superhuman, madmen are subhuman, according to Fichte: "The two deviate from the customary standpoint of man; genius . . . is divine and is far above that point of view, but madness is animal and is below that point."[25] Hence why genius is rightly revered, and madness deplored.

Even as a lowly student, Schopenhauer was unconvinced. He was suspicious, first, of Fichte's assumption that intelligence is an unbroken line ascending from animals through humans to the gods. And even if he were to accept that, it was not obvious to him that the mad belong at the lower end of this spectrum. A clever dog, he noted, has more in common with a person of average intelligence than with one of unsound mind. (Schopenhauer's lifelong personal affection for dogs was almost certainly playing a role in this argument that promotes their intellectual powers.) Conversely, the madman has more in common, superficially at least, with a person of genius than with even a very clever canine. Characteristically, and disarmingly, Schopenhauer defended both animals and the insane at the expense of the mediocre human.

Schopenhauer seemed to base his stance on a mixture of casual observations (i.e., the general behavior of a clever dog, perhaps his own), on the one hand, and some romanticized notions of the bond between genius and madness, on the other, which he had picked up from literary and philosophical sources. He quoted Seneca: "There has been no great mind without an admixture of madness"; he pointed to Shakespeare's *King Lear*, "a picture of madness with a touch of genius," and Goethe's *Torquato Tasso*, "a picture of genius with a touch of madness."[26] To supplement these—at best—anecdotal forms of evidence, Schopenhauer added some provisional theoretical reasoning. Like animals, he proposed, "the man of sound intelligence is firmly encased in the bodily conditions of our consciousness and thinking."[27] In other words, an animal and an average human being are alike in intelligence insofar as their quantity of intellect is strictly proportional to the amount required for fulfilling their basic physical needs. The madman and the genius, by contrast, both display an intelligence disconnected from their needs, but for different reasons. The genius has intellect in sheer abundance, and consistently demonstrates it through piercing visionary insights. The madman's thinking, by contrast, is deranged and dysfunctional, making it, nevertheless, occasionally flash with apparent brilliance as it violently tears itself away from its service to the body.

This rationalization notwithstanding, Schopenhauer's association of madness with genius may seem to us just as questionable, if not as derogatory, as Fichte's dehumanizing association of it with animals. Madness is not, after all, a condition to be glorified. With his next move, however, Schopenhauer set himself apart from Fichte in yet another way. Unsatisfied with mere theory, he went in search of the only place to find answers.

:::

Schopenhauer began visiting patients in the psychiatric wing of Berlin's Charité hospital.[28] The hospital was already a century old, but psychiatry as we know it was still in its infancy: the German word *Psychiatrie*, from which other languages would get their versions, had been coined by Johann Christian Reil only a few years before Schopenhauer arrived in Berlin.[29] It combined the Greek words for soul (*psukē*) and healing (*iatreia*). A distinctive feature of the German approach to this new official branch of medicine was its close ties to university research. At the time that Schopenhauer visited, the Charité was not yet associated with the university; by 1828, however, it would be (and still is). Perhaps the most widely recognized name to go on to study there would be Alois Alzheimer. Decades before that, however, Schopenhauer was conducting his own informal inquiries.

Minus the therapeutic intent, it could be said that Schopenhauer pioneered the talking method later associated with Freud, for that's all he appears to have done: he simply spoke with the patients. The people that he met were indeed often fragile, afflicted, and disturbed, but, contrary to what Fichte had professed, not to his mind subhuman. As he later reflected in his notebook: "Often when observing the *insane* I do not find . . . that with them *the best in man* suffers."[30] It is clear from their occasional appearances in his later published writings, too, that these conversations with the insane had a lasting and shaping influence on all of Schopenhauer's subsequent thinking about mental health and illness.

This is not to say, however, that he managed to transcend all of the assumptions of his day. For example, he once recalled a "completely imbecilic boy of about eleven years who lived in an asylum," to whom he had paid multiple visits:

> He was rational (since he could both speak and understand) but had a less developed understanding than many animals. Every time I visited he would stare at a monocle I wore around my neck: it reflected the windows of the room and the tops of the trees so that they appeared to be behind my neck. This he regarded with great surprise and joy every time I was there, and looked at the glass with unwavering astonishment: he could not understand the absolutely immediate causality of reflection.[31]

In the version of the story that he tells in his manuscript notes, Schopenhauer poignantly adds that the boy, incapable of grasping that the magical image captured in the monocle was a mere reflection, never turned around to see the trees themselves.[32]

In the first line, Schopenhauer seems to perpetuate the same dehumanizing comparison as Fichte: he claims that the boy was even less developed than an animal. But in fact, while any comparison of this sort is regrettable, Schopenhauer intended to make a slightly different point from Fichte's. He did not recall the boy as an example of *madness* at all, but rather—and this may only make matters worse—the "best example of stupidity that I have come across."[33] Stupidity, according to Schopenhauer, was a dysfunction not of reason, but of the understanding. By "the understanding" he meant the mental faculty that is responsible for perceiving causality: that is, why things are the way that they are. More specifically, then, the boy who marveled at the trees that were captured in Schopenhauer's monocle had failed to understand the causality of reflection, an ability that even some nonhuman animals seem to demonstrate. Schopenhauer's evidence that nonhuman animals can understand different forms of causality was often, as ever, charmingly anecdotal:

> A short while ago, I had installed in my bedroom large curtains, reaching to the ground, of the sort that part in the middle when one draws the cord. In the morning upon arising, as I drew these for the first time, I noticed to my surprise that my very intelligent poodle stood there quite astounded, and looked around, upwards and sideways, for the cause of the phenomenon.[34]

Rather than change his mind about madness, then, Schopenhauer's meetings with the "imbecilic" boy only confirmed to him a claim that he had already made in his critical annotation to Fichte's remarks: "The weak-minded imbecile . . . is closer to the animal."[35] There is evidence that he never changed his mind about this view: though there were three editions of *The World as Will and Representation* in Schopenhauer's lifetime, including one as late as 1859, the year before his death, and though he made several changes, including substantial revisions and deletions, he never altered these remarks on the boy in the asylum.

He did, however, at least credit the boy with a different, and working, mental capacity. Philosophers in the Kantian tradition, like Schopenhauer, commonly distinguished the understanding from reason, as reflected in Schopenhauer's claim that although the boy failed to understand causality he was nonetheless perfectly rational. The boy's rationality was evident to Schopenhauer in his ability to hold a conversation at all. This is not to suggest that Schopenhauer thought rationality consists in speech itself. Rather, according to Schopenhauer, rationality consists in the ability to form, grasp, and follow the links in a logical chain of abstract thoughts, on which much language depends. It was this ability, he observed, that the mad, as distinct from the merely stupid, genuinely struggled with.

:::

Meeting with more psychiatric patients prevented Schopenhauer from drawing the overly simplistic conclusion that madness is the complete absence of reason. On the contrary, the evidence of rationality among the mad was to him so striking that it even raised the possibility that these patients were not insane at all:

> While we are speaking to them, the insane appear to be astonishingly rational in their looks and gestures, and it often seems to us as if they were pretending and had the advantage over us. Thus they have the complete use of their faculty of reason and their ailment is simply that they *do not speak the truth*.[36]

The problem, according to Schopenhauer, was that the insane could provide rich and cogent narrative histories of themselves, suggesting that the proper exercise of reason was within their grasp—but all of their stories were demonstrably, absurdly untrue. "It is so difficult to ask a mad person about his earlier life," he wrote. "The true and the false become increasingly blended in his memory."[37] Assuming that they were not simply barefaced liars, the insane appeared to be making earnest claims about invented versions of themselves.

It dawned on Schopenhauer that the connection between madness and memory must be important: "Might not *madness*," he conjectured, "consist in the *will having lost causality concerning cognition*? Consequently, might not *madness* be a mere derangement of *memory*?"[38] Again, it was not the case that the insane lacked memory, for they at least attempted to recall their past experiences. What they appeared to lack, rather, was controlled, accurate, and reliable use of this rational function. Considering how much of ourselves is made up of our past experiences, a dysfunction of this kind had significant ramifications for a person's ability to connect with themselves, the world, and other people.

This much had crystallized in Schopenhauer's mind by 1814, but in 1816 he finessed his working theory of madness once more, inspired once again by his own observations: "I thought for a long time that madness was really only a disease of the memory," he noted, "This, however, is not so, for many insane people have good memories."³⁹ He didn't doubt that madness must have something to do with memory, but he abandoned his initial assumption that it was primarily due to a lack of control. Many insane people, in his experience, controlled their memories very effectively—almost *too* effectively. Control over memory seemed, if anything, itself to play a role in the origin of madness. As a result, Schopenhauer finally settled on his official view, which he would present in *The World as Will and Representation*. Madness, he wrote, is "the *torn* thread of memory."⁴⁰

On this view, it was no accident that he discovered gaps, muddles, and even pure fictions in the personal stories spun by the insane. These "errors" were, in fact, well motivated, although still not conscious lies. They were rooted, Schopenhauer surmised, in a general unwillingness to commit unwanted experiences to memory, which was nothing extraordinary in itself:

> how loath we are to think of things that are detrimental to our interests, pride, or desires, how hard it is for us to decide to lay them before our intellect for a precise and serious examination, how readily we unconsciously break off or slink away from this study instead.⁴¹

For some, however, assimilating certain painful experiences becomes simply *too* difficult: "it reaches the point where the operation simply cannot be carried out,"⁴² leaving significant holes in their recollection that go on to be plugged with fictions and fantasies. Madness to Schopenhauer was, in short, a controlled but subconscious misuse of memory to conceal threatening facts about ourselves from ourselves.

From this point onward, Schopenhauer firmly stood by his memory-based theory of madness. A chapter in the 1844 edition of *The World as Will and Representation*, titled "On Madness," begins: "True mental health consists in perfect recollection of the past."⁴³ If we did not know better, this would be a highly perplexing claim, for the ability to forget—specifically those things that are worth forgetting—is surely also the sign of a healthy mind. His point, however, was that mental health consists in a reliable and accurate ability to recall, not *everything*, but the significant things that, for better or worse, make up who we are. A good few decades since his first visit to the Berlin Charité, he continued to illustrate his views by drawing on his own personal experiences of observing the insane:

> My own experience over many years has led me to suspect that madness emerges most frequently in actors. And how these people abuse their memories! Every day they learn a new role or refresh an old one: and these roles have no connection to each other, and every evening the actor needs to forget himself entirely to become someone completely different. This leads straight to madness.[44]

> I have presented the psychic origin of madness due to a great unhappiness as it affects someone who, to all other appearances, is healthy. With someone already strongly disposed to madness on somatic grounds, a very slight aggravation will be enough: so for instance I remember a person in a madhouse who had been a soldier and went mad because his officer addressed him in the third person.[45]

The soldier in question might have been Ernst Hoeffner of the Prussian Brigade, whom Schopenhauer had met in the Charité and later sent a copy of the Bible—a curious gift from an atheist. Hoeffner gave Schopenhauer some of his own written reflections on the nature of madness, which voiced the distress of someone torn from himself and the world: "There is nothing more dangerous," Hoeffner wrote, "than a human who is suddenly separated from all that wherein he sought and found his life."[46]

∴

Madness, thought Schopenhauer, sometimes made the difference between life and death. It descends upon us not only when our past is too painful to bear, but also when our passions might otherwise drive us to utter self-destruction. He offered the Shakespearean example of a doomed love affair that can only end in a double suicide, "unless nature saves the life by allowing madness to enter, which then wraps its veil around the consciousness of that hopeless state."[47] This self-protective mechanism is triggered whenever necessary.

In this respect, Schopenhauer was a precursor to the Austrian psychiatrist Sigmund Freud, father of modern psychoanalysis. Freud, too, put self-protective psychical mechanisms at the forefront of his thinking about mental dysfunction. He developed a theory of repression according to which thoughts, memories, and desires that we cannot admit to ourselves, because they are destructive, traumatic, humiliating, or forbidden, are buried deep in the unconscious mind. Although Freud often denied any immediate influence, even Schopenhauer's wording clearly foreshadowed his theory:

> If . . . certain events or circumstances are fully repressed from the intellect because the will cannot bear the sight of them, and if the gap that then arises is patched up with some invention due to the need for coherence—then there is madness.[48]

The difference with Freud was not only that he sought to treat this illness, but also that, to do so, he developed various methods of plumbing the psychological depths of the unconscious mind, including dream analysis and the famous "talking cure." So far as we know, Schopenhauer never delved in this therapeutic direction.

Freud was only four years old when Schopenhauer died in 1860. In fin de siècle Vienna, however, when Freud's career was ascending, Schopenhauer's name would have been well known in intellectual circles, as is evident from the smattering of references to Schopenhauer in *The Interpretation of Dreams* (1900). Still, Freud claimed to have devised his own theory of repression without any help from Schopenhauer. The similarity between the two, he professed, was only later brought to his attention by a fellow psychoanalyst:

> The theory of repression quite certainly came to me independently of any other source; I know of no outside impression which might have suggested it to me and for a long time I imagined it to be entirely original, until Otto Rank . . . showed us a passage in Schopenhauer's *World as Will and Representation*

in which the philosopher seeks to give an explanation of insanity.... What he says there about the struggle against accepting a distressing piece of reality coincides with my concept of repression so completely that once again I owe the chance of making a discovery to my not being well read.[49]

Schopenhauer, for his part, was quite familiar with the roots of a tradition that helped to train Freud, which was neither German nor Austrian, but French. Schopenhauer rarely cited authorities on mental illness because, clearly, he preferred to come to his own conclusions. But when he did cite any authorities, it was most likely to be the work of the French *aliéniste* Jean-Étienne Dominique Esquirol. The alienists were psychiatrists avant la lettre. In contrast to Germany's academic approach to mental health research, they were asylum superintendents as much as physicians. They therefore had more frequent personal contact with the patients. The alienists held, furthermore, that the therapeutic aims of their practice could not be achieved without improvements to the general living conditions of the asylum residents: Esquirol, for example, following his teacher Philippe Pinel, limited the use of personal physical restraints. With their more humane and hands-on approach, it is no surprise that Schopenhauer liked their style.

By aligning himself with the French alienists, Schopenhauer also leaned to one side of a debate about madness going back at least as far as the seventeenth-century English philosopher John Locke. The debate was between "psychists," on the one hand, who focused on the psychological origins of madness, and "somatists," on the other, who focused on its physiological origins, although neither side could entirely deny the psychogenic factors in mental illness nor its organic basis, and so the real question was where to place the emphasis. Locke had argued that madness is a confusion of ideas received through the senses, putting him more on the side of the psychists. His views found their way into Pinel and Esquirol's thinking via the work of the Locke-inspired radical empiricist Étienne Bonnot de Condillac.[50]

In Schopenhauer's Germany, the somatists were winning the day. One of its leading exponents, Wilhelm Griesinger, became the director of the Berlin Charité not long after Schopenhauer's death and himself took a step toward more humane treatment by moving from long-term hospitalization to the beginnings of community-based care. There is even a hint of evidence that Schopenhauer kept up to date with the latest developments in German psychiatry: his personal library contained an 1829 issue of the *Magazine of Philosophical, Medical and Forensic Psychology*, edited by J. B. Friedreich, another leading German somatist. Although in his own theorizing he tended to emphasize the psychic factors that explain madness, Schopenhauer fully accepted that "the psychic will involve the somatic." This was especially so, he surmised, in the case of a subject painfully close to his heart and home: namely, the predisposition toward suicide:

> it is grounded in a certain bodily distress, and an external cause is required in proportion to the level of such distress; only at the highest level is none required. Thus, there is no unhappiness so great that it would move everyone to suicide, and none so small that something similar to it has not already done so.[51]

"The hereditary nature of the tendency to suicide," he wrote in his notebook in 1828, "proves that the subjective part of the decision to commit it is indeed the stronger."[52] Tellingly, perhaps, this entry appears just before a draft of his book dedication to his father. Of the heritable traits, he wrote, "Most heritable of all is the tendency to suicide."[53]

Nevertheless, as a source of authoritative insight on matters of mental health and illness, Schopenhauer almost always preferred to cite the French psychists over the German somatists, if anyone. His theory of madness followed suit: like Freud later, it was primarily, though not exclusively, concerned with the dynamics of the mind, rather than preconditions of the body.

Freud traveled to Paris in 1885 to study under Jean-Martin Charcot at the Salpêtrière hospital as part of his general medical training, the very place where Pinel and Esquirol had implemented their humanitarian reforms.[54] Charcot, however, had not taken forward his predecessors' psychist leanings. Although he treated patients that today we might regard as mentally ill, and treated them using methods we might regard as psychotherapeutic, such as hypnosis, Charcot considered himself a neurologist first and foremost rather than a psychiatrist. His ultimate career goal was to find the organic basis for hysteria—a goal he never achieved. Freud always respected Charcot, but his own studies in hysteria, published a decade after his visit to Paris, put the psychical origins of mental illness back on the map. Both the cause and the cure for madness, he argued, were found mainly in the mind. Acknowledgment of traumatic early incidents in a patient's case history, for instance, was crucial to understanding and treating their condition. This may seem obvious to us now, since we live in a post-Freudian age. But Charcot never quite made the same connection, despite knowing deeply intimate details of his patients that frequently included childhood sexual abuse.[55] Instead of exploring the psyche, the Salpêtrière school quested fruitlessly for a lesion in the brain.

Despite the decades between them, many of Freud's revolutionary findings would not have surprised Schopenhauer: that madness is essentially connected to memory, meant in a highly specialized sense; that it is triggered mainly by the unconscious rejection of painful life events; that it is as much a self-protective function as it is a general dysfunction—and that, for all these reasons, it can readily befall any one of us.

:::

Schopenhauer's intrepidness had taught him a lot about madness since that long annotation written as a student in defiant response to his teacher's casual dehumanization of the insane. There wasn't even a mention of the role of memory in his initial strenuous denial of Fichte's point that madness is animalistic. It seems only to have dawned on him after his trips to the asylum. Ironically, however, it might have been Fichte in the first place who planted the first seed that there was even a connection between madness and memory worth exploring.

In the winter semester of the same 1811–12 course, according to Schopenhauer's notes, Fichte lectured on a phenomenon he called "reproductive invention."[56] The idea referred to our ability to create fictions by reassembling components of things that we have perceived in the past, as distinct from recollection that reproduces our perceptions of things exactly how they were or as close as we can recall. Using reproduction invention, we can create for ourselves a pleasant world of fantasy—but only if we do not mistake it for our perceptions of the real world. "Now," Fichte finished his thought, "if in this way reproduction takes the place of sense of perception, then this is called *madness*."[57] According to Fichte, then, the insane lived in fantasy worlds due to a confusion between invention and recollection. Except for some finer technical details, unlike before, Schopenhauer did not note down add any significant interjections or objections to Fichte's point.

None of Schopenhauer's experiences, however, led him to doubt his main anti-Fichtean thesis that madness is, or can be, close to genius. "In frequent visits to madhouses," he later wrote, "I have found individual subjects with unmistakably great talents, whose genius was clearly visible through their madness."[58] On this basis, he theorized that what genius and madness share is a disrupted relationship with time: the mad lose their sense of themselves in time through the evident dysfunction of memory, whereas geniuses lose it through their extraordinary ability to perceive the eternal essence of things, thereby making themselves into pure, timeless subjects. To the keeper of the Dresden Zwinger who found a babbling Schopenhauer absorbed in contemplation of the plants, therefore, it was unclear whether the man who stood before him was a genius or simply mad.

Schopenhauer gave no further details about the great talents that he saw on display in the madhouses, aside from those quoted so far. We do know, however, that he exchanged some poetry with a patient at the Berlin Charité, a young theology student named Traugott Schultze.[59] Schultze's poem contained a touching tribute to Schopenhauer's sympathetic approach to patients like himself:

> To the noble one, who appears fair
> to him who cries in the cell
> the suffering friend of human beings.[60]

It is a reminder of how Schopenhauer, in defiance of his teacher Fichte, truly discovered the humanity that survives madness: not in his conclusions, that is, so much as his methods. By talking with those whom he met in the asylum, Schopenhauer engaged with them as people, not merely as specimens. Rather than simply study the insane, he attempted to get to know them—as best as anyone could.

CHAPTER 5

Live First, Then Philosophize

How Schopenhauer Left Academia

On March 13, 1820, Schopenhauer traveled back to Berlin for the second time, not as a student but as a teacher. Hopefully. He had applied to become a *Privatdozent*, an unsalaried university lecturer, which required him to give a test lecture to the faculty. By then Fichte was long gone—killed by typhus on January 29, 1814—and on October 5, 1818, Hegel had ascended to the vacant chair of philosophy after several jobbing stints in Jena, Bamberg, Nuremberg, and Heidelberg. Even though Schopenhauer already had his magnum opus *The World as Will and Representation* to his name, there was no reason for Hegel to see this barely known newcomer, eighteen years his junior, as any sort of threat. And so, as if to make the threat clear, Schopenhauer had suggested to the dean of faculty that, were he to be hired, his lectures could be scheduled at the exact same time as Hegel's.

Magnanimously, or perhaps indifferently, Hegel granted Schopenhauer's lecture a pass. First, however, he tested the newcomer's mettle.

The lecture took place on March 23. With Hegel's approval, Schopenhauer had selected a philosophical topic going as far back as Aristotle: the so-called four causes. It was comfortably within

Schopenhauer's field of expertise: his doctoral dissertation and first book, *On the Fourfold Root of the Principle of Sufficient Reason* (1814), had been a fresh but historically literate investigation of the various forms of causal explanation. Among other things, the book took an unusual stance on animal minds, which Schopenhauer now aired for his prospective colleagues. First, he professed, animals possess not only sensation but also the faculty of understanding: they perceive not only sight and sound, and so on, but also cause and effect. Second, and more contentiously, animals are responsive to motives. In fact, according to Schopenhauer, that is precisely what it is to be an animal, as distinct from matter, which is only moved by force, and plant life, which is at most moved by stimulus.[1] What distinguishes humans from nonhuman animals is the ability to be motivated by abstract thoughts as well as immediate perceptions, which requires the additional faculty of reason. But a motive in general, Schopenhauer declared, is any sort of mental representation that gives rise to an action, conjoined with a desire that sets the goal of the act.

"When a horse lies down on the street, what then is the motive?" Hegel inquired.

"The ground, which it finds beneath it, in connection with its fatigue, a disposition of the horse," Schopenhauer answered. "If it stood next to an abyss, it would not lie down."

"You consider animal functions likewise as motives? Therefore the beating of the heart, the circulation of the blood, et cetera, follow as the results of motives?"

"These are not properly called animal functions. In physiology, one calls 'animal functions' the *conscious* movements of the animal body."

"Oh, but one does not understand *those* as animal functions . . ."[2]

From here the lofty philosophical discourse on the nature of causality could only descend into a pedantic technical dispute over what zoologists typically count as animal functions. Schopenhauer had a more specific meaning in mind, referring only to the functions that are distinctive of animals as opposed to vegetables and minerals. A cardiovascular system, even if it is only ever found in animals, is still not what *makes* them an animal. That, he thought, was some sort of conscious motivation, even of the most primordial kind.

Luckily, there was a zoologist on hand to clear things up—and, doubly lucky for Schopenhauer, it was a sympathetic friend, Martin Hinrich Carl Lichtenstein. Lichtenstein was not in attendance by chance: he had effectively lined up the job. Schopenhauer attended Lichtenstein's lectures as a student, and before that they had met at his mother's salon.[3] Lichtenstein sided with Schopenhauer, not out of undue partiality, but rather a wish to see the standoff end before either philosopher could embarrass himself any further.[4]

∷∷

Schopenhauer had been away from Berlin for close to seven years. His student days ended abruptly in the middle of 1813 when he became fearful of a French invasion of the city, and more specifically of being drawn into the conflict. (No such invasion occurred: like his father before him, Schopenhauer was just as prone to base his movements on potential perils as actual ones.) For twelve days, he fled south to Dresden, briefly stopping at a small Saxon village named Hoyerswerda. But after sensing, correctly this time, that another military clash was on the horizon, he headed west to his mother's home in Weimar.[5] A lot would happen for him in the seven years before he returned to Berlin, both personally and philosophically.

On the personal front, by 1820, Schopenhauer was no longer on speaking terms with his mother and just barely with his sister. Pressure had been building ever since his father's death, but waves of rancorous quarreling pushed it past its breaking point. The fallout would make the period when Johanna helped Arthur to escape his apprenticeship—which, with all his brooding and her berating, was hardly a treasured time—look as though the two had never been closer.

The first wave hit as soon as he got back to Weimar in May 1813. Johanna had taken on a liberally named lodger, Georg Friedrich Conrad Ludwig Müller von Gerstenbergk, whom many suspected was something more than a friend to her (Christiane Vulpius von

Goethe, among others, fanned the flames of hot gossip).[6] Gerstenbergk's presence in the Schopenhauer household unsettled both Arthur and Adele in different ways. To Arthur, he was further confirmation of his mother's failure to honor her late husband. For Adele, who was almost sixteen, things were a little more complicated. Gerstenbergk was over a decade younger than Johanna, and only a decade older than Arthur, making the age gap between him and Adele roughly the same as the one that had stood between her own father and mother.[7] He thus became her first romantic infatuation, and the start of a series of unrequited loves.

Unable to think and write in the midst of such a tense domestic atmosphere, Arthur retreated further south again to Rudolstadt, a small town on the edge of the mountainous Thuringian forest. There he found the peace of mind to complete *The Fourfold Root*, which he successfully submitted for a doctorate from the University of Jena. Any personal pride he might have felt, however, was quickly eclipsed by Johanna's latest achievement. Shortly after he returned to Weimar in November 1813, she published an edition of her travel diaries, including her recollections of the grand tour. The two books were brought out with the same publisher, but met with opposite receptions.[8]

Overshadowed and outnumbered, Arthur invited a close friend from Berlin, Josef Gans, to stay with them at the start of 1814, as if Johanna's house wasn't crowded enough. She belittled Arthur's failed first book, suggesting the title sounded more like an apothecary manual, a quip that Gerstenbergk riffed on by referring to it as a laxative (in a written note peppered with distasteful references to Gans's Jewishness).[9] Arthur retorted with a prediction that his works would still be around long after hers had been consigned to the scrap heap of history. Johanna drily agreed: "Of yours, the entire first printing will still be available."[10] Inevitably, she found her son's judgmental attitude toward her, and his inhospitality toward her companion, intolerably oppressive. On Monday, May 17, 1814, she took herself and Adele to stay in nearby Jena, leaving Arthur with instructions that he should be gone by their return on Thursday.[11] Obediently he never saw his mother again.

He was, however, remotely drawn back into one more family crisis before the rupture was complete. Back in 1809, when Arthur had received his share of the inheritance, Johanna encouraged him to invest it, as she had done, with a Danzig banker named Abraham Ludwig Muhl. Wisely, it turned out, Arthur only invested around a third of his portion, whereas his mother and sister had gone all in.[12] On May 28, 1819, Adele sent Arthur a panicked letter to report that Muhl's bank had collapsed, leaving her and Johanna in utter financial peril. Out of desperation, Johanna and Adele accepted a settlement that reduced their funds by roughly 70 percent. Arthur, having less at stake, managed to hold his nerve for over two years until Muhl had recovered well enough to pay out with interest. Saved only by his own fiscal foresight, he was disappointed that Johanna had failed to protect Adele's inheritance, and part of his own, remarking in the midst of the crisis that she "had honored the memory of her husband, of my father, neither in his son nor in his daughter."[13] All the same, he offered to divide up the remainder of his share between the three of them. Out of pride, Johanna of course declined.

:::

At the same time, philosophically, Schopenhauer had come into his own. His student days had brought him up to speed with the latest developments in post-Kantian philosophy. Apart from attending lectures by Fichte and the theologian Friedrich Schleiermacher, he conducted extensive independent studies of Fichte's written works as well as those by Friedrich Heinrich Jacobi, Jakob Friedrich Fries, and Friedrich Wilhelm Joseph Schelling. Schelling had once lived with Hegel at a seminary in Tübingen in 1790, and many years later would himself take up the chair of philosophy at Berlin after his former roommate's death. Schopenhauer thus often treated, or rather mistreated, the three Berliner professors as a set: "*Fichte, Schelling* and *Hegel* are not philosophers," he later wrote, "lacking as they do the first requisite for being counted as such, seriousness and honesty in research."[14]

To supplement his post-Kantian diet, Schopenhauer filled several notebooks with staples from the Western canon, both ancient (Plato and Aristotle) and modern (Francis Bacon, John Locke, and Gottfried Wilhelm Leibniz). In this respect, one notebook stands out from the rest: a collection of excerpts from the periodical *Asiatic Researches*, kept from November 1815 to May 1816. Here Schopenhauer transcribed choice proverbs, annotating them with glosses in his own contemporary nomenclature:

"The eyes opened: from the eyes a glance sprung; from that glance the sun was produced."
 [Schop.] Dependence of the object on the subject.
 "These deities being thus framed, fell into this vast ocean: and to Him they came with thirst and hunger: and him they thus addressed: 'Grant us a smaller size, wherein abiding we may eat food.'"
 [Schop.] The macrocosm demands the microcosm.
 . . . "That, whence all beings are produced: that, by which they live, when born: that, towards which they tend; & that, into which they pass; do thou seek, for that is Brahma."
 [Schop.] The will-to-live is the source and essence of things.[15]

Serious research into classical Indian philosophy was perhaps the best thing to have come out of the tense few months that he had spent in the Schopenhauer-Gerstenbergk Weimar residence. Following a recommendation from Friedrich Majer, a former student of the revered historian Johann Gottfried Herder, he borrowed an edition of the Hindu text the Upanishads from a library in Weimar on March 26, 1814.[16] His facility with languages did not yet extend as far as Sanskrit, so instead he relied on a peculiar version composed by the French explorer Abraham Hyacinthe Anquetil-Duperron, titled the *Oupnek'hat*—which was not even in German, but rather Latin, and furthermore was based on a selective Persian translation from 1656 by the Indian Mughal prince Dārā Shukoh.[17] Despite the distance this put between Schopenhauer and the original source, he felt a strong and immediate affinity with Indian thought. After Johanna had expelled him from Weimar, he borrowed another copy of the *Oupnek'hat* from the library in Dresden, where he settled for next four years or so. His co-lodger at Große Meißensche Gasse 35, Karl Christian Friedrich Krause, who would spend nine months studying Sanskrit in Paris, must have given him plenty of conversation on this recondite topic.[18] Soon he acquired his own copy of the *Oupnek'hat*, which from then until his death he treated like a daily prayerbook, reading at least a few passages most nights before bed.[19]

With all of these streams of influence pouring into Schopenhauer's thoughts, and his notebooks filling up with reflections, extensions, disagreements and departures—and still only in his midtwenties—he was ready to start writing his masterpiece.

∴

Modestly, but deceptively, Schopenhauer prefaced his book with the claim that it only contained "a single thought."[20] In truth, as its title suggested, his real aim was to set out an entire worldview; it thus contained uncountably many thoughts. What he really meant to say by "a single thought," then, was how all his thoughts hung together. He hesitated to call it a system because of the structure that this word would imply. A system, he explained, is an architectural construction: it is built like a house, brick by brick, arising from a solid and independent foundation. Instead, Schopenhauer encouraged his reader to think of his philosophy as organic, rather than systematic: instead of an artifice, it was an animal, with integrated, inseparable, mutually dependent organs and limbs. It was singular and unified, therefore, but not small or simple. If he only had "a single thought," it was rather in the manner that a blue whale is "only" a single creature.

After the preface, the book began: "The world is my representation."[21] The decision to use a first-person possessive pronoun was significant. Schopenhauer never meant, of course, that the world was specifically *his* representation—not even he was that egotistical. Nor, however, did he mean that each of us lives in our own little world; in philosophical terms, he aimed to keep us from sliding over from idealism, the view that the world is constituted by minds, into solipsism, the view that only the mind that constitutes the world exists. By proposing that the world is *my* representation, however, rather than *a* representation, he instead indicated something important about what representation even is. It could be taken to mean the entity that forms the object of experience, but that, to him, would be incomplete. According to Schopenhauer, the object of experience never stands alone; it is always accompanied by the subject who has the experience. Representation is thus the relationship between a subject and an object: or, more concretely, that we are "not acquainted with either the sun or the earth, but rather only with an eye that sees a sun, with a hand that feels an earth."[22] Representation includes, and is conditioned by, us the representers too.

On this point, Kant's influence on Schopenhauer was at its most evident. Kant's most revolutionary theoretical idea was that the experienced world is shaped by the mind. This made him a kind of idealist, but instead of assuming that minds passively receive impressions of an independent reality, he contended that they also play a constructive role too. Many of the basic features of the world as we know it, Kant argued, such as space, time, the constitution of objects, and the causal relations between them, are all forms of knowledge that we bring to it. Without them, we could not even begin to apprehend the world as an organized and integrated whole in the first place. It followed, however, that we lack access to the world as it is in itself. While this may sound like a major problem, especially for those of us who are eager to know the world beyond appearances, there is another way of putting Kant's point that makes it sound more obvious, or perhaps even trivial: we cannot know what the world is like in the absence of the very conditions of knowing it.

But if the limits of our knowledge were so obvious and unbreachable, then how do we explain our constant habit of trying to overstep them? Much philosophy the world over is, after all, animated by the desire to know reality itself as opposed to mere appearances. Hence Schopenhauer's next key proposition: "The world is my will."[23]

If we were no more than the Kantian knowers described so far, our experience of the world would be very different from how it actually is. All there would be is cognitive relations between the subject and object of knowledge. We would be like an *Engelskopf*, Schopenhauer wrote: angelic heads hovering over and above the world.[24] But we are far from that: we are "rooted in this world" and "completely mediated through a body whose affections . . . are the starting point for the understanding as it intuits this world."[25] We are embodied creatures, who not only know the world but reside in it, want things from it, and are affected by it. The latter as much as the former determines the world in which we live.

Our embodied experience, Schopenhauer thought, is also the source of an indispensable metaphysical insight. Unlike everything else in the world, which we only ever know as mere representations, we appear to have a dual experience of ourselves. On the one hand, we know ourselves like any other object: we have a certain shape, a certain look and feel, and we stand in certain causal relations and histories with other objects. On the other, we also know ourselves from the inside. We know not only how the movements of our bodies manifest, but also what it is to be the thing that moves.

Schopenhauer's proposition "The world is my will" referred to this insight. It was such an important insight for a couple of reasons. First, it forms the basis for our metaphysical need to know the world beyond appearances. There are many possible motives for such a need, and Schopenhauer, for one, linked metaphysical speculation to our fear of death and the search for consolation. But whatever its origin, we must first have some sense that there *even is* a world beyond appearances for us to know. Our metaphysical need, then, aims at knowledge of something like the deeper, immediate knowledge that we appear to have of ourselves. Second, the world as will also offers a key to unlocking the very riddle that it reveals: we must assume (Schopenhauer proposes) that all appearances other than ourselves are nevertheless related to their inner essences as our own bodies are related to our own will.

> When it comes to objects other than our own body, objects that have not been given to us in this double manner but only as representations in our consciousness, we will judge them on the

analogy with our body, assuming that, since they are on the one hand representations just like the body and are in this respect homogeneous with it, then on the other hand, what remains after disregarding their existence as representation of a subject must have the same inner essence as what we call *will*.[26]

Building on this analogy, Schopenhauer proposed to carry out a comprehensive interpretation of the world, from the complicated drama of human life, through animals and plants, down to the most insignificant and unassuming items of existence: "if it were a mote in a sunbeam, it would still exhibit that unfathomable something, at least as gravity and impenetrability: but this, I say, is to the mote what a man's *will* is to the man."[27] Just as we know ourselves as will and representation, in other words, with some deep reflection we can come to know the whole world as will and representation.

(A word of warning: by giving the name "will" to the inner essence of all things, Schopenhauer never meant to attribute volition, or willpower, to everything that exists. Only animals, who are responsive to motives, have a will in this literal sense. His point, rather, was that if we want an insight into the relationship between an appearance and its essence, then we have no better—indeed no other—model than the relation between our own body and will. He insisted, nevertheless, that we retain the potentially confusing word "will" for this insight, as opposed to, say, force or energy, in order to remind ourselves of the introspective origins of the newly extended concept.)[28]

True to his goal of giving a full and integrated worldview, Schopenhauer proceeded to expand on his philosophy's aesthetic and ethical dimensions. Both his aesthetics and ethics are premised on the ramifications of a world driven by the will. To begin with, our experience of the will, Schopenhauer argued, is exclusively painful:

> All *willing* springs from need, and thus from lack, and thus from suffering. Fulfilment brings this to an end; but for every wish that is fulfilled, at least ten are left denied: moreover, desire lasts a long time and demands go on forever; fulfilment is brief and

sparsely meted out. But even final satisfaction itself is only illusory: the fulfilled wish quickly gives way to a new one.[29]

Even if we do manage to satisfy all our needs, then we only swing over to the other form of our unending suffering: boredom. Aesthetic experience, however, can provide us with a little relief: when we calmly contemplate natural beauty or works of art, the demands of the will are temporarily forgotten. Additionally, when we perceive the world in a way that is free from the concerns of the will, as well as getting a welcome psychological break, we also get deeper cognitive penetration into the things we are perceiving. Instead of attending to their individual features, we attend to their universal qualities: "The first," Schopenhauer wrote, "is like the countless, violently moving drops of the waterfall, which always change and do not stand still for a single instant: the second is like the rainbow that rests peacefully on top of this raging tumult."[30] For these timeless essences, he borrowed the term "Idea" from Plato, and in doing so he turned Plato's view of the arts on its head. Plato was famously cautious about the value of the arts. Rather than silencing the will, the arts according to Plato gave free rein to our irrational passions, and, rather than revealing deeper truths, art was usually an inferior source of knowledge compared to philosophical discourse. For Schopenhauer, it was quite the opposite: aesthetic sensibility was something close to saintly wisdom.

Close, but still not all the way there. In the final movement of his philosophy, Schopenhauer proposed a more permanent form of escape from the will to life. For the aesthete, pure contemplation of beauty becomes a goal in itself; but such a state of mind is ultimately unsustainable, and soon the demands of desire regain the upper hand. For others, however, a deeper apprehension of the true nature of the world has a more direct effect on the will: it "intensifies his powers to the point where he finally grows tired of the game and seizes upon serious things."[31] Instead of knowledge providing yet more motives for the will, it now "becomes a *tranquillizer* that placates and abolishes all willing."[32] This difference marks a transition from *aestheticism* as a form of salvation to *asceticism*, the "*deliberate* breaking of the will by forgoing what is pleasant and seeking out what is unpleasant, choosing a lifestyle of penitence and self-castigation."³³

Asceticism, Schopenhauer noted, is represented as the highest spiritual ideal in most world religions, but especially, of course, in those that came out of India. The following are the very last lines of Schopenhauer's book, which, judging by his manuscript notes, he settled on as early as 1816, two years before it was actually published:

> We can look at the lives and the conduct of saints; of course we rarely encounter them in our own experience, but they are brought before our eyes in their recorded histories as well as in art, which is vouchsafed by the mark of inner truth; and this is how we must drive away the dark impression of that nothing that hovers behind all virtue and holiness as the final goal, and that we fear the way children fear darkness. We must not evade it through myths and meaningless words as the Indians do, words such as "re-absorption into *Brahman*," or the *Nirvana* of the Buddhists. Instead we confess quite freely: for everyone who is still filled with the will, what remains after it is completely abolished is certainly nothing. But conversely, for those in whom the will has turned and negated itself, this world of ours which is so very real with all its suns and galaxies is—nothing.³⁴

It might seem like the ultimate nihilist statement: to end his magnum opus on the word "nothing." Schopenhauer's stated aim, however, was to drive away the "dark impression" given by this nothingness; even the Hinduism and Buddhism that he so loved, when they tried to give positive names to nothingness, were too evasive on this point for his liking. Asceticism is nothingness, but only from our side of things, we who are "still filled with the will." We fear it rather as we fear the unknown, but we need only witness the calm serenity of those who are on the other side to see that there is really nothing to fear.

Perhaps the most troubling part of this ending, in fact, was Schopenhauer's claim that we "rarely encounter" such spiritual salvation. It can be approximated, but next to no one achieves it in full, himself included. This limitation seems to have occurred to Schopenhauer before he had started in earnest to write *The World as Will and Representation*. In a notebook from late 1813, before his retreat from the domestic disturbances in Weimar to the civil quiet of Dresden, he wrote:

> What is to be desired?—An eye that sees the sun from a prison as well as from a palace; this is desirable and nothing else.—Who can have it? Anyone.—Who would like it?—Everyone. Who wills it?—One in a hundred thousand.[35]

∷

In March 1818, Schopenhauer sought a publisher for his masterpiece. Through Johanna's connections, he persuaded Friedrich Arnold Brockhaus to take it on. As it happened, she also had a book coming out with Brockhaus, a reedition of her grand-tour travelogues titled *Tour Through England and Scotland*.[36] As before, Johanna's book strongly outperformed Arthur's. A decade later, by which time F. A. Brockhaus was dead and his sons had taken over the family business, Schopenhauer approached them with the proposal of a second edition.[37] They replied that there were still around 150 copies left from the original printing, fulfilling the cruel prediction that Johanna had made after his first book was published. The handful of reviews that it received were lukewarm to hostile. All agreed that he wrote beautifully, but none accepted his doctrines, and some even fiercely rejected them—or, perhaps worse, assimilated them to other existing systems of thought.[38]

The burden of this reaction was lightened only a little by a warmer response from Goethe, who received his copy via Adele on January 18, 1819. Reportedly, as Adele learned from Ottilie von Goethe, he dipped into it on several occasions, especially, naturally, its many pages on artistic genius.[39] Emboldened, Schopenhauer paid Goethe an unannounced visit on August 19, 1819, which turned out to be their last-ever meeting. Initially, it was a cold and awkward encounter, as Goethe was entertaining a guest at the time, and so he had to send the philosopher away at first. In his diary, however, Goethe wrote that he enjoyed their eventual conversation later that day, adding that "Dr. Schopenhauer" was "usually misjudged, but also a difficult to know, meritorious young man."[40]

By then it had already dawned on Schopenhauer that a book was not the speediest method to disseminate his philosophy. "The wide gulf between the populace and books," he wrote, had taught him "how slowly (though surely) acknowledged truths reach the populace, and therefore with regard to the velocity of the propagation of physical light nothing is less like it than the light of the mind."[41] He had not given up on the power of the written word altogether, but he queried the age-old association of truth with light, at least with respect to the speed of travel. Perhaps teaching, he thought, would be a quicker and more effective way of transmitting his ideas. To that end, he got in touch with a former classmate from his days at the gymnasium in Gotha, Ernst Anton Lewald, now a professor of theology at Heidelberg.[42] He made the same inquiries with Johann Friedrich Blumenbach, whose lectures on comparative anatomy in Göttingen had helped shape his views on animal cruelty, and finally also with Lichtenstein in Berlin. Notably, none of Schopenhauer's connections were insiders from the world of philosophy. He even avoided reestablishing contact with Schulze, his once inspiring philosophy professor at Göttingen, who was among those to have published a middling review of *The Fourfold Root*.[43]

Of these three opportunities, Schopenhauer decided to pursue Berlin. At first he leaned toward it on the grounds of its typical student, who tended to be more worldly and experienced, in his view, having come to Berlin after undertaking professional studies, such as medicine, or being of independent means and thus able to devote themselves entirely to education for its own sake. (In these respects, Schopenhauer based his assumptions on his own student experience.) But in the end Lichtenstein clinched the decision with a purely numerical argument: Berlin now had over one thousand students, making it much larger than the other candidates. Lichtenstein tempered his argument with the caveat that while Hegel's presence had reinvigorated interest in philosophy, those large audiences only flocked to his lectures, leaving junior staff with a smaller, poorer—financially and intellectually—proportion of the student body. Even the illustrious Fichte's son, Immanuel, who started teaching at Berlin not long after graduating in 1818, struggled to make ends meet and depended on the occasional government subsidy. Schopenhauer, however, was unfazed by these omens, as he explained in his reply to Lichtenstein on December 8, 1819. First, despite the financial shock of the Muhl banking crisis, which at that point was still unresolved, his primary goal in going into teaching was never to make a living for himself. And as for the issue of attendance, he took Lichtenstein's warnings under advisement, confidently adding that "I trust myself completely in this respect and want to create an audience for myself."[44]

On the final day of 1819, Schopenhauer sent a dossier of materials to the dean of faculty at Berlin, August Boeckh. The package included not only his published works so far and his infamously impudent scheduling suggestion ("I ask you to choose the hour according to your best judgement: the most suitable is probably the one where Professor Hegel reads his main lectures"), but also a rather extraordinary curriculum vitae. Having no professional academic experience to speak of, Schopenhauer instead told his version of his entire life story so far. He included nearly everything: his almost-birth in England, the family's flight from Danzig, the happy two years at Le Havre, Dr. Runge's school, the grand tour, Reverend Lancaster's academy, the miserable apprenticeships, the Gotha gymnasium, the first move to Weimar, the university years in Göttingen, and then Berlin, with extra details here for obvious reasons, the circuitous journey back to Weimar, the writing retreats to Rudolstadt and Dresden, right up to the present moment when, "I, who until then had only been driven by the desire to learn, was seized by the desire to teach."[45]

There were two notable deceptions. First, while Heinrich Floris's tragic demise was too pivotal to omit entirely, Schopenhauer described it as "a sudden, bloody death that happened by accident."[46] With a little more candor, he depicted Heinrich Floris as "a strict, violent man, but of irreproachable integrity, honesty and unbreakable loyalty, and gifted with excellent insight in commercial transactions." He even admitted that his father "didn't hesitate to attack me with cunning," referring to the tactical deployment of the grand tour.[47] Nevertheless, Schopenhauer paid tribute to Heinrich Floris, as he always would, first for his ardent—if misguided—desire to set his son up with a job for life, and second for the accidental benefits of his death: "namely free time and a completely carefree existence."[48]

By contrast, his other omission was any real acknowledgment of his mother's helping hand. She too was not excluded altogether: he noted that she was still alive and well known for her own writings, but the only other role that he assigned her in his story, apart from providing the occasional place to stay, was listening to his woes when he wanted to leave his last apprenticeship. Instead, he gave Fernow most of the credit for strengthening his resolve to quit his job for a life of the mind, as though Johanna hadn't actively solicited Fernow's intervention.

Schopenhauer's relationship with his mother was at its nadir when he wrote his curriculum vitae. Her contribution to his life did not fit the narrative he was constructing. It suited him to mention the occasional assistance, and implicit endorsement, that he received from learned men like Fernow; he made much of his work on color theory with Goethe, yet another collaboration facilitated by Johanna's connections. Otherwise, however, the story as Schopenhauer told it was one of steering himself off the road that his father, however well meaning, had misguidedly mapped out for him. Despite his enormous privilege in certain obvious respects, Schopenhauer's route into academia, he underlined, had been "hindered and blocked." He had worked hard to repurpose those privileges toward the life that he felt it was his sole purpose to live. At the same time, with more than a touch of embarrassment, he was effectively apologizing for his late development. Twice he referred to his "advanced age." He was only in his thirties, but then so was Boeckh, who had been a professor at Berlin since Schopenhauer was a student there and was now the dean of faculty. It was Schopenhauer's first official assertion of his somewhat paradoxical status as a highly privileged outsider. While it was a selective interpretation, it was not a total fabrication either. Of his family's move from Danzig to Hamburg, he wrote: "So I became homeless in my tender childhood (I was then five years old); since then I have never acquired a new home." He was never literally homeless, of course, but he still felt out of place wherever he went.

Boeckh duly circulated Schopenhauer's petition among his colleagues, disdainfully noting the "arrogance and extraordinary vanity" of the applicant's insolent scheduling suggestion. Hegel raised no objections to a test lecture; the date was set, and the infamous showdown ensued.[49] Arrogance and vanity notwithstanding, Schopenhauer's strategy was sincere, if naive. It wasn't purely a stunt or deliberate self-sabotage; if it was a challenge, it was as much to himself as to current academic trends and tastes. His personal animus toward Hegel wasn't even all that strong—yet. For all he knew, pitting himself against the big name on campus could be his breakout triumph, a return on the investment of his inheritance in himself. Was he a late-blooming wunderkind? It was one way to find out.

But the gamble never paid off, not even close. A grand total of five students attended Schopenhauer's lectures in the summer of 1820—and that, it seems, was his peak audience. He continued to offer classes in Berlin at various points throughout the 1820s, until his flight from the cholera outbreak of 1831.[50] The outcome was always the same: audiences countable on one hand and none of them seriously interested in philosophy or else they'd be in Professor Hegel's class. The road to recognition still had a long way to go.

A letter to Adele, dated January 15, 1822, offers a window into Schopenhauer's state of mind during this period. He had decided he would move back to Dresden, he tells her, at least for the summer, but perhaps for the rest of his days, "most of which," he claimed almost correctly, "were already over." Aside from his unattended lectures, he also disliked Berlin as a city: it was too expensive, and unbearably hot in the summertime. It was getting him down; he hadn't read a single book in over a year and a half. But he had at least accomplished all that he ever really wanted from life, he thought, namely, the writing his own book. Plus his personal wealth was more than enough to live off. Probably he would continue conducting his studies in Dresden. Maybe he would come back to Berlin in winter, if and when—he added with uncharacteristic optimism—"someone appoints me to a chair."[51]

:::

As the road to recognition only grew longer, Schopenhauer leaned further into his outsider status. If he ever had any respect for university philosophy, it was short-lived, as his almost immediate disillusionment with Fichte had shown. But his notoriously open hostility toward it, and Hegel in particular, developed gradually before reaching its full pitch.

Schopenhauer's earliest interaction with Hegel's work had been facilitated by the publisher Carl Friedrich Ernst Frommann, who happened to be a family friend of both the Schopenhauers and the Hegels. In the summer of 1813, Frommann loaned Schopenhauer a copy of Hegel's recently published *Science of Logic*. On November 4, Schopenhauer returned the book with a note to say that he would have done so sooner "had I not known that you were as little inclined as I to read it," suggesting that it had spent all those months in his possession unread.[52] Schopenhauer was thus always at least cool toward Hegel, but for a time he was still capable of tactful—or perhaps tactical—cordiality: on March 18, 1820, he wrote to dean Boeckh about how kind it had been for Professor Hegel to approve the topic of his test lecture. This was, crucially, before their public face-off.[53]

In 1827, when a second edition of Hegel's *Encyclopaedia of the Philosophical Sciences* was published, Schopenhauer venomously took to his notebook:

> The *Hegelian philosophy* is made entirely for a lucrative and profitable professional wisdom, for instead of ideas it contains mere words, and the lads want to have words to repeat mechanically, to write down and take home; they cannot use ideas.[. . .] On the whole, Hegel's philosophy contains *three-quarters sheer nonsense and one-quarter spurious notions.*[54]

A choice quotation from Hegel to illustrate his point—"Being as existence which mediates with itself through the negativity of itself, is the reference to itself only by its being a reference to something else which is direct only as something posited and mediated"— suggests that Schopenhauer had at least opened the book on this occasion. In the meantime, attendance at his lectures continued to dwindle. His winter 1826–27 lecture course was attended by just three medical students.[55] With increasing frequency, Schopenhauer's later writings contained scattershot attacks on Hegel and other elite university philosophers. Kant's profound but technically difficult prose, Schopenhauer thought, had enabled all sorts of stylistic mischief among the next generation of German philosophers:

> The public had been compelled to realize that what is obscure is not always senseless: so senseless things immediately took refuge behind obscure modes of presentation. *Fichte* was the first to seize upon this new privilege and make vigorous use of it; *Schelling* was at least his equal in this, and soon they both were overtaken by a host of hungry scribblers devoid of both spirit and honesty. Still, it was *Hegel* who ultimately showed the greatest audacity in dishing out pure nonsense, slapping together senseless, raving tangles of verbiage such as had only ever been heard in lunatic asylums; he became the instrument of the most ponderous, universal mystification that the world has ever seen, and this with a degree of success that will seem utterly incredible to posterity and will remain a monument to German foolishness.[56]

Though personal and petty, Schopenhauer composed his diatribes with undeniable verve. The prefaces to subsequent new editions of his books were similarly dedicated to outbursts of splenetic rage about the conspiracy of silence around his own work.

As with many of Schopenhauer's lifelong preoccupations, he nursed his grudge at its greatest length in his final book *Parerga and Paralipomena*. Toward the end of an infamous chapter titled "On University Philosophy," he confessed to being "in favour of philosophy ceasing to be a trade," although he pulled back from this extreme stance with the limited provision that the teaching of philosophy at university should stick "strictly to lecturing on logic, as a completed science capable of strict proof, and to a history of philosophy, succinctly delivered and to be completed within one semester."[57] Later he took the even harder line that students should only be taught formal logic, "which absolutely belongs at the university."[58] University philosophers, in Schopenhauer's opinion, could not even be trusted to teach the history of their own discipline.

Schopenhauer's position on university philosophy was not, however, a stance against academia in general. A meager provision though it was, his grounds for retaining logic at universities, namely, that it was a provable science, indicate what sort of thing he thought really belonged there. Though like many German philosophers of his generation Schopenhauer assumed that philosophy was, or ought to be, the queen of the sciences rather than its handmaiden, he otherwise had the utmost respect for genuine scientists and scholars of all sorts. After all, his old teachers to whom he turned when he went job hunting were not themselves philosophers but two biologists (Blumenbach and Lichtenstein) and a classicist (Boeckh). The problem, rather, was that philosophy does not mix well with the university environment. It lacks the standards of objectivity that protect other disciplines from abuse. With the important exception of logic, philosophy had no agreed method for conferring the status of knowledge other than the critical judgment of one's peers and the public—which, of course, could always be swayed in ways other than speaking the truth.

From this perspective, Schopenhauer's critique of philosophical style was not purely aesthetic. His point was not only that such empty verbiage made a tangled cacophony of the German language—although that too.[59] Rather, the deeper problem was that the uninitiated must simply take it on trust that sense can be made of what would otherwise appear to be utter gibberish. "The writer," he wrote, "who himself has nothing distinct and determinate in mind, heaps words upon words, phrases upon phrases and still says nothing, because he has nothing to say, knows nothing, thinks nothing, but nonetheless wants to talk."[60] Droplets of insight, assuming there are any, are rationed out in the tiniest doses:

"Following the homoeopathic method, the weak minimum of a thought is diluted with a fifty-page torrent of words and now, with limitless confidence in the truly German patience of the reader, quite unperturbedly, it prattles on page after page."[61] In this way, professors built entire careers on tottering towers of words.

University philosophers, moreover, were incentivized to comply with the abuse of their discipline for the obvious reason that, if they were lucky, it could make them a fairly decent living. They lived, according to Schopenhauer, by the motto *primum vivere, deinde philosophari*—live first, then philosophize. They lived, that is, *from* their discipline rather than *for* it.[62] The entry-level teaching position at German universities, the *Privatdozent*, who was expected to eke out a living from stipends and student donations, was the ideal training scheme for such an ignominious trade.

The insinuation that it is in some way disreputable to be paid as a philosopher goes all the way back to Plato's famous contrast between his impecunious tutor, Socrates, on the one hand, and the fee-charging Sophists, on the other. In this respect, slightly disingenuously, Schopenhauer held himself up as a model against his peers: "I have sought truth, not a professorship; this is at bottom the basis of the distinction between me and the so-called post-Kantian philosophers."[63] His personal financial security gave him a vital advantage, of course. He did better, however, by pointing to the Dutch philosopher Baruch Spinoza, who was "so clearly aware of this that he declined the professorship offered to him just for this reason" and instead continued to earn his living as a lens grinder.[64]

Schopenhauer's vantage point on university philosophy, not to mention his personal experience of it, is too partial for us simply to take his word for it. If his showdown with Hegel had worked out, and he went on to enjoy ascending academic success, would he have attacked university philosophy with quite the same ferocity? Or would he instead have seen it as the very device for disseminating philosophical truth that he initially hoped it would be? Who can know. But Schopenhauer's essay on university philosophy is perhaps best read as a manifesto of his own intellectual values, rather than the diagnosis of a scholarly disease. His lyrical, anecdotal, untechnical style; his witty collusion with his readers, his only real students, against the powerful enemies that he was unafraid of making; his limitless range of subject matter, and lack of any agenda other than the one that he devised for himself—it is indeed hard to see how these virtues could have flourished inside a university atmosphere.

CHAPTER 6

Love Stories Without Love

How Schopenhauer Never Married

"True love, like a ghost, is much talked about but seldom seen," wrote the French aphorist François de La Rochefoucauld.¹ Schopenhauer disagreed. In his view, love could be seen almost everywhere. The real problem, however, was that it is seldom seen correctly. In this respect, he thought of himself as a kind of realist in not one but two ways. He was opposed, on the one hand, to La Rochefoucauld's skepticism: love is real, not fictional or even rare. On the other, he was equally opposed to idealism about love: high romantic ideals *are* fictions—indeed, are the subject matter of much fiction. Love exists, then, just not as we like to think. There is perhaps no better illustration of the difference between, and dangers of, such realism and idealism than the love lives of Schopenhauer and his sister, Adele.

:::

In late April 1819, or perhaps it was early May, Schopenhauer's first child was born. At the time of arrival, he was halfway through a long overdue trip around Italy. He had been desperate to depart for the past two years, but delayed until *The World as Will and Representation* was completed, delivered, and almost ready for distribution.

He set off via Vienna, arriving first in Venice, followed by Bologna and then Florence. By the time his author copies were available to collect in December 1818, he was already in Rome, so he entrusted them to a family friend, the art historian Johann Gottlob von Quandt. He stayed in Rome until May, except for an excursion further south to Naples where he explored the crumbling ruins of Pompeii, Herculaneum, Baiae, and Pozzuoli. At the coastal town of Paestum, he visited a temple to the sea god Poseidon, erected long ago by the ancient Greeks. He marveled at the thought of a monument that had not been shaken in the course of twenty-five centuries, wondering whether Plato's feet had once trodden the path where he now stood. On his way back north, he retraced his steps through Florence and Venice, but then went west through Padua, Vicenza, Verona, and Milan. He crossed the Alps into Switzerland through the Gotthard Pass, before finally returning to Dresden in August 1819. In total, he spent eleven months away.[2]

Just like when he was a teenager on his grand tour, Schopenhauer kept a travel diary during his Italian sojourn. But unlike then, most of the entries were philosophical thoughts that still lingered in his mind after finishing his book. In Naples in March 1819, at the castle Capo di Monte, he saw a fine painting by a young Venetian artist named Francesco Hayez, which reminded him of his theory of weeping.[3] In the picture, the epic hero Odysseus is welcomed at the court of the Phaeacian King Alcinous: a rhapsode delights the other courtiers with tales of the carnage that Odysseus had wrought upon Troy, but Odysseus himself buries his face into his cloak and sobs bitterly at the story of his own embattled life. It perfectly illustrated Schopenhauer's thesis that weeping is noble self-pity—so well, in fact, that the same passage from Homer's *Odyssey* would later be added to the second volume of *The World as Will and Representation*.[4]

Naturally, Schopenhauer's thoughts also turned to the virtues of travel, which he was beginning to view with renewed appreciation. In Venice on November 1, 1818, he wrote:

> Whoever is suddenly moved into an entirely foreign country or city where a way of life very different from his own and even the

language prevail, at first feels like one who has stepped into cold water. He is suddenly brought into contact with a temperature far different from his own; he feels a powerful superior impression from outside which makes him anxious. He is in an element that is foreign to him and in which he is unable to move with ease. Moreover, he is frightened because everything surprises him and he is afraid of being conspicuous to all. But as soon as he calms down somewhat and has become acclimatized to his environment and has taken on some of its temperature, he begins to feel extraordinarily well like the man in cold water. He has assimilated the element and then no longer has to concern himself with his own personality. He now turns his attention purely to his surroundings and precisely through an objective and disinterested contemplation of them he now feels superior to them instead of being depressed by them as previously.[5]

Paradoxically, the further Schopenhauer got away from home, the less homeless he felt. He felt most at home, he found, among strangers: "To me close acquaintances often become and are strangers and strangers are often familiar, and to them all I speak the same language, whereas others make a great difference in this respect."[6] Over time he perfected his Italian, so that he could speak the language of strangers literally as well as figuratively. When in Italy, he was about as comfortable in the world as he ever would be in his adult life.

In part, he was buoyed by the still-live prospect that the book he had just released into the world was going to make his name. Letters from Adele with reports of its reception, however—or rather lack thereof—gradually eroded his hopes away. In Rome in April 1819, he penned a poem full of self-defensive braggadocio:

> From long and deeply harboured pains
> 'Twas unfolded from my very heart.
> Long did I strive to hold it firm and
> Yet I know success is finally mine.
> Howe'er you view the work,
> Its life you cannot imperil.

It you may hold up but never will destroy.
Posterity will erect ~~monuments~~ a memorial to me.[7]

Failure to capture an audience apparently hadn't damaged his levels of self-belief too much.

Adele lived for and through her brother's Italian letters. Like Arthur, she had always admired Italy from afar and had been learning its language for some time. One day, in fact, she would spend more time there than he ever did; between 1844 and 1849, she lived in Genoa, Rome, and Naples, and even wrote a guidebook to Florence. For the time being, however, she was still sharing a roof with the man who was both her first serious crush and her mother's rumored lover. Any form of escape was welcome.

Before Arthur's trip, most of Adele's impressions of Italy had come from a young councillor in Weimar named Hans Heinrich von Könneritz. Könneritz (as Adele always referred to him, at least in writing) had described Rome to her in such minute detail that, between his account and Arthur's, she feared there would be no surprises left for her if she were to visit for herself someday. On Könneritz's advice, she asked Arthur to bring her back some sepia pigment from a specialist art shop in Milan, along with songs for the guitar and mosaic tiles, which were so expensive to buy at home but had barely any value over there. There were rumors that Adele and Könneritz were an item: "People gossip when I'm friendly with him," she wrote to Arthur.[8] But while she admitted that he was very attractive—in the same letter, she refers to him as the "town Adonis"—and though he was in every way more suitable than Gerstenbergk, ultimately she was repelled by his vanity. Her feelings had in fact been vacillating in this way for over a year: in a diary entry of March 27, 1818, she wrote: "Yesterday I wrote a little poem on Könneritz. It's kind of a dumping because I feel quite definitely that my interest is waning. I have placed him so high that now I hate to see him act in a way that puts him on a par with ordinary young men. It tormented me, and so inside I suddenly withdrew."[9] After May 1819, Adele's concerns with Könneritz completely dried up, partly because she became consumed by the collapse of Muhl's bank, and partly because he left Weimar to become director of the royal theater in Dresden, and from there went on to have a distinguished diplomatic career.

Over in Italy, Arthur was entangled in his own romantic affairs. Sweetly, but also strangely, he used his letters to manage and augment his sister's impression of his prowess in this domain. First, to her great disappointment, he led Adele to believe that he simply hadn't encountered Lord Byron in Venice at all. In truth, of course, he had seen Byron but lacked the courage to introduce himself. His excuse was that he feared Byron would seduce his "*dulcinea*" (his Italian sweetheart), who, upon seeing Byron, had cried out after him, "*Ecce il poëta inglese!*"–Behold the English poet![10] When Schopenhauer confessed this presumably truer version of events in later life, he smacked his forehead with regret at his own cowardice, but added that Byron was only "the second, not the first English poet" (as none could rank above Shakespeare). At the time, it seems, he just could not have his sister know that he was ever romantically intimidated.

It was at least true that Arthur even had a Venetian *dulcinea*, although we cannot be sure it was the very same *dulcinea* that led to his studied avoidance of Byron. Her name was Teresa Fuga. On the return leg of his trip, he let Teresa know that he would soon be revisiting Venice, to which she enthusiastically replied:

> I received your letter with great pleasure and learned that you have not forgotten me and that I am much in your thoughts; but believe me, my dear, I too have not forgotten you. . . . I love you and wish to see you, do come, I am looking forward to embracing you and spending a few days with you. I have a friend already, but he is forever leaving Venice and only visits me now and again—in any case he leaves for the country on Sunday, where he will be staying for fifteen to twenty days; you can therefore come without fear, I await you with all my heart; I no longer have a relationship with the "impresario," I have long had this other friend; and as for Englishmen who have fled England and come to Venice out of desperation, I have no flirtations with them any more either.[11]

Evidently, however, his relationship with Teresa was not exclusive. She can't have recalled him quite so well as she makes out either, since she addressed her letter to "Arthur Scharrenhans."[12]

Arthur also told his sister tales of a mysterious highborn woman whom he intended to bring home to marry, but even Adele was skeptical at this prospect: "Your beloved is rich, she is of good standing, and yet you think she will want to follow you?"[13] She too was Venetian, or at least that was Adele's understanding. According to some later accounts, Schopenhauer claimed that his rich beloved was in fact from Florence, and that it was he who had—rather ignobly—broken off their engagement when he discovered that she had a lung disease.[14] Probably none of these facts is quite straight, but in any case the blend of truth and half-truth let Arthur project a somewhat swashbuckling image back home.

Only one of Arthur's liaisons was backed by evidence that Adele could have verified. In a letter to him dated February 5, 1819, Adele wrote: "I feel sorry for the girl you mentioned; I hope to God that you have not betrayed her, since you are *true* to everyone, why not to a poor, weak thing like her?"[15] Adele's remarks referred to a housemaid in Dresden with whom, it seems, Arthur had conceived a child just before he left for Italy. In her diary on April 27, 1819, Adele wrote: "His girl in Dresden is *enceinte* [i.e., pregnant]; I am appalled—but he is meanwhile behaving correctly and well."[16] By behaving well, she meant that he had at least admitted paternity and offered financial support. She encouraged him, however, to consider going beyond what she regarded as the bare minimum, and even offered up her own assistance in this regard: "Can I do something for the girl? Say so frankly, and take your duty not in the usual narrow sense to which the baseness of men like you reduces it. I wished that the child would not have been born, but it is here, so care for it according to the degree of the needs that it will develop later in its life."[17] Adele's offer of help was perhaps the tenderest way that any member of the Schopenhauer family ever handled the trouble with being born.

By September 8, 1819, Arthur's child, a little girl, had already died. Adele regretted the child's death almost as much as she had initially regretted her birth: "That your daughter is dead, I am sorry; since if the child had lived, it would have given you joy. You would not be so alone. You would have had someone for whom to care."[18] The grief that Adele felt on her brother's behalf—for she made no reference to the fact that the child was, or could have been, her niece too—sheds a different light on her desire that he should have done more for his daughter. To her mind, it had always been more than a matter of doing the decent thing, and not only for the sake of the child, or the mother, but for Arthur himself. There were precious few opportunities for men of his nature to cherish and nurture another human life, and he, in her eyes, had just thrown one away.

Much as Arthur might have tried to impress Adele with his many dalliances, then, in reality it only ever left her feeling more saddened for him. The one thing that united all his tales was the complete absence of any depth. After she joked about the likelihood that his wealthy Italian lover would ever follow him back to Dresden, she added: "Oh, I make stupid jokes and yet it really hurts me inside that in one of your letters there are two love stories without love, and that all this is not what I would have wished for you. These tendencies have already taken a sad turn for the unfortunate girl in Dresden."[19] There was, admittedly, more than a trace of snobbery to Adele's wishes: "May you not lose the ability to value a woman by continuing to waste your time with the vulgar and common ones of our sex." She thought her brother deserved a higher class of woman than the ones with whom he had evidently been successful. But she also thought that he deserved a higher class of love too, something over and above mere lust: "May heaven lead you one day to a woman for whom you could feel something deeper than that agitation *that I never once understood.*"[20]

As she herself admitted, Adele knew little of lust; but, to her credit, she knew that it differed from love. This much was evident in her final dismissal of Könneritz, on grounds that prioritized moral qualities over physical ones: he may have been handsome, but he was vain. It seems, as well, that she was not interested in making compromises. At one point Arthur had wanted her to marry Quandt, the friend to whom he had entrusted his author copies of his book while he was still away in Italy, who had first met Adele and Johanna in Karlsbad in 1815. She was briefly tempted—Quandt was cultured, kind, and, not that it seemed to matter to her, rich—but she didn't pursue it. With irksome persistence, Arthur proposed the idea again over twenty years later, implying perhaps that she had made a mistake. She wrote back to him forcefully on January 23, 1836: "As far as marriages like that with Quandt are concerned, I beg you, don't tell me about it, regret is not in my nature, I had reasons *that still stand*, so I don't regret anything of the kind. Respect that, dear Arthur!"[21] With regards to what Adele could have meant by marriages "like that," it might be no coincidence that most of the rest of her letter concerned her worsening financial situation. Just as she would not marry for looks, on principle Adele would not marry for money. She would marry for love or not at all, where love, to her, meant "to a man whom I particularly and thoroughly respect and place spiritually above or beside me."[22]

Some men recognized Adele's intellectual gifts, by then an established family trait, but often only to contrast them unkindly with her physical appearance. As the Hanoverian surgeon Georg Friedrich Ludwig Stromeyer said: "Fräulein Adele was a person of a special kind. Except for a slim figure and delicate hands, she had nothing that could draw the eye; her physiognomy was just as plain. And still she pleased men by her intelligence, culture, and diffuse knowledge."[23] Louis (as he was known to his friends) strung Adele along with love poems and letters, but in 1831, like they all did, he married someone else. Her anguish at never finding the right person sometimes drove Adele to regret her very existence—yet another established family trait. On October 27, 1831, she wrote to Arthur in despair:

> I don't like living, I dread old age, I dread the loneliness that is certainly part of my life, I don't want to get married because it would be difficult for me to find a man who was right for me. I only know one whom I could marry without reluctance, and he is *married*.[24] I am strong enough to endure this desertion, but I would be heartily grateful to cholera if it relieved me of the

whole history without severe pain. Therefore your fear is strange to me, since you also feel unhappy and have often wanted to get out of life by taking some violent step.[25]

Adele's last remark reveals much. Evidently Arthur had at some point confessed that he too had struggled with self-destructive urges, although likely not on the same grounds.

: : :

If Schopenhauer was a realist about love, then he was also a reductionist. All love—or more precisely, all *romantic* love—was reducible, in his view, to sexual desire. "All instances of being in love," he wrote, "however ethereal they might pretend to be, are rooted solely in the sex drive."[26] He later developed and published this view in a chapter titled "Metaphysics of Sexual Love" in the second and expanded edition of *The World as Will and Representation* from 1844. But, for obvious reasons, the matter of sexual reproduction was clearly on his mind by the end of 1819 too, the year in which his first daughter was born and died. In his travel journal, which he continued to use even after returning home from Italy, he wrote: "A man's life with its endless suffering is nothing but the explanation, the paraphrase of the *act of procreation*, i.e. of the most distinct affirmation of the will to life."[27] Here he was concerned less with the question of what love is, and more with how to view acts of love from the perspective of his pessimism. To bring new life into the world was, after all, to condemn it to relentless pain and misery, and who else could be blamed but the parents who did the deed? In this respect, Schopenhauer may have regarded the brevity of his own daughter's life as a kind of mercy or even a sign of nascent wisdom. He was impressed by the example of the German Enlightenment philosopher Gotthold Ephraim Lessing, who when his child died only moments after being born, was "amazed by the understanding of his son who had not wanted to come into the world at all."[28]

Whatever love is, then, its force must be strong enough to override the obvious fact, to Schopenhauer's mind, that procreation only adds more sufferers to the world. Indeed, it often felt to him as though the power of romantic attraction and repulsion transcended both parties, as though it were a command prenatally issued by their merely possible offspring:

> The affection of two person of different sexes for each of *is already* the will to life of the new individual that they can and would like to produce; this will is already stirred with the meeting of their glances.—Antipathy between them indicates that what they would inevitably produce, if it materialized, would be a badly formed, sorrowful and luckless being not in harmony with itself.[29]

Schopenhauer recorded this thought in his travel notebook in early 1820. But judging by the conclusion of his 1844 chapter on sexual love, the thought of a conspiratorial glance between two wanton lovers clearly stuck with him over the decades:

> If we now look into the bustle of life . . . we see everyone occupied with its cares and troubles, striving with all their might to satisfy life's endless needs and to ward off suffering in its many forms without anything to hope for other than to sustain this tortured individual existence through a short span of time. But in the middle of this turmoil we see the gaze of two lovers looking with longing at each other—but why so secretively, furtively, nervously?—Because these lovers are traitors, secretly plotting to perpetuate all this need and vexation, which would otherwise quickly come to an end.[30]

If blind sexual urges were still not strong enough to push two people to procreate, then the pull of illusory romantic ideals could always lend assistance.

In case Schopenhauer's realism should seem cynical, it should be noted that to him the deeper goal of procreation, namely, the fine-tuning of the next generation of human beings, was among the highest of callings: "Isn't the precise determination of the individualities in the next generation a much loftier and worthier goal than their extravagant feelings and supersensible soap bubbles?" he asked. "Indeed, could there be a greater or more important goal on earth?" Plus, he added, if his theory was right, then it would explain and justify the seriousness with which people conduct their romantic affairs. Unbeknown to them, or just barely known, they carry out a deed of the utmost importance.

Another way to defend Schopenhauer's realistic stance would be to reconsider the question that his theory best answers. In response to the question "What is love?" Schopenhauer's theory—that it is no more than the sex drive in a cunning disguise—admittedly reduces it down to the basest of instincts. However, in response to questions like "Why is it so hard to find happiness in love?" there is something undeniable about his view. We are, after all, often romantically drawn to people for reasons that not only elude our consciousness, but go far beyond our personal interests. It may be the goal of procreation, or, less reductively, it may be a multitude of other physical, social, or cultural forces, each with their own aims and often working at cross-purposes. At any rate, the interests that our romantic matches serve may not be limited to our own; and what is good in the eyes of the species, or society, or whatever else it might be, may not be good with respect to one's own personal happiness. Romantic ideals and instincts are there precisely to mask this otherwise obvious fact, according to Schopenhauer, or else the high cost to ourselves, and perhaps to all of humankind, might put us off even bothering altogether.

Furthermore, just as he wasn't a skeptic about love, Schopenhauer was not a complete cynic either. Occasionally, he suggested a kind of partnership that was, if not real love, then something comparably meaningful:

> Precisely because amorous passion in fact turns on the child to be conceived and its traits, and because these are at its core, a friendship can arise between two young and well-constituted young people of the opposite sex, a friendship based on an agreement of temperament, character, and the tendency of their minds, without the admixture of sexual love; there might even be a distinct aversion between them in this respect.[31]

Thus, Schopenhauer at least believed in friendship between those who are unsuited to be lovers. If this is friendship instead of romance, then is friendship *within* romance also possible? Luckily—and perhaps surprisingly—Schopenhauer also answered yes:

> We can comfort tender and loving minds by adding that passionate sexual love is sometimes accompanied by a feeling that is of a completely different origin, a feeling that is actually friendship grounded in harmony of temperament, although this usually only comes to the fore when genuine sexual love has been extinguished by its satisfaction. This friendship will stem mostly from . . . the mutually corresponding and complementing physical, moral and intellectual qualities of the two individuals from which sexual love arises.[32]

This really is a matter of luck. Such friendship does not automatically emerge from romantic love, Schopenhauer thought, but rather from the same source as any good friendship, namely, harmony. It is therefore entirely fortunate if the qualities that make for a romantic match, which are not necessarily the qualities that would make for a good friendship, nevertheless happen to be complementary and harmonious. If happy marriages are possible, then this is how—although, with a trace of La Rochefoucauld's skepticism, Schopenhauer added that these marriages are "famously rare."[33] By contrast, the unluckiest in love are those repelled by enmity yet compelled by desire: the recipe for a truly tempestuous affair.

:::

How lucky in love were the Schopenhauers by these standards? To start with Arthur and Adele, neither of them, it seems, ever found a lover who could also be a friend. The difference between them, however, was that this didn't stop Arthur, who evidently had at least a few lusty liaisons nevertheless, but it did stop Adele, who was after something more. Their situations were of course vastly different in regard to their genders too; in almost every respect, Adele simply wasn't granted the liberties in life that Arthur enjoyed. But they also clearly had different values and temperaments when it came to romantic matters.

As for their parents, whether Johanna and Heinrich Floris made a good match depends on how their relationship is viewed. With respect to their own happiness and friendliness, at least initially they were surprisingly well matched, given such shared values as cosmopolitanism and republicanism, and their common passion for world travel and high culture. Obviously, however, their marriage did not have a happy ending, and not just because of Heinrich Floris's premature death, but also, it seems, the unlivable domestic environment in the lead up to it. The end of Johanna's marriage, however sad and abrupt, gave her a new lease on life—not that she ever put it quite that way—which would have been even happier had she not been constrained by financial troubles further down the road.

But, on Schopenhauer's theory, this is not the only way to judge the success of his parent's marriage. Aside from the couple's own happiness, a romantic match can be judged with respect to its main product: that is, the quality of the offspring. Were Arthur and Adele themselves evidence that Johanna and Heinrich Floris were well matched? At first, it might seem that the answer is no. After all, as just mentioned, the Schopenhauer children were even less lucky in love than their parents. Additionally, at times, both were severely unhappy in life, as shown by Adele's intimation that both had contemplated a violent end. In these respects, Arthur and Adele might seem like the epitome of the "badly formed, sorrowful and luckless being not in harmony with itself" that really ought to have generated antipathy, rather than romance, between their parents.

On the other hand, Arthur and Adele were both intelligent, talented, and—each in their own way—sensitive people, which had to count for something. Arthur even became mildly obsessed with identifying the origin of these qualities, if not in himself specifically, then in other noteworthy figures. For obvious reasons, perhaps, he became passionately committed to the theory that intellectual qualities are inherited from the mother. For decades he collected evidence for this view. In one collection of notes marked

Berlin, January 1826, he began to compile a list of academic sources for this theory, as well as anecdotes of outstanding men with intelligent mothers.[34] He updated these notes throughout the 1820s, the 1830s, and even into the early 1840s, including an article called "Mutterwitz," which appeared in the *Blätter für literarische Unterhaltung* on October 4, 1841. From this source alone, he learned that Francis Bacon's mother was a distinguished linguist and translator, and Walter Scott's a published poet.[35] A recent biography of Kant had described his mother as "a woman of great natural understanding,"[36] and in his autobiography Hume claimed that his mother was "of *singular merit*."[37] Aside from these examples, it was also well known among Schopenhauer's social circle, such as it was, "what an uncommonly clever, quick-witted, and superior woman *Goethe's* mother was," and the same was said of Schiller.[38] In short, almost all of his intellectual icons had, like him, an intelligent mother. All of this evidence made it into the second edition of *The World as Will and Representation* in a chapter titled "The Heritability of Traits." Although Schopenhauer stopped short of proposing himself as yet another example, in his own indirect and egotistical way, it was a rare, if veiled, tribute to his mother.

There was another side to this popular theory, however, to which Schopenhauer assented with greater hesitancy. One of his main sources also hypothesized that, while intellect comes from the mother, character comes from the father.[39] Though he found fewer academic sources in support of this view compared to the alleged matrilineal inheritance of intelligence, in the end Schopenhauer saw enough of his father in himself to agree with it:

> I refer everyone to his own experience. To begin with, let him consider himself, admit his own inclinations and passions, his character flaws and weaknesses, his vices as well as his merits and virtues, if he has any: and then let him think back on his father, and no one will ever fail to notice those same personality features in his father as well.[40]

There were, of course, many qualities that Arthur admired in Heinrich Floris—for instance, the man's sheer industriousness. But there were also many qualities he may have regretted inheriting from his father—if that is really where they came from—such as his paranoid suspicion of others, his violent eruptions of temper, and his melancholic moods.

Regrettable or not, similarities between a father and his child enhanced the basis for another sort of love, Schopenhauer claimed. In one of few the specific remarks about fatherly love in his published works, he wrote:

> Paternal love is based on the fact that the begetter recognizes himself in the begotten, and this love is what makes the father ready to do more for his child, to suffer more, to hazard more, than for himself, and at the same time recognize this as his debt of guilt.[41]

A father recognizes that he has brought his child into the same struggle and strife as himself. With others, he merely happens to share the fate of humanity, but with his children, he has inflicted it upon them, giving him a stronger sense of responsibility for their welfare. (And there is of course no reason why this should not apply to mothers too.) If this is true, then, for all his faults, it was a form of love more evident in Heinrich Floris's approach to fatherhood, at least for a time, than in Arthur's treatment of his own abandoned child.

In notes from 1821, Schopenhauer mused on a more chilling version of fatherly love—if it can even be called that: "From time to time cases constantly occur in which *suicide concerns also the children*," he wrote, and proceeded to list several examples taken from the news, including a joiner in Frankfurt in 1817, who killed his wife, their five children, and then himself. If, as Schopenhauer had proposed, a father recognizes himself in his children, then it might explain how one could even begin to imagine that "without their deaths there is no liberation for himself." Even on this explanation, however, Schopenhauer regarded the act as utterly deluded. If suicide was no solution, then murder couldn't be either.

:::

So far, on matters of love and sex, it might seem as though Schopenhauer only ever had relationships between opposite sexes in mind. At first, indeed, he said little publicly about same-sex relationships, and when he did say anything it was tasteless: for example, "the sense of beauty that instinctively directs the choice of the object of sexual satisfaction is easily misled when it degenerates into a pederastic tendency."[42] However, Schopenhauer later revised his views on same-sex relationships in two important ways.

First, for the third and final edition of *The World as Will and Representation*, published in 1859, he added an appendix to his chapter on sexual love that retracted his remark that the sense of beauty can "degenerate" into a "pederastic tendency." His retraction did not start off well: "Viewed in itself, pederasty presents itself not merely as an unnatural monstrosity but also as disgusting and repulsive to the highest degree . . ." (the quotation continues in this vein). Then, however, he turned another corner: "But if we now turn to experience, we find the opposite to be the case: we see that this vice, in spite of its repulsiveness, has been in vogue and frequently practised at all times and in all countries of the world."[43] True to his worldly outlook, Schopenhauer conceded that a practice found at every point in history and in all corners of the globe simply cannot be "unnatural" in every sense of the word. Anything so ubiquitous cannot be a freak of nature. He therefore challenged himself to explain why such "unnatural" sexualities are, in some sense, natural after all. In his explanation, he never dropped his assumption that nature's ultimate aim is to produce offspring; instead, he attempted to figure out how certain kinds of same-sex relationships could serve that aim. He also stuck with the classically Greek model, namely, sex between young boys and men, hence why he persisted with the (now archaic) term "pederasty." With these assumptions in mind, he finally settled on the view that pederasty is nature's way of simultaneously satisfying the sex drives of boys, who are too young to reproduce, and men, who are too old, by getting them to have sex with each other instead.

By today's standards, this is unsatisfactory for any number of reasons, not least because it reinforces a pernicious conflation between gay relationships, on the one hand, and sex between adults and minors, on the other.⁴⁴ Nevertheless, Schopenhauer was at least undogmatic enough to put the assumptions of his day to the test of experience and find them lacking. He knew, furthermore, that he took a risk by publishing anything even faintly encouraging on this topic: "I wanted to do a small favour for the philosophy professors," he wrote sarcastically at the end of his addendum, "who are now very disconcerted by the increasingly wide popularity of my philosophy, which they have so studiously ignored: I have given them the opportunity to slander me by saying that I have defended and recommended pederasty."⁴⁵

Similarly, the second way that Schopenhauer revised his views on same-sex relationships was partly misguided, partly enlightened. As before, it started when he made some hasty comments about pederasty, which he then went back to change. This time, the comments appeared in his 1841 work *The Two Fundamental Problems of Ethics*, which was a combination of two long essays, one on free will and the other on morality. In the essay on morality, he paused to consider the ethics of a range of "unnatural lusts," once again meaning sex acts that do not aim at procreation, including "sodomy, pederasty and onanism."⁴⁶ He asked himself whether these lusts are immoral, and initially answered no, they are not. His logic was practically identical to his argument that suicide is not immoral. Like suicide, these acts of "unnatural lust" only concern the people who perform them. In the case of onanism, in fact, they only concern one person, but even if they involve more than one person, so long as everyone involved assents, then there can be no harm in it. Consent, then, is a necessary condition, but other than that, "unnatural" lusts are simply not a matter for moral judgment.

However, in the 1860 edition of the same work, Schopenhauer altered his argument. First, he revised his brief list of unnatural lusts to "onanism, pederasty and bestiality,"⁴⁷ thereby dropping the mention of sodomy and adding bestiality (for reasons unclear). Second, he changed his stance on pederasty. By 1860, incidentally the year of his death, Schopenhauer believed that pederasty *was* immoral after all. The change of mind seems to lie in the matter of consent. In the 1841 version, his grounds for not deeming pederasty immoral were the principle *volenti non fit injuria*: no injury is done to him who wills it.⁴⁸ In 1860, however, he was clearly of the view that mere willingness, or rather *apparent* willingness, does not remove the injury in this case. He clarified why this is so: "for the injustice lies in the seduction of the younger and inexperienced party, who is physically and morally corrupted by it."⁴⁹ Once again, by pederasty, Schopenhauer evidently had in mind sex with young boys, and here youth and inexperience decisively changed the ethics of the situation. Expressions of willingness do not remove the injury here because, to do so, consent from participants must be properly informed, rather than seductively obtained. Even if they do consent, that is, if the young and inexperienced do not know what they are consenting to, then it becomes a real moral matter. By implication, if it were between two well-informed and consenting adults, the situation would be entirely different.

At first sight, Schopenhauer's change of mind about pederasty might have seemed retrogressive, making a moral matter out of something that he previously thought was really nobody's business. But, first, the moral factors that produced his change of mind were not to do with the genders of the participants but only their stages of life. He was never against same-sex relationships, it seems; he was only against what today might be called grooming. (Again, an objectionable part here is the potential conflation of these two different things.) Second, and relatedly, Schopenhauer never even entertained the argument that same-sex relationships are immoral simply because they are same-sex. According to his moral principles, consistently applied at any rate, the kind of sex that two adults consent to have with one another is simply not a moral issue.

As with his arguments on suicide, however, Schopenhauer's argument for why most unnatural lusts are not immoral came with a caveat that applied to any and all forms of lust. Even if it they are not immoral, he thought, unnatural lusts still aren't recommended. Asceticism was, after all, the highest, if virtually unachievable, ethical ideal in Schopenhauer's view. For this reason the sex drive, however it manifests, should be the first thing to go, hence why true ascetics practice voluntary chastity among other forms of strict self-denial.⁵⁰ From this higher perspective, abandoning sexual lust is really no loss, for such lust was only ever "the quintessence of the whole fraud of this noble world . . . it promises so unspeakably, infinitely and extravagantly much and then delivers so pitifully little."[51]

Rightly or wrongly, it is one principle that Adele and Arthur could have agreed on—not that Adele ever advocated chastity, nor that Arthur practiced it, but that lust (as distinct from love) meant very little, and that it was certainly not a direct way to redeem existence. They still differed, of course, on the promise of its product. To Arthur, parental love was just one more instinct among others that masked the overwhelming costs of procreating. To Adele's mind such love could, perhaps, have deepened and enriched a man like Arthur's life.

::::

On December 10, 1836, Schopenhauer reconnected with his best friend from childhood and French counterpart, Anthime Grégoire de Blésimaire. It was almost two decades since they had lost touch, but in that time Anthime would often search the newspapers for any mention of Schopenhauer's name. In the fall of that year, he was delighted to find an advertisement for a book by a lady novelist named Schopenhauer. By his own admission, Anthime didn't read a lot of novels, but on this occasion he hurriedly ordered it. Mistakenly assuming that Adele was its author, Anthime found a way to write to her, and he took the opportunity to inquire about Arthur. She duly passed on the message, and in his reply to Anthime, Arthur corrected his error about the novel's author. "It's not my sister," he wrote, "it's my mother who writes the novels, she became very famous & saw 2 editions of her complete works in 24 volumes. She is a good novelist, but a bad mother."[52]

Schopenhauer, too, had been looking for signs of life from his old friend. For the past three years, he had checked the lists of travelers arriving into Frankfurt in case there were any from Le Havre who might happen to know Anthime. Only two such travelers passed through, but too quickly for Schopenhauer to track them down for questioning. He was pleased to hear that Anthime was surviving and apparently thriving:

> I see with great pleasure that, according to all appearance, you have not only life, but also the kind of life that I have always seen as the most beautiful of all, to be in the countryside, lord in his castle, surrounded by his family & all the eases & amenities, especially many books, & far, far from the rest of men.[53]

Almost every part of this description was indeed Schopenhauer's idea of happiness: natural beauty, self-governance, basic comforts, interesting things to read, and, above all, complete seclusion. Everything, that is, except for being surrounded by family, which did not usually feature anywhere on Schopenhauer's list. Normally, he regarded family life as something to be sacrificed for the sake of his philosophy. "How," he once asked, "should someone who seeks an honest living for himself and wife and child devote himself to the *truth*?"[54] But, not being a philosopher, a family life was what his oldest friend had chosen.

At first, Arthur and Anthime had been on much the same path in life. Their fathers were both shipping merchants, who died within the same year.[55] Both sons soldiered on with their vocational training: Anthime even moved to Hamburg in May 1806 in order to study German for business purposes. Although by then Johanna and Adele had vacated Hamburg, Arthur was still there on his own apprenticeship, and so in January 1807 Anthime moved in with Arthur.[56] In the period that the two young men were housemates, both took the opportunity to sow their wild oats, including a visit to a brothel where Anthime later recalled the "embraces of an industrious whore."[57]

After their youth ended, only Anthime settled into the life laid out before him. In contrast to the idyllic picture that Arthur later drew in his letter, however, for a long time family life had been a source of deep sorrow to Anthime. He had married in 1813, but shortly after the two friends stopped corresponding, Anthime's wife died. In that time they had three children together, although only one survived: a girl named Eugénie. In 1819, Anthime took Eugénie to live in Paris, to get away from his business in Le Havre and devote himself to his last surviving daughter. In 1827, Eugénie died too, leaving Anthime completely bereft of his first family. To escape his awful loneliness he remarried, and in 1829 they bought a château in the countryside just outside of the city. Along with a great deal of love and happiness, Anthime's second marriage brought him another daughter, Marie, who was eight years old at the time when he reestablished contact with Arthur.

Meanwhile, as he himself summarized to Anthime, Arthur had been living the bachelor's life, "having neither wife nor children: 2 bastards, whom I had, died young."[58] Judging by a letter from Adele to Ottilie on January 16, 1836, his second illegitimate child was born in Frankfurt the previous year. Other than the fact that she was another daughter who also died in infancy, even less is known about this child than the first. The closest Arthur came to marrying, he told Anthime, was to a woman in Berlin with whom he been having a secretive liaison for over ten years.[59] She was a dark-haired dancer named Caroline Richter, although she went by Ida, and when Arthur first met her she was only nineteen years old. The relationship was not exclusive: during their affair Ida became pregnant at least three times, not by Arthur. All of her pregnancies interfered with her stage career, two of them came to term, and only one survived: a son named Carl. When Arthur fled Berlin in 1831, Ida promised to follow him but never did. "No doubt she had some family ties," he wrote to Anthime, understatedly referring to the fact that he had asked her to leave Carl behind in school rather than bring him along to Frankfurt.[60] It pained Arthur to lose Ida, since she was, he told Anthime, the only woman who was ever truly attached to him. Still, the couple remembered one another later in life: on Arthur's seventieth birthday in 1858, she sent him a pair of embroidered slippers, while he, in a codicil to his will, left her—but pointedly not Carl—the princely sum of 5,000 taler.[61]

The divergence between the two boyhood friends, by now so very unalike, became clear to them both when Anthime and his daughter came to visit Frankfurt in July 1845. Schopenhauer had gone to the trouble of booking them two rooms on the third floor of the Englischer Hof.[62] When they met up for dinner, however, according to Anthime's account, Schopenhauer arrived late and quarrelsome:

We were already at the table when someone came to tell me that my friend had finally arrived. He is a short, white-haired man who looks very old. . . . He is of such disagreeable character that we quarreled quite seriously. He professes, he says, the religion of the Hindus [Anthime and his second wife were strict Christians]. It's an eccentricity to add to all the others. He is considered mad, and indeed he must be.[63]

The unfriendly feeling was mutual. As he later recalled, Schopenhauer's last meeting with his "French brother" only reminded him that "one diverges more and more, the older one becomes. Finally, one is completely alone."[64]

: : :

On top of everything else, even by this time, Schopenhauer's gamble on becoming a philosopher, at the price of being a confirmed bachelor, still hadn't paid off. On January 23, 1836—the year after Arthur's second child was born and died; the same year that they received word from Anthime about his eventual domestic bliss; and in the very same letter that she reaffirmed her decision not to marry Quandt—Adele professed that she could not truly judge her brother's life choices until their consequences came to light. Only time would tell, she said, whether or not the world would ever embrace his thought. "For one hour of your faith," she wrote to him, "I would give my whole existence. And you have bought it cheaply, if you have only risked the quiet middle-class happiness of having a house, a farm, a wife and a child—I envy you!" As much as Adele coveted her brother's wasted opportunities for love, family, and happiness, above all she envied the life for which he sacrificed all those things. If, that is, this long-awaited life would ever come to pass.

CHAPTER 7

The Second Sex
How Schopenhauer Underestimated Women

Schopenhauer was never settled in Berlin. He lived there for over a decade, on and off, but he never quite felt at home. Apart from anything else, he always hated noise. "Knocking, hammering and ramming," he wrote, "has been a daily pain to me my whole life through."[1] Street noise especially bothered him. Like any metropolis of the early nineteenth century, the air in Berlin was filled with the sound of coachmen cracking their whips. He had a visceral aversion to these snaps and cracks, as though the tip of the lash sliced cleanly through his brain, he said, banishing all thought from his mind.

> Coachmen, porters, errand boys and so on are the beasts of burden of human society; they should by all means be treated humanely with justice, fairness, consideration and care, but they should not be allowed to obstruct the higher endeavours of the human race through impudent noise. I would like to know how many great and beautiful thoughts these whips have already cracked out of the world.[2]

Only a thinker of Schopenhauer's persuasion could contend that workers deserve humane treatment not on the grounds that they are human, but rather because society makes them into animals. When the *Bulletin of the Munich Animal Protection Society* reported that Nuremberg had outlawed all superfluous cracking and whipping of horses, he applauded the news—a triumph of humanity, but also of peace and quiet.³

His Berlin years saw him through his thirties and into his forties. The disillusionment of middle age hit him almost as soon as he arrived. All he wanted to do was close his front door behind him and forget about the world. In his notebook, he wrote of happiness: "If, when I was young, there was a ring or a knock at the door, I was pleased, for I thought now it might come. Today, when there is a knock on the door, I am frightened, for I think: here it comes!"⁴ Now he only expected trouble at his door.

Toward the end of April 1820, after moving his lodgings twice in as many months, Schopenhauer rented rooms from a widow named Dorothee Marie Becker at Niederlagstrasse 4, a street just off Berlin's bustling boulevard Unter den Linden. Initially he occupied three rooms, but in early 1821 he reduced it to just two: a study at the front, and a bedroom at the back. The third room came to be occupied by an unmarried seamstress named Caroline Luise Marquet, though he had no cause to learn her name until later.

One day in late July 1821, Schopenhauer returned home to find three women in the entryway to his rooms, including Marquet. It hadn't happened before: as he understood it, access to this entryway was exclusive to him and another man who also rented a room at the front. Although Marquet's room at the back of the house adjoined Schopenhauer's bedroom, she had her own entrance beside the stairs, and so had neither the right nor the need to congregate with her friends outside his door. Rather than confront them, however, on this occasion Schopenhauer complained to his landlady. At the time, the widow Becker confirmed that only he and his gentleman neighbor had official access to the entryway. It would not happen again, she reassured him.

But on August 12, it did happen again. The same three ladies were back. Once more, Schopenhauer intended to complain to his landlady and asked the housemaid to find her, but this time she wasn't home. He decided to take matters into his own hands by asking the women to leave. Two of them were ready to comply, but Marquet refused. He stormed off into his rooms, instructing them to be gone by the time he reemerged. But when he did, there they still were. Since he was on his way out again anyway, he offered Marquet his arm to lead her away. She insisted on staying put. At this point, Schopenhauer lost his temper and grabbed Marquet by the waist to forcibly remove her. After he had deposited her outside, she threatened to sue him for assault and demanded the belongings that she had left behind. He threw them out the door, but neglected one item, which Marquet charged back in to retrieve. He picked her up and threw her out again, calling her a bitch as he did so. This time she fell to the floor—on purpose, Schopenhauer thought.

This, at least, was his version of events. According to Marquet, he was much more violent. When he reemerged from his rooms, she claimed, he did so brandishing a stick. Later Schopenhauer explained that this was only his walking stick, which along with his hat he always took out with him, and already had in hand when he had first arrived home. Marquet testified that he did not merely lift her out by the waist, but by the neck with both hands. Schopenhauer doubted that he was even physically capable of this feat. Marquet alleged that he tore off her hood, that she fainted, and that he kicked and punched her. Schopenhauer denied touching her again after successfully throwing her out, and he added that if she had really fainted, then she couldn't have heard the name he called her. He accepted blame for the name-calling and the forcible removal, but no more.[5]

The day after the incident, Marquet sued as promised. In doing so, she started a protracted legal battle that lasted almost six years from August 13, 1821, to May 4, 1827. In that time, several further claims and counterclaims were made. The widow Becker now revealed that, in fact, she had granted Marquet access to a chest of drawers located in the entryway. The two of them, it turned out, were close friends—or in cahoots, as Schopenhauer saw it. He rebutted, first, that his landlady's new testimony contradicted her initial reassurances about who had rightful access to the entryway; second, that such limited permission still didn't grant Marquet or anyone else the right to congregate outside his door; and third, that he should not be held responsible for acting on what turned out to be inadequate information. Later, Marquet further claimed that not only was she injured in the tussle but she now also suffered from lasting damage, including mental distress and a tremor that made it impossible for her to work. On the other hand, Marquet's own witnesses, her two friends, cast some doubt on her credibility by denying that she had really fainted after being thrown out.

At first, the decision went in Schopenhauer's favor. On March 1, 1822, Marquet's suit was dismissed. According to the initial ruling, he was within his rights to expel Marquet from the entryway, and though he had caused some minor injuries, he had not used excessive force. Marquet appealed; Schopenhauer submitted a counterargument, and in April he applied to expedite the process, as he was about to embark on a second escape to Italy that he was not willing to delay. Satisfied that he had done enough, he went away in early May as planned. With much the same complacency, he continued not to defend his case with quite the same doggedness that Marquet prosecuted it.

Later in May, to his surprise, Marquet won her first appeal. Encouraged and emboldened, she submitted further claims, and in the end Schopenhauer was made to pay her an annual alimony of sixty taler until such time as she was fit to work again, as well as most of her legal costs. Marquet never did work again, however, so Schopenhauer made payments to her until she died in 1842. When he received a notice of her death, he scrawled across it: "*obit anus abit onus*"—the old woman is dead, the burden is lifted.[6]

:::

Though there were no more physical altercations (as far as we know), Schopenhauer's interactions with women were rarely admirable. Perhaps his best female companion was his own sister. Communication with Adele was strained at times, but not as tense and sporadic as with his mother. To the very end, it was sustained by deep affection.

After two decades apart, Arthur and Adele were briefly reunited in Frankfurt in late 1842.[7] In the intervening years, she had followed in her mother's footsteps by publishing her own novel, collections of short stories, and an opera libretto.[8] Her health, however, had seriously declined. She required almost constant care from a close friend, Sibylle Mertens-Schaaffhausen, an art collector and archaeologist who had been widowed from a miserable marriage with six children, and who became Adele's belated live-in life partner. They had traveled around Italy together throughout the late 1840s, and it was only Adele's worsening condition that brought her permanently back to Germany in May 1848. With Sibylle's help, she managed to see Arthur again one last time in March 1849, about which little is known except that it was hastily planned at short notice.[9]

On August 11, 1849, Ottilie von Goethe met Arthur in Frankfurt with news of his sister's illness, which was now becoming extremely grave. She had traveled directly from Adele's sickbed in Bonn. The following day, Ottilie wrote to Sibylle about how he had taken the news. She had wanted to write immediately, but "Arthur came so late and stayed so long that I wasn't even able to write a single line. He was deeply saddened to know Adele is so ill, and he praised the good fortune that she had your care." A few days later, Ottilie sent an almost identical report to Adele herself: "Your brother, dear Adele, gave me a good old impression again. He was deeply saddened to know that you were suffering."[10]

Becoming increasingly moribund in late August, Adele dictated a letter to Arthur about putting her affairs in order. Among other things, she bequeathed to him her share of the family silver. The rest of her belongings, cherished but worthless, she instructed Sibylle to disperse among her childhood friends. This included her unsold copper engravings, miniatures painted by her mother, a few pieces of furniture, some costume jewelry, and a "ladies' library." She thanked her brother "from the bottom of my heart for all the kindness of the last few months."[11] He replied with hopes that all these end-of-life administrations would turn out to be unnecessary. He assured her, nevertheless, that he would "follow your desired instructions as stated by you in your letter, in case that you should, as we Buddhists call it, exchange life."[12] By the time Adele received his reply, however, she was already too unwell to read it herself. Sibylle read it to her instead, and Adele signaled her gratitude with a look and a nod. She died on August 25, 1849.

On September 9, Arthur wrote to Sibylle with some of the details for settling Adele's estate. While he somehow could not remember the exact date, he could vividly picture the day of Adele's birth. He recalled receiving a large bag of marzipan that he was led to believe his new little sister had brought along specially for him. Correctly detecting that Sibylle was devastated by Adele's death, he counseled her to let time heal her melancholy. He kept his solemn promise to Adele by not interfering with Sibylle's initial decision-making about the estate. Sibylle, in return, graciously released to him some precious family items: a miniature portrait of him at the age of twenty-one by the Dresden artist Karl Ludwig Kaaz, which had been commissioned by his mother, and his father's notebooks from 1803–5, the years of the grand tour. She also sent him a commemorative coin marking the one hundredth anniversary of Goethe's birth, which happened to coincide with the funeral service that Sibylle had arranged for Adele. (For reasons unclear, Arthur did not attend.) It brought back memories of one family Christmas in Weimar when Goethe was there to see Adele receive her gifts.[13]

Arthur had been far less wistful over his mother's death. Johanna Schopenhauer died not long after she and Adele had moved from Bonn to Jena in 1837, having left expensive Weimar in 1829. Despite Johanna's literary success, their finances had continued to dwindle ever since the Muhl crisis. A modest pension from the Grand Duke of Saxe-Weimar-Eisenach, Charles Frederick, enabled her final move to Jena.[14] Like Adele, Johanna's health declined in the years leading up to her death; during the first long period of silence between her and Arthur, she suffered a sudden attack that paralyzed her feet and left her permanently ailing and weak.[15] The moment of death itself, however, was reportedly peaceful. On April 17, 1838, Johanna drank a cup of tea and went to bed at around half past eight. At eleven o'clock, she suffered a little breathing difficulty, but then gently closed her eyes and passed away, apparently without pain.

This, at least, is what Adele was told. For when the moment came, Adele was visiting Weimar, and subsequently hurried home about two hours afterward. In the letter she wrote to break the news to Arthur, it was evident that Adele felt terrible for not being there at the end. "I will never forget it and never completely get over the fact that I was fetched too late. . . . I really can't write anymore."¹⁶ Arthur's reply is not extant, but he must have found the right words to console his younger sister, who, on April 23, thanked him for his kind and gentle letter, and reassured him that today she felt much calmer. That the death was reportedly swift and unexpected, Adele conceded, was perhaps even a piece of good fortune for Johanna.

Other than that, the Schopenhauer children did not spend long commiserating the loss of their mother. "Let mother rest," Adele advised Arthur. "What she did to both of us may be forgotten."¹⁷ The remainder of their correspondence on this matter concerned itemizing the inheritance, all of which was allotted to Adele, and settling as many debts as possible. All the large items of silverware were sold in Bonn to pay off debts; the rest of the small items, such as the cutlery, went to Adele (and so eventually to Arthur). If there was anything he wanted to keep for himself, she told him, then he was welcome to have it, but there is no evidence that he took anything. The only possession of his that signaled any lasting affection for his mother was a portrait of her, which Adele was surprised to find hanging on his wall during her reunion visit to Frankfurt in 1842. Adele herself owned four portraits of Johanna, although none, along with this one, were at all to her taste.¹⁸

:::

If, at his sister's behest, Schopenhauer left the final word on his mother unwritten, the same cannot be said of his wider views on women. Those he made all too clear. Women, he wrote, are "the second sex that lags behind in *every* respect."¹⁹ They are "destined neither for great mental nor physical works."²⁰ Women should therefore be accommodated by society, but never revered. They are suitable only as lovers, wives, and mothers, or nurses and governesses.

Schopenhauer made these flagrantly sexist remarks in the chapter "On Women" in 1851's *Parerga and Paralipomena*. Although they may seem aimed at women in general, in fact his criticisms had a specific and recent version of womanhood in mind. It was the modern European woman, or "the lady" as Schopenhauer referred to her, who had been put in a false position by being granted ever greater equality with men. Most ancient and some non-European societies, by contrast, had things right (in his view): "Accordingly," he wrote,

> it would be highly desirable if Europe also assigned this No. 2 of the human race her natural position once again, and put a stop to this lady-nonsense about which not only all of Asia is laughing, but Greece and Rome would have laughed in the same way; the results in the social, civil and political context would be incalculably beneficial.[21]

Charitably, Schopenhauer seems to have thought that the benefits of putting the lady back in her place would fall to women as much as to men. Women, he thereby suggested, were incapable of acting independently in anyone's best interest, including their own.

There was, however, another side to Schopenhauer's critique of the lady. Even in modern European society, he noted, not every woman, but only the lady, enjoyed such an advantageous position. Even the lady herself enjoyed her position on one important condition: marriage, or at least the potential for it. Aside from limiting the lady herself, this left unmarried women undersupported and underprotected, which could manifest in one of two ways. "In the upper classes," Schopenhauer wrote, "they vegetate as useless old spinsters, but in the lower classes they are subjected to inappropriately hard labour, or becomes prostitutes."[22] The sale of sex was, Schopenhauer thought, the seedy underbelly of ladyism: "What else were they," he asked, "but women who have been shortchanged in the most terrible manner by the monogamous tradition, genuine human sacrifices on the altar of monogamy?" As for the so-called spinster: "She is usually uncared for and in any case more or less unhappy due to the fact that she has failed in the mission of her sex."[23]

Difficult though it is to disentangle the sympathy from the misogyny, Schopenhauer was evidently concerned that the relative security and dignity of the lady had the side effect of worsening the conditions of women in more vulnerable social positions, thus adding to the world's general quantity of misery. In the case of spinsterhood, his own sister was a case in point. It was challenging enough for Schopenhauer to maintain and manage his rentier lifestyle as a bachelor, never mind realize his other high-minded ambitions. For Adele, it was doubly harder, and ultimately hopeless, to do the same as a spinster.

Not to mention widows. In this respect, like Adele, Johanna Schopenhauer's social position appeared in her son's essay on women. Perhaps for this very reason, having spent all his sympathies, he came down hard on the women who outlive their husbands:

> That widows burn themselves with the corpse of the husband is of course revolting, but it is also revolting when they afterwards squander on their lovers the wealth the husband has earned through ceaseless hard work his whole life, consoling himself that he was working for his children.[24]

Inherited wealth, he argued, should be managed by the men in the family. The surviving women of the family should be allotted a lifetime annuity secured by a mortgage, but never the real estate or capital.[25] Once again, he assumed that this was only in their best interest. Generalizing from his own experience may have led Schopenhauer to this conclusion: while it was patently fallacious to infer that women in general are naturally less financially responsible than men, it was beyond doubt that Arthur was better with money than Johanna and Adele. The Schopenhauer women's finances were so dire by the end of their lives that one of the last few letters he ever received from his mother, co-signed by his sister, happily transferred to him full responsibility for managing an inherited family property in Ohra, Danzig (now Orunia, Gdańsk) from which all the Schopenhauers jointly collected rent.[26]

Patriarchy was natural, in Schopenhauer's view, but not like this. As a solution, he proposed not the abolition of marriage but a radical revision to it: in one form or another, he was in favor of polygamy instead of monogamy. In print, he advocated a well-known existing model: "The Mormons," he wrote, "are right."[27] If men could marry multiple wives, it would ensure that no woman lacks the male support that he felt they needed.

In earlier private notes, however, Schopenhauer had already devised a more dynamic and even-sided model of polygamy, one that even leaned toward polyandry rather than polygyny, at least at first.[28] On his second Italian tour, Schopenhauer stayed in Florence from September 11, 1822, to May 4, 1823. In his travel notebook—just below an entry on his visit to the Palazzo Riccardi, the former palace of the Medici, where he was unimpressed with the allegorical style of its ceiling paintings—he devised a novel solution to the marriage problem. Instead of one husband with multiple wives, he proposed that each young woman marries two young men. The two husbands share responsibility for supporting their wife, and she in return is solely responsible for satisfying their sexual and reproductive needs. When (Schopenhauer continued) she is no longer attractive and fertile, the husbands jointly marry a second, younger wife, expanding the threesome into a foursome. At this point each husband, presumably more financially secure by now, fully supports one of the two wives, while the first wife offloads her reproductive duties on to the second.[29] Schopenhauer's unusually extensive knowledge of classical Indian literature gave him a precedent for such polyandrous marriages: "On *tetragamy* it is to be noted that in the *Mahābhārata* the five Pandanas or sons of Pandu have one spouse in common, Draupadi."[30]

When Schopenhauer sketched out his model of tetragamy, he did not explain what happens next to the second wife when she one day effectively becomes a double-widow with potentially several dependent children. Perhaps he assumed that she would still be young enough to remarry a second pair of husbands. He did, however, forestall other problems. First, he admitted that on his proposal a man could never know for sure which of the children were his; but he argued that an educated guess could be made on the basis of resemblance, and with a strong air of suspicion added that "even now it is not always certain."[31] Second, with three to four participants in the marriage, there were of course bound to be many quarrels and rivalries. His answer here was, once again, that this already happens within and between supposedly monogamous relationships.

One thing to glean from Schopenhauer's proposal of tetragamy is that his attraction to polygamy was not, or not always, about giving a man more than his fair share of wives. Instead it was about the mismatch between men's and women's needs and abilities (as he understood them) at their different stages of life, which monogamy, in his view, failed to address. Although he continued to assume that women, for their own good, require the custodianship of a husband, in his ideal world this requirement would at least be met in the case of every women, even if it meant sharing a wife for a while. "Accordingly," he concluded, "for the female sex as *a whole* polygamy is a real benefit."[32]

In addition, Schopenhauer argued, monogamy underpinned versions of sexual honor that were inevitably harmful or even lethal to women. For women, monogamous sexual honor meant chastity before marriage and fidelity after. The social price of sexual dishonor was high: "every girl that has betrayed the entire female sex through illicit intercourse is expelled and shamed . . . this girl has lost her honour. No woman may have anything to do with her; she is avoided like the plague."[33] To evade being shunned, some women resorted to deadly and self-destructive methods: "the many bloody sacrifices made to the female principle of honour—in infanticide and suicide of mothers—testify to its origin's not being purely natural."[34] By contrast, protection of male sexual honor primarily victimized not men but women again: for men, abstaining from adultery was less important than avenging instances of it in women, on women. As an example, Schopenhauer gave Othello's jealous murder of Desdemona. In this case, punishment is meted out on the wife and not her alleged lover, which to him was evidence that the entire honor code was ultimately rooted in men's control over women's bodies rather than the self-control of either gender.[35] And the double standard did not end there, Schopenhauer noted: the stigma of a husband's failure to exact his revenge, namely, that of being a confirmed cuckhold, was still nowhere near the social disgrace assigned to any woman who disobeyed monogamy.[36]

To those who still objected to polygamy he pointed out that, as far as he could see, it was already the norm. There already was, in his words, "a publicly sanctioned class with the special purpose of protecting from seduction those women favoured by fate who have found husbands or those who could hope to"—namely, prostitutes, not to mention the other extramarital options that men were also permitted.[37] "Where are there real monogamists anyway?" he asked, rhetorically.[38] Whatever the merits or demerits of Schopenhauer's schemes, his proposal was never to introduce polygamy, but rather to regulate it.

:::

Beyond this, the less said about Schopenhauer's official views on women, the better. But it is an ironic quirk of history, or perhaps only right, that Schopenhauer, often considered philosophy's arch misogynist, who so long awaited any recognition from his peers and the public, in fact owes much of his renown to the work of women. His first English biography, for instance, was written by a Jewish German-British woman named Helen Zimmern.

In 1850, when she was four years old, Zimmern's family emigrated from Hamburg to Nottingham, England, before settling in London in 1856. Like Schopenhauer, her father was a merchant and she had one sibling, a sister named Alice. Zimmern was reportedly a sickly child, sometimes taken out of school and educated at home. From the age of fourteen, she attended a finishing school in Bayswater. In the year she turned eighteen, when she became a British citizen, she resolved to become a writer.[39] She succeeded. Her *New York Times* obituary on Saturday, January 13, 1934, described her as a "writer and leading member of the British colony . . . in Florence where she had lived since 1887." It continued: "She afforded in her writings a valuable interpretive link of Italy and Germany to England and the United States."[40]

Zimmern's biography of Schopenhauer appeared in 1876, making it among the first of her numerous books and articles on everything from the German Enlightenment to Italian football.[41] At a time when there were still no full-length English translations of Schopenhauer's work, it gave readers an indispensable insight into his life and work. "The book, sympathetic yet critical, and excellently composed," wrote one reviewer of a revised edition from 1932, "will serve as an attractive introduction for students of literature to one of the finest writers of the German language, and will help students of philosophy to approach his thought with more patience and understanding."[42] It brought attention not only to Schopenhauer, but also to Zimmern herself.

On the strength of her biography, Zimmern was invited by the composer Richard Wagner to the northern Bavarian town of Bayreuth, where he had erected a festival hall dedicated to his own music.[43] There Zimmern met the philosopher Friedrich Nietzsche, who at the time was just as enamored with Schopenhauer as Wagner himself. They walked and talked together after lunch, Nietzsche having spent most mornings at his writing desk.[44] She must have made a good impression on Nietzsche, for on April 25, 1876, she wrote to him with thanks for sending a copy of his new collection of essays, *Untimely Meditations*. A decade later, Zimmern was evidently still important enough to Nietzsche to appear on his list of people to receive his later work *Beyond Good and Evil*, a book that she went on to translate in 1906 (although publication was delayed until 1910, partly due to rancorous negotiations between the editor and Nietzsche's sister Elisabeth, the executor of his estate).[45] Before the end of his working life, cut short by a decade of debilitating psychosis starting in 1889, Nietzsche had more or less anointed Zimmern as his official English translator. On December 9, 1888, by which time Nietzsche was opposed to Schopenhauer's philosophy, though no less obsessed, he wrote to his friend and amanuensis, the composer Heinrich Köselitz: "She introduced Schopenhauer to the English, why not his antipode?"[46]

In the decade or so between first meeting Zimmern and electing her as his translator, Nietzsche had become a trusted friend. Nietzsche, like Schopenhauer, acquired a reputation for misogyny based on his published works; but in person, she later recollected, he was beyond a gentleman.[47] Both Nietzsche and Zimmern enjoyed spending their summers in the Swiss Alps, including stays at Sils Maria 1884 and 1886, when the two could frequently be seen discussing his work while strolling beside Lake Silvaplana. They were also spotted by Meta von Salis, another of Nietzsche's many female friends, sitting in a corner of the Alpenrose Hotel, engrossed in conversation: he famously mustachioed, she beneath a mound of thick black hair, both of them with deep dark pools for eyes.[48] At first, admittedly, she was unsure of what to make of him, but quickly she detected his desperate need for friendship: "I listened with more or less feigned interest, for, to tell you the truth, I understood only little then of what he spoke about. But it seemed to give him such relief to talk to a human being! The man seemed to me so lonely, so unspeakably lonely!"[49]

Zimmern never met Schopenhauer; in the years that their lives overlapped, she was still a child living in England. But, just as she later did for Nietzsche, in her biography she made an attempt to explain and mitigate Schopenhauer's reputation as a misogynist. She mainly put it down to an abject lack of experience:

> It will be remembered that Schopenhauer, so far as we know, was an utter stranger to intimacy with intellectual or distinguished women, and that he seems never to have met one capable of reflecting his ideas. Had this been the case, he might not have so roundly denied the very possibility of genius to women.[50]

It may seem like the wrong excuse, given Johanna Schopenhauer's distinguished reputation in her day, as Zimmern well knew. Even Arthur rated her ability as a novelist, albeit not as a mother. But apart from the fact that her reputation had long since waned even by Zimmern's time, Johanna's own internalized sexism may have contributed to Arthur's specious distinction between the mere talents of women like his mother and his sister, on the one hand, and the evident genius of men such as himself, on the other. As Johanna once wrote in the introduction to an edition of her diaries: "I repeat my request, not to take up this book with too great expectation. It contains a woman's simple tales of what she has seen and observed, written to entertain pleasingly, and not to instruct deeply."[51]

:::

If not Helen Zimmern, then Schopenhauer did at least meet a couple of the women who were responsible for cementing his renown.

One of them, a woman of many names, even had a few things in common with Zimmern.

Jessie Taylor—also known as Jessie Laussot, also known as Mrs. Karl Hillebrand—was born in London on December 27, 1826. Like Zimmern, later in life she settled in Florence, where she conducted an acapella choir, played piano, and wrote articles on Italian music.[52] Also like Zimmern, Taylor was drawn into Wagner's orbit—or rather, perhaps, she drew Wagner into hers.

Taylor's first encounter with Wagner was in Dresden in the late 1840s, when he was working on the production of his opera *Tannhäuser*. On March 24, 1850, she invited him to Bordeaux, where she lived with her husband, a wine merchant named Eugène Laussot.[53] Both Taylor and Wagner were unhappy in their first marriages and saw each other as a way out. Together they hatched a plan to escape to Greece and then onward to the Near East. On April 5, Wagner returned to work on the score for *Lohengrin* in Paris, where he lived in exile after his involvement in Dresden's doomed May Uprising of 1849. Over letters they continued to map out their escapade, with Wagner suggesting setting sail from Marseilles to Malta. By the time he returned to Bordeaux, however, the plan was already foiled. Taylor had told her mother about it, who immediately reported it to Eugène, who in turn threatened to murder Wagner. The police promptly expelled Wagner from Bordeaux.[54]

Schopenhauer had his own brief encounter with Taylor, who came to visit him in Frankfurt in 1859. Little is known about the trip, except that she was clearly already familiar enough with Schopenhauer's work to give him her opinion to his face. Reportedly, she told him she found it "too wordy." Sternly, he replied: "Not one word too many!"[55]

In 1889, Taylor published her own translation of two works by Schopenhauer: *On the Fourfold Root of the Principle of Sufficient Reason* and *On the Will in Nature*. She did so, however, not under her own name, but that of her husband since 1879, Karl Hillebrand, despite the fact that Hillebrand had died five years before her translation was published. Taylor was not alone in publishing Schopenhauer in English under her husband's name: in 1897, for example, a Mrs. Rudolf Dircks—whose actual name is now hard to find—

published selections from across Schopenhauer's works, including his essays on women, love, noise, and suicide, among others.[56] It was this translation, in fact, that would one day introduce the novelist D. H. Lawrence to Schopenhauer, whose realism about sexual desire Lawrence found intensely liberating.[57] Schopenhauer's views on sex were noticed by other Englishmen too, from Charles Darwin to the progressive sexologist Havelock Ellis, who, along with his coauthor John Addington Symonds, pioneered research into same-sex relationships.[58]

As a translator of Schopenhauer, Taylor was something of a trendsetter too. Although translations of Schopenhauer were already being released between 1883 and 1886, their translators, R. B. Haldane and John Kemp, had rendered the title of his main work as *The World as Will and Idea*. In her translations, however, instead of "idea"—liable to be confused with its better-known Platonic version—Taylor translated the German word *Vorstellung* as "representation," which has now become the scholarly standard.[59]

:::

Jessie Taylor's encounter with Schopenhauer did not appear in Helen Zimmern's biography; if Zimmern even knew of it, it was perhaps all too brief. But Zimmern did include Schopenhauer's final encounter with a woman who, had his life not ended less than a year later, might one day have changed his mind entirely about the so-called second sex.[60]

Elisabet Ney, born on January 26, 1833, in Münster, Westphalia, was known to Schopenhauer as the grandniece of Michel Ney, one of Napoleon's bravest commanders and a marshal of his empire. In her own right, however, she was a sculptor. When she first announced her artistic ambitions, her family were aghast. Before she was finally given permission to study sculpture, it was necessary to go on weeks of hunger strikes: "If you do not let me go," Ney warned her mother, "I will die."[61] At eighteen, she got her own way and left to study in Munich—a compromise with her parents, as her first choice was Berlin. Only two years later, however, she moved to Berlin anyway to study with the founder and leader of its school of sculpture, Christian Daniel Rauch. Rauch was sufficiently impressed with Ney to recommend her for a scholarship at the Berlin Academy of Art, in the face of protestations that the tall, slender, female artist with a mass of short auburn curls would only distract the male students.[62] Rauch died on December 3, 1857, leaving Ney without a champion in Berlin, but with, fortunately, the opportunity to complete some of his more distinguished commissions, including a bust of the naturalist and explorer Alexander von Humboldt. When Humboldt died on May 6, 1859, Ney was once again without a patron, so she left in search of another.[63]

On October 1, 1859, aged twenty-six, Ney descended on Schopenhauer in Frankfurt with the proposal to sculpt his bust. She almost didn't get past his housekeeper, who passed on Ney's calling card—"Elisabet Ney, Sculptor, Berlin"—and announced: "there is a beautiful young woman dressed in white at the door; she came from Berlin to see the master."[64] Forever cautious of people at his door, Schopenhauer initially refused her entry; but then, for reasons known only to himself, he changed his mind. Ney was seen through to his library, and at first he was still unconvinced: he had no interest in commissioning a bust of himself, least of all, he said, by a bold and unknown girl.[65]

Nevertheless, Ney somehow prevailed. Just an hour later, the two were striding from room to room in his apartment to find a suitable spot for Ney's temporary studio.[66] By early November the bust was already complete, and it might have been done even sooner had Schopenhauer not denied Ney's request to make a plaster cast of his head, afraid that it might damage his eyes. To his delight, she even had time to make a model of his poodle.

In those few weeks, and indeed for months afterward, Schopenhauer barely sent a letter without proudly mentioning his remarkable artist-in-residence. He was clearly impressed and deeply flattered, and he didn't mind who knew about it. When Ney moved on to an even more prestigious assignment in Hanover, a bust of none other than George V, Schopenhauer eagerly awaited a duplicate that was being prepared in Berlin. After much anticipation, it finally arrived on August 18, 1860, giving him approximately one month of life left to enjoy it. His resemblance to the sculpture had

Figure 5. Schopenhauer (1859) by Elisabet Ney.

already begun to fade around the mouth and jaw, however, as by then he had lost all his teeth.

Apart from an insight into the artist's studio, Ney had belatedly given Schopenhauer the novel experience, to him, of living with a women whom he respected and even suited. "When I come back from taking my meal, we drink coffee together and sit next to one another on the sofa, and then I feel like a married man," he told a close friend, clasping his hands together in delight.[67] Sometimes they sent out for lunch from the restaurant above his apartment, or went for walks over hills and dales near the river.[68] His admiration for her artistic ability tested the limits of his misogyny—although never quite beyond its breaking point. During one sitting, she looked up from her work to find an amused expression on his face. "Why are you looking at me like that, Herr Doctor?" she inquired.

"I'm doing my best to spot even a hint of a mustache on you," he replied. "It seems to me more and more unbelievable that you are a woman every day."[69]

On the Woman Question, the two were not in fact opposed on every issue. On the one hand, Ney was living disproof of Schopenhauer's opinion that no woman could achieve any profound kind of excellence, and she was proud of it. On the other, however, she too was disappointed by the examples of womanhood in her day. She detested how women with the same potential as her would neglect it for things that she considered fatuous and childish, like dressing up and dancing, or simply for the sake of their husbands.[70]

Schopenhauer did not appear to be aware that Ney had already found her real partner in life—although at that point, perhaps, she didn't quite know it either. In Heidelberg in 1853, Ney met the Scottish-born physician and philosopher Edmund Montgomery. It may even have been Montgomery, in fact, having grown up partly in Frankfurt, who suggested to her the idea of seeking Schopenhauer as a client.[71] Like Schopenhauer, Ney was initially opposed to the institution of marriage in its current form, albeit on different grounds: in her view, marriage for women was virtually a form of slavery, and any love worthy of the name was free rather than contractually reinforced.[72] Ney and Montgomery married eventually, however, on November 7, 1863, at the British consulate in Madeira, where he had set up a medical practice. She insisted at least on keeping her name. Later, they uprooted to the United States, sailing first to New York in January 1871, then joining friends at a commune in Thomasville, Georgia, and finally settling on a plantation in Waller County, Texas.

Even at that great distance in time and space, however, it is unlikely that Ney ever forgot Schopenhauer, and not just because of one memorable October in Frankfurt in 1859. In the year that Ney emigrated to America, she gave birth to her first son with Montgomery. The boy, who did not live long, dying at the age of two, was named Arthur.[73]

CHAPTER 8

Metaphysics into Action
How Schopenhauer Expanded Ethics

When the time came, there was little to keep Schopenhauer in Berlin. To say that he had succeeded in nothing would be no exaggeration. His academic career was dead on arrival; his love affairs, such as they were, lacked any real meaning; and to top it all off, having fought a lawsuit and lost, he was saddled with decades of debt to a woman he barely even knew, or only enough to despise. As for his philosophy, publicly at least, it was a fallow decade. Although he continued to fill up his notebooks with material that he would one day harvest for later books, he published no new work.

Throughout these years, he attempted to escape his many failures in various ways. Only one form of escape could be classed as a success, and that was his return to Italy. Ever since his first visit he had often dreamed that he was back in Rome or Naples, only to wake and find himself still lying in his two-room lodgings on Niederlagstrasse. The second trip, when it finally came, turned out to be even happier than the first. Although he was only in Italy from August 1822 to May 1823, he padded it out on both sides with visits to towns and cities in Germany and Switzerland, beginning with Leipzig, Nuremberg, and Stuttgart in June, and then Schaffhausen and Vevey in July.[1] Once in Italy, he stayed first in Milan and Venice, before overwintering in the warmth of Florence. Unlike the previous time, he did not send any letters to Adele; their relationship had not yet recovered from the Muhl crisis, and it wouldn't until his Berlin years were over. He did, however, send at least one letter, on October 29, 1822, to an old friend from Weimar days named Friedrich Gotthilf Osann. It painted a vivid picture of Schopenhauer's luscious Italian lifestyle.

"Again," he wrote, "the Great Bear stands low on the horizon. Again, dark green foliage stands still in the air, sharply cut out against the dark blue sky, serious and melancholy. Again, olives, vines, pines, and cypresses make shine the landscape in which countless villa swim. Again, I am in the city whose pavement is a kind of music."[2] Every day, he continued, he crossed the piazza, passing statues, cathedrals, bell towers, and baptistries—enormous, colorful, marble jewels, he called them, washed clean by the rain and gleaming in the sunshine. Oranges grew in the monastic courtyard of the Basilica di San Lorenzo, even in late October, as though the trees didn't know the seasons. It was after dark when he wrote his letter, by the light of a tall, brass, three-flame lamp, lit by a servant who dished up heaps of fresh figs, grapes, and lemons, and wished him a good night. His room was modestly furnished, with iron beams high overhead and stone floors underfoot.

Of the Italian people, Schopenhauer was more ambivalent. They were even louder, he discovered, than those of Berlin, although he did find their voices much more agreeable in the theater, where they sung out sonorously. He found Italians attractive but hard to trust: "such beautiful faces," he said, "and such bad dispositions." He was charmed, nevertheless, by their infinite cheerfulness, which he attributed to good health and clement weather. One Italian, a complete stranger, even paid him a prescient compliment: "Sir, you must have created something great; I do not know what it is, but I see it in your face."[3] On balance, he preferred Florence's untameably romantic character to the bland banality of Berlin: "With Italy, one lives as with a beloved, today in violent quarrel, tomorrow in adoration:—with Germany, as with a housewife, without great anger and without great love."[4]

Schopenhauer hadn't contacted Osann just to submit a travel

report, however. His ulterior motive was fresh academic gossip. Although Osann was six years Schopenhauer's junior, he was already much further along in his career as a professional classicist, having come from a cultured Weimar family that valued scholarship. Not by coincidence, Osann and his brothers were all academics, who at one point were considered by Adele as marriage material. Had anyone been talking or writing about him, Schopenhauer asked? If anything had appeared in print, then he requested to be sent copies immediately. ("As far as I know," Osann would write back, "nothing has appeared that concerns you.")[5] He was also keen to hear about recent job movements: "Three philosophical chairs had to be filled in Heidelberg, in Breslau, in Berlin: with which subjects did they fill them?" Osann confirmed that Fichte the younger had been effectively ousted from Berlin on the alleged grounds of holding liberal views, which Schopenhauer must have received with mixed emotions. He had no sympathy for any Fichte, but little for academic censorship either.[6]

Before he left for Italy, Schopenhauer had inquired about a position for himself at Giessen, which made for a couple of odd coincidences. First, the job went to Joseph Hillebrand, father of Karl, who later married Jessie Taylor, Schopenhauer's eventual translator.[7] Second, Osann himself would be offered a full professorship there in 1825. On his return, Schopenhauer made further inquiries at Würzburg and Heidelberg, neither of which would pan out. By this time, if he had made any name for himself at all, it was a thoroughly bad one. In the backroom conversations between the various officials who vetted him for the Würzburg job, the Bavarian envoy to Berlin claimed that "he has no reputation whatsoever as a writer or teacher" and "would not be a great gain for the University." Worse still, the minister of culture, who admitted to having no firsthand knowledge of Schopenhauer's writings, nevertheless said of his person that "he has always appeared to me to be very arrogant, and I have heard more against than for him."[8] He was as good as blacklisted.

An alternative occupation, given his excellent language skills, would have been as a translator. Schopenhauer attempted in vain to secure contracts to translate some of his favorite authors across several different languages: Hume from English into German; Kant from German into English; Sterne from English into Italian (or German, he offered either); Giordano Bruno from Italian into Latin; Baltasar Gracián from Spanish into German.[9] He even prematurely drafted a preface to his Hume translation in which he advertised the rather casual, but no less true, qualification that "since my stay in England when I was a boy, I have become very fluent in English."[10] A Germanified Hume and an anglicized Kant, rendered by someone so philosophically literate as Schopenhauer, ought to have been a tantalizing proposal for any publisher; but none were interested.

After Italy, Schopenhauer dragged his feet back to Berlin. He could only dread what awaited him there: "The climate and mode of life in Berlin do not agree with me," he wrote, "One lives there as on a ship; everything is scarce, expensive, difficult to get, and provisions are desiccated and dried up. On the other hand, roguery and deception of all kinds are worse than they are in the country where lemons grow."[11] The contrast was stark between Italy's sheer abundance and Germany's meager scarcity; and the characters back home, perhaps thinking of Caroline Marquet specifically, were even less trustworthy.

Progress was slowed down further by illness. Leaving Florence in the spring of 1823, he visited Rome and Venice one last time, before crossing the Alps at Tyrol in Austria. After that, he spent almost a year in Munich, perhaps involuntarily: six weeks after his arrival, he was laid low by all manner of unpleasantness—hemorrhoids, fistulae, gout, and various nervous disorders. He went completely deaf in his right ear, and his nerves were so racked that his hands trembled. When he was finally fit to move again, he convalesced for a while in the spa waters of Gastein. From August 1, 1824, he stayed in Dresden, a place he fondly recalled ever since taking refuge there to complete *The World as Will and Representation*. But things in Dresden felt very different now. Apart from the fact that his old acquaintances had moved away, the city was no longer suffused with all the excitement of writing a book that he trusted would open up his future.[12]

In *The World as Will and Representation*, Schopenhauer had

briefly written about what he called "the acquired character."[13] He gave it this name because, unlike moral character, it was not, in his view, inborn and unchanging. Acquired character is less to do with the qualities we are given, and more to do with what we make of those qualities. Ideally, he argued, each of us should find a station in life that suits our natural abilities and thereby allows us to enjoy our talents, rather than face the frustrations of trying and failing at things we were never cut out to do. The journey, however, is rarely a straight line; it takes experimentation and self-discovery, as we cannot even know where our best qualities lie until they are revealed in life. Eventually, acquiring character requires strict focus and discipline: "we can only seriously and successfully pursue one particular project—whether it is pleasure, honour, wealth, science, art, or virtue—by giving up all claims that are foreign to it and renouncing everything else," Schopenhauer advised.[14]

When Schopenhauer returned to Berlin in May 1825, he had already acquired several defective conceptions of himself, which he had to abandon for the sake of his happiness. "When at times I felt unhappy, this was more by virtue of a mistake, of an error in my personality," he wrote in the midst of his Berlin years.

> I then took myself to be other than I was and then deplored that other person's misery and distress. For example, I took myself to be a lecturer who does not become a professor and has no one to hear his lectures; . . . or to be the defendant in that assault case; or to be the lover who is not listened to by the girl with whom he is infatuated; or to be the patient who is kept at home by his illness; or to be other persons who are afflicted and burdened by similar miseries. I have not been any of these; all this is the stuff from which at most the coat has been made which I wore for a while and which I then discarded in exchange for another. But then who am I? I am the man who has written the *World as Will and Representation* and has given a solution to the great problem of existence which perhaps will render obsolete all previous solutions, but which in any case will exercise the minds of thinkers in the centuries to come. I am that man, and what could disturb him in the few years in which he has still to draw breath?[15]

One upside of his unsettled status in Berlin was the preservation of his freedom: "That which of my external things lies nearest to my person," he wrote, "as close to my body as my shirt, is my independence which does not allow me ever to forget who I am and to play the part of someone else, for example that of a literary hack or a professor."[16] With nothing tying him down except various misfires at making himself, when cholera broke out in 1831, Schopenhauer was poised to launch yet another escape.

He was not only escaping his failures, or even disease, but also almost certain death. On New Year's Eve in 1830, Schopenhauer had a strange dream that he interpreted as portending his demise at some point in 1831:

> From my sixth to my tenth year I had a bosom friend and constant playmate of exactly the same age who was called Gottfried Jänisch and who died when I in my tenth year was in France. In the last thirty years I had very rarely thought about him.—But on the night in question, I arrived in a country unknown to me; a group of men was standing in a field, and among them was a tall, slim, grown-up man who had been introduced to me, I do not know in what way, as that very Gottfried Jänisch, and who greeted me.[17]

He took the dream as a bad omen, and the cholera as proof. "Had I remained there [in Berlin]," he later reflected, "I should have died of cholera." After arriving in his new home city of Frankfurt, he had a second dream: "In it (I think) were my parents and it indicated that I would now outlive my mother who at that time was still alive; my father who was already dead was carrying a light in his hand."[18] This dream he interpreted as vindication of his decision to flee.

:::

> Healthy climate. Beautiful area. Amenities of large cities. Variety of large cities. Better reading room. The Natural History Museum. Better acting, opera and concerts. More Englishmen. Better coffee houses. No bad water. The Senckenberg Library.

No flooding. Less observed. The friendliness of the place and its entire surroundings. You are more unrestricted and less bothered by the society that chance, not your choice, gives you, and have the freedom to cut off and avoid unwelcome dealings. A skilled dentist and fewer bad doctors. No such unbearable heat in the summer. The physics exhibit.[19]

These were Frankfurt's key selling points, as methodically listed by Schopenhauer in his accounts book. After Berlin, he wavered for a few years between Frankfurt and Mannheim, spending some time in each in the early 1830s, including those first months of 1832 that he spent in isolation from the cholera-ridden outside world. In June 1833, however, he settled in Frankfurt for good, never to leave it again, aside from the odd excursion.

In the decades to follow, he occupied a few different Frankfurt addresses—Alte Schiesingergasse 32 (1831–36), Am Schneidwall 10 (1836–40), Neue Mainzerstrasse 3 (1840–43)—until he moved, for the remainder of his life, to the riverside street Schöne Aussicht (translation: Beautiful View). He furnished his rooms with extreme simplicity, having no fondness for lavish domestic adornments; he was fifty before he even bought his own furniture. It gave off the impression to visitors that he didn't intend to stay; it was, some said, an apartment for strangers on earth.[20] Only two features indicated long-term inhabitation. First, his books, which spilled out into the hallway between the library and study. Second, in later years, a bronze-gilded statuette of the Buddha, which he asked a friend to buy from a Parisian antiques dealer in 1856.[21] Enthroned on a marble console, adorned with freshly cut flowers, Schopenhauer's Buddha sat in full lotus position, upright and cross-legged, his left hand opened toward the sky and his right resting on the earth. "He sits there like a tailor," remarked Schopenhauer's strict Catholic housekeeper Margarete Schnepp, with a laugh. "Have I ever blasphemed your Lord God?" Schopenhauer replied.[22]

Although Frankfurt suited him well, there was still some unrest in the years ahead. 1849, for one, got off to an inauspicious start: on February 22, almost nobody remembered his sixty-first birthday. Nobody, that is, except for a young man named Julius Frauenstädt.

"Your care to remember my birthday touched me immensely," Schopenhauer wrote to Frauenstädt on March 2, 1849, "since you're probably the only one who thought of it. But evidently a single celebration, springing solely from true esteem, is worth more than a hundred prompted by mere courtesy, or hypocrisy, such as are offered to the great and rich."[23] Frauenstädt was not a Frankfurt resident but a devoted fan based in Berlin. One morning in July 1846, at around eleven o'clock, he summoned the courage to call upon Schopenhauer in person. When he knocked, a dog barked loudly back. When Frauenstädt entered, Schopenhauer was dressed in a light-gray housecoat, reclining on a sofa opposite the door with a book in his hand. These were normally his hours for work and study, but, making an exception, he leaped up off the sofa with a cordial greeting. The two chatted for over an hour, and Frauenstädt quickly became one of Schopenhauer's first followers. Optimistically, but not inaccurately, Frauenstädt predicted that one day many more people besides him would celebrate Schopenhauer's birthday.

Along with his thanks for the solitary birthday letter, Schopenhauer sent Frauenstädt greetings from his dog, Atma. By the end of 1849, however, he had some sad news to report on this front too. "My dear, dear, big beautiful poodle: he died of old age, not quite ten years old," Schopenhauer wrote on December 9.[24] It saddened him for a long time; he once confessed to Frauenstädt that if there were no dogs, then he would not want to live.[25] Atma's successor was a young, energetic, brown poodle, also called Atma, but nicknamed Butz, who never quite replaced his soulful white-furred predecessor in Schopenhauer's heart.[26] It capped off a year of grief for Schopenhauer: earlier in 1849, Adele had also died.

Other disturbances besides personal grief interrupted Schopenhauer's peace of mind in Frankfurt. The years of 1848 to 1849 were, after all, a time of constant revolution across Europe, not least in Frankfurt, where a newly appointed National Assembly convened in Saint Paul's Church on May 18, 1848, tasked with devising a unifying constitution for the German confederation. The conflict came to Schopenhauer's doorstep on September 18, 1848, as he explained in the very same letter to Frauenstädt. Two days previously, the National Assembly had narrowly approved, on its second attempt, a controversial peace treaty that, contrary to its own founding aims, obstructed the goal of German unification. Radical insurgents, disillusioned with the assembly, took to the streets in protest and built barricades, including one on the main bridge into the city, right next to Schopenhauer's apartment. The National Assembly requested Prussian and Austrian military assistance, and fighting broke out.[27] As gunfire shook the walls of his building, Schopenhauer heard voices and banging at his locked door. At first, thinking that it was the revolutionary insurgents, he barred it shut; but then, when his housekeeper saw that, in fact, it was a troop of twenty blue-trousered Austrians, he eagerly invited them inside. The soldiers shot at insurgents from his windows before moving on to the next apartment for a better vantage point. To assist the commanding officer, who spied a pack of rebels at the barricade, Schopenhauer—like a caricature of his social class—loaned out his double-barreled opera glasses.[28]

The National Assembly lasted little over a year before it was finally expelled from Frankfurt. It had already suffered a significant blow, however, not long after the skirmish outside Schopenhauer's apartment. A left-wing member of the assembly, Robert Blum, had been drawn into leading a violent and unsuccessful uprising while on a parliamentary mission to Vienna. For his part in the rebellion, Blum was executed by firing squad on November 9. He lived on in the hearts, and the songs, of many radicals and liberals, but not in Schopenhauer's.[29] In life, Schopenhauer had so disliked Blum, whom he saw as the enemy of all law and order, that when the two of them were once seated opposite each other in the Englischer Hof, he got up and moved to another table. (In another version of the same story, Schopenhauer didn't even know that the man at whom he took offense was Blum. Instead, he simply detested Blum's unappealingly bearded appearance, full beards being, to him, the sure sign of a troublemaker, and asked the waiter to be reseated.)[30] He thought that death by firing squad was too good for Blum: hanging would have been better. Schopenhauer was known to raise a toast, instead, "to the noble Prince Windisch-Grätz," the Austrian field marshal responsible for crushing the Vienna Uprising that Blum had led. Even the aristocratic officers in the Englischer Hof found this ghoulish sort of behavior from Schopenhauer distasteful.[31]

∴

The revolutions of 1848–49 turned many into migrants (like Helen Zimmern and her family) and exiles (like Richard Wagner). Earlier in his life, Schopenhauer was evidently prone to take flight from conflict too, but oddly not in this case. For once he stayed put, suggesting that in Frankfurt there was finally something worth staying for. Philosophically speaking, however, he was always fearful of political unrest. For Schopenhauer, peace, order, and stability, not necessarily liberty, equality, and democracy, were the primary political goods.

As a political theorist, by his own admission, Schopenhauer fell somewhere in the lineage of the seventeenth-century English philosopher Thomas Hobbes. He even told the same story as Hobbes about the origins of civil society. In the state of nature, everyone has an original right to everything but an exclusive right to nothing, which is ultimately an unlivable situation.[32] Unless you are very powerful, or very lucky, anything you gain is at immediate risk of being taken away. Any prudent person should therefore be willing to moderate their claim to all things on the understanding that others will do the same.

Like other state-of-nature theorists, Schopenhauer did not propose this transition as a literal and historical happening; he gave neither the state of nature nor our exit from it any specific time or place. But, if evidence be needed, it was enough to observe what happens when the fabric of civil society starts to unravel: "As soon as any group of people is released from all law and order," Schopenhauer pointed out, "then at once we clearly see the war of all against all."[33] The Hobbesian origins story, therefore, revealed the self-interested stake that we all continue to have in maintaining a stable order.

Of course, human beings can as little be trusted to respect this prudent arrangement as they can be to respect justice for its own sake. If they can get around the law, they will. Citizens must therefore endow some form of government with the power to enforce the contract that they hold with one another. Of all the possible forms of governance, Schopenhauer, like Hobbes, but unlike his republican parents, preferred monarchy:

> Republics tend towards anarchy, monarchies towards despotism, and the constitutional monarchy, which was then devised as a middle ground, tends towards factional control. To found a perfect state, you must start by creating beings whose nature allows them all to sacrifice their own well-being for the public good. Until then, something can be achieved by having *one* family whose well-being is inseparable from that of the country; so that they cannot promote the one without the other, at least as far as the most important issues are concerned. This is what gives the hereditary monarchy its advantage and its strength.[34]

Schopenhauer's reasoning reveals his political values. To each of the possible forms of government, he assigns a form of disorder that it tends toward, even including his own preferred option of monarchy. None of them is completely perfect, mainly because perfect order would require perfect beings, which, in Schopenhauer's view, we are decidedly not. But the nearest to perfection is whichever one is the least liable to collapse into the form of disorder to which it tends. Schopenhauer settled on hereditary monarchy because at least in this case—at least in theory—the royal family's interests are bound up with those of the public, which holds them back from the pure self-interest of the absolute despot.

Governments enforce the terms of the political contract by means of punishment. But Schopenhauer was adamant that retribution is not punishment's proper aim; in fact, he found the very idea repulsively vengeful and bloodthirsty.

> When you retaliate for a wrong by inflicting pain without any future purpose, this is revenge; it can have no goal other than that of comforting yourself for your own suffering by looking at the suffering you have caused in someone else. This is wickedness and cruelty and it is ethically unjustifiable. If someone

wrongs me, this in no way authorizes me to wrong him. Repaying evil with evil, with no other purpose, is neither moral nor otherwise justifiable through any rational ground.[35]

Punishment, in Schopenhauer's view, should be oriented toward the future, not the past. Specifically, it is the primary way that a government ensures its people will continue to obey the political contract to which they have assented.

As disgusted as Schopenhauer was by retribution, however, he was not altogether opposed to the most severe punishments, including even capital punishment.[36] The motives to commit the most extreme crimes, murder, for example, could only be outweighed by the threat of equally extreme consequences. In fact, Schopenhauer took an even harder line than this: even *attempted* murder, if it could be proven, he thought should carry a death sentence.[37] He did at least accept that such measures should be reserved for the very worst offenses, and so any lesser crimes should not be punishable by death. When Schopenhauer rejoiced in the execution of Robert Blum, therefore—assuming that this expressed his considered stance and was not just for show or out of hypocrisy—he must have believed that revolutionaries like Blum endangered more lives than they defended. Admittedly, the bloodshed in Frankfurt alone, to which Schopenhauer had borne witness, included thirty dead insurgents, sixty-two military fatalities and causalities, and two conservative members of the National Assembly, Felix Lichnowsky and Hans von Auerswald, who were cornered and killed by mobs in the street.[38] In fairness to Blum, as himself a concerned member of the National Assembly, even he did not condone the violence on that occasion.

So far, so Hobbesian. But Schopenhauer also departed from Hobbes in important respects. First, although he sided with Hobbes on political matters, on moral matters Schopenhauer sided with perhaps Hobbes's greatest critic, the Genevan philosopher Jean-Jacques Rousseau. Rousseau was, in Schopenhauer's words, "the profound knower of the human heart."[39] Like Rousseau, Schopenhauer disagreed with Hobbes that human affairs are exclusively born of self-interest. On the contrary, every human being is, to some degree or other, also moved by fellow feeling. The "innate repugnance at seeing someone like himself suffer" (a favored phrase of Schopenhauer's from Rousseau's 1755 *Discourse on the Origin of Inequality*) constrains and moderates our otherwise destructive ego. Even in times of great turmoil—indeed especially so—noble selflessness always stands out:

> Who would dare to deny for a moment that in all ages, among all peoples, in all life's circumstances, even in a state of lawlessness, even in the midst of the horrors of revolutions and wars, and in things great and small, every day and every hour, it manifests a decided and truly miraculous effectiveness, daily prevents many a wrong and calls into being many a good deed without any hope of reward and often quite unexpectedly, and that where it and it alone has been effective, all of us unconditionally grant the deed true moral worth with emotion and deep respect.[40]

If Schopenhauer thus aligned himself with Rousseau, then why was he such a Hobbesian in so many other respects? In one way, in fact, Schopenhauer was opposed to both Hobbes and Rousseau. All state-of-nature arguments, he thought, rest on a flawed assumption about the universality of moral character. "For there are human beings," Schopenhauer argued, "in whom the sight of another immediately excites a hostile feeling, such that their innermost being cries out: 'Not I!'—And there are others with whom that sight immediately stirs up friendly interest, and their innermost being says: 'I once again!' In between there lie innumerable degrees."[41] Hobbes and Rousseau were thus partly right and partly wrong: right that human beings have at least these two basic dispositions toward self-interest (as per Hobbes) and fellow feeling (a la Rousseau), right even that one disposition is bound to dominate the other, but wrong to overlook the decisive differences in the proportions of individual moral character.

Even if Hobbes is only partly right, however, it is still prudent, Schopenhauer thought, to come down on his side over political matters. If *everyone* were kindly disposed toward each other, then of course we could place our trust in the rest of society, and we might even do away with governance altogether. But since many of us, or rather all of us at some point or another, are not always so kindly disposed, it is sadly necessary to seek some other sort of security. "If *justice* reigned in the world it would suffice to have *built* one's house," Schopenhauer said. "But because *injustice* is the order of the day, it is required that whoever built the house also be in a position to protect it."[42] A well-founded fear of being harmed is sufficient to make Hobbesians of us all, even among the most noble-hearted.

:::

Schopenhauer had laid out his Hobbesian political theory as early as the first edition of *The World as Will and Representation* in 1818. His Rousseau-aligned morality of compassion, however, awaited a later occasion. It proved more controversial than he anticipated.

On July 26, 1839, Schopenhauer anonymously entered an essay competition set by the Royal Danish Society of Sciences. The question asked, in so many words, about the metaphysical source of morality. He was confident in his answer, to say the least. Along with his submission, he enclosed a sealed letter to be opened if—or rather when—his entry was crowned as the winner. It also contained a few requests and suggestions. If he won, then he requested first to be informed immediately of his victory. Second, he suggested that he could be awarded his prize when the Danish royal ambassador was next in Frankfurt. Third, he announced his intention to publish his (soon-to-be) prizewinning essay in Germany along with another essay that, by chance, had already been awarded a prize by the Royal Norwegian Society of Sciences on January 26 of the same year. The Norwegian essay, on the topic of free will, paired nicely with his Danish submission.

It may have been the Norwegian win that supercharged Schopenhauer's confidence. With greater humility, in his long acceptance letter to the Royal Norwegian Society, he came clean that his level of recognition in Germany did not quite match his age or, in his view, his achievements: "You must know," he wrote, "that I am now in my fifty-second year: I have not yet attained the celebrity of which, as I frankly confess, I believe myself worthy."[43] He was once again apologizing for his lateness, while still insisting—to arguably the first academic institution ever to recognize it—on his worthiness.

If the Norwegians raised his hopes, then the Danes dashed them. On January 30, 1840, the Royal Danish Society issued the judgment that it could not, in good conscience, award Schopenhauer the prize—despite the fact that he was the competition's sole entrant. At the end of their judgment, the Royal Society added that it should not go unmentioned "that several distinguished philosophers of recent times are mentioned in such an indecent fashion as to provoke just and grave offence."[44] Naturally Schopenhauer suspected foul play, specifically a Hegelian bias. Many years after the fact, he was told as much by a Swedish scholar named Adolf Leonard Nordvall, who was introduced to Schopenhauer's work by Frauenstädt in 1852, and even came to visit him in Frankfurt over two days at the end of July 1856.[45] Nordvall was of the belief that the prize had been judged by Hans Lassen Martensen, a well-known Hegel sympathizer and later the Bishop of Zealand. Nordvall was wrong, however, or at best partly right. Martensen was not even a member of the Royal Society at the time, and claimed to have no inside knowledge of the incident.[46] One of the judges was, indeed, the incumbent Bishop of Zealand, Jakob Peter Mynster; but the head judge was Frederik Christian Sibbern, who once recalled meeting Schopenhauer as a student in Berlin in 1813, and since then only knew of his work through reviews and the largely unfavorable opinion of others.[47]

On November 18, 1839, Sibbern wrote out a confidential verdict that included the main points of the judgment that Schopenhauer later received. On the one hand, the private verdict confirms that the "very brutish and coarse expressions" in question were indeed those aimed at "men like Fichte the elder, Hegel, [and] Schelling"—figures with whom, as it happens, Sibbern had associated while on his trip around Germany from 1811 to 1813. On the other hand, however, Sibbern himself was no Hegelian; rather, he put Hegel in the same bracket as Schopenhauer, whose "barely half-ripe philosophy could have found much support in the Hegelian philosophy."[48] Mynster, who shared his own private verdict a few days later, agreed with the Sibbern's negative opinion: "despite the vitality and force which the style of the author sometimes has," he wrote, "it constantly passes into rudeness."[49]

Despite losing the Danish contest, Schopenhauer published his two Scandinavian essays anyway. In fact, not for the first time, he wore his rejection as a badge of honor. The title page of the book, published in 1841, read as follows:

> *The Two Fundamental Problems of Ethics*
> *Treated in two academic prize essays*
> *by Dr. Arthur Schopenhauer,*
> member of the Royal Norwegian Society of Sciences
> I. On the Freedom of the Human Will, *crowned with a prize*
> by the Royal
> Norwegian Society of Sciences, at Trondheim, on 26 January 1839.
> II. On the Basis of Morals, *not* crowned with a prize
> by the Royal Danish
> Society of Sciences, at Copenhagen, 30 January 1840.[50]

It perfectly illustrated Schopenhauer's cantankerous, comical, and perhaps not altogether consistent character. He took almost as much pride in being rejected by a prestigious academic institution as he did in being recognized by one.

Schopenhauer did not register his discontent in the title page alone, however. In a lengthy preface, he deconstructed the Royal Danish Society's official judgment brick by brick, convincingly explaining where they had gone so terribly wrong.

In the Danes' judgment, the problem was not just that Schopenhauer was rude about other philosophers. On their reckoning, they had clearly set a question about the connection between metaphysics and ethics. They were forced to clarify this because the exact wording of the question—"Is the source and basis of moral philosophy to be sought in an idea of morality that resides immediately in consciousness (or conscience) and in an analysis of the remaining basic moral concepts that arise out of it, or in another cognitive ground?"—hardly excluded ambiguity. (It did not even mention metaphysics, for a start.) They alleged that Schopenhauer had instead spent the majority of his essay arguing, not terribly well, for his own ethical principle of compassion, and only a minor part on the connection between ethics and metaphysics, which if anything ought to have been his first priority.[51]

Schopenhauer disagreed with every point.[52] On his interpretation, the Royal Society had in fact asked about the source of morally praiseworthy actions. He had, he claimed, completed this task in two steps. First, he had strenuously argued against the widespread view, associated with Immanuel Kant, that the source of morality was dutiful obedience to unconditional moral laws. On Schopenhauer's view, such a lawlike ethics of obligation only made sense in a theistic context where there was some authority—namely, God—to underwrite moral commands, much as a monarch underwrites political obligations. Putting God aside, Schopenhauer then turned to the second, positive part of his case, in which he aimed to reveal the real source of moral value. For this, at least initially, he adopted not a speculative metaphysical method but an empirical one. When one person praises another's actions as morally good, he asked, what exactly is it that they praise? The feature common to all the actions that we tend to praise, he observed, was a high degree of selflessness.[53] Contrariwise, if we detect even a hint of self-interest in someone's action, this tends to taint its moral praiseworthiness. Mere self-interest does not make people bad, of course, unless we also detect something worse, like positive malice. But, as natural born egoists, we tend to expect, rather than esteem, self-interested action. The motive to act on the suffering of others as though it were our own, Schopenhauer named compassion. The principle of compassion, he thought, and of morality as a whole, was best captured in the following maxim: "Harm no one; and helps others to the extent that you can." It comprised, therefore, two forms: the passive act of letting other living beings be, and the active one of lending them assistance.

The rejection of theological ethics alone may have been enough to raise the hackles of the pious Danish Society; the panel of judges included a bishop, after all. However, in their defense, so far Schopenhauer had only given the empirical grounds of his own ethical principle, rather than its metaphysical basis. In their official judgment, the panel claimed that they had clearly asked for the latter. But on this point too, Schopenhauer disagreed. He had, in fact, proceeded to provide a metaphysical basis for his ethics—and not merely as an appendix or afterthought, as the Royal Society claimed, but rather as the climax and culmination of his argument. So far, Schopenhauer's arguments had explained what quality makes an action worthy of moral praise, namely, compassion, but the next step was to provide a deeper explanation of what compassion is and where it comes from.[54] For this task, Schopenhauer's metaphysics turned out to be tailor-made. On Schopenhauer's view, the things that appear to separate us as individual beings—space, time, and causality—are not, in the end, metaphysically deep. In reality, we are all manifestation of one and the same thing, namely, the will to life. Those, therefore, who take on the suffering of others as their own are, to this extent, more enlightened beings. Instead of seeing others as a "Not I," compassionate people see them correctly as an "I once more."[55] Elsewhere, Schopenhauer put the point succinctly: "To be just, noble, and humane is simply to translate my metaphysics into action."[56]

(Sibbern and Mynster snippily dismissed Schopenhauer's Buddhistic metaphysics. "The author's Buddhism is not of much use," wrote Mynster in his private verdict.)[57]

Thoroughly vanquishing the Danish Royal Society's judgment never quite exorcised Schopenhauer's animus against them, however. In the month of his death, September 1860, he brought out a second edition of *The Two Fundamental Problems of Ethics*. The second preface, though shorter than the first, was no less outraged: "If the purpose of academies were to suppress truth as much as possible, to suffocate mind and talent to the best of their ability and bravely uphold the reputation of windbags and charlatans," he wrote, "then on this occasion our Danish Academy would have fulfilled it exceptionally."[58]

:::

Schopenhauer's contribution to ethics is noteworthy for other things besides his spectacular Danish defeat. In contrast to the assumptions of classical ethics, he did not think that ethical theory made ethical theorists any more moral than the rest of us. But his own theories turned out to have real applications for matters of intense public debate and social change. In one instance, in fact, there was yet another curious connection to Scandinavia.

Not long after his visit to Frankfurt in July 1856, Adolf Leonard Nordvall, the Swede who had misinformed Schopenhauer about the Danish judging panel, published a pamphlet titled *Should and Can Something Be Done to Prevent Mistreatment of Animals?* It called for a Swedish society for the protection of animals, and as its model Nordvall recommended the association established in Munich in 1842 by a pioneer of the German animal welfare movement, Ignaz Perner. Schopenhauer and Perner were known to one another from afar and respected each other's work. Through a mutual associate, Schopenhauer sent Perner a copy of his book on ethics in 1850, to which Perner reportedly responded with enthusiastic praise.[59] Of Perner, Schopenhauer said in *Parerga and Paralipomena* that he "shines for all of Germany as a beacon for the protection of animals against brutality and cruelty," not long after which he received yet another admiring letter from Perner.[60] Nordvall's own ambitions were realized in 1870, when he founded Sweden's first animal welfare association in his home town of Strängnäs. In 1882, he was appointed chair of the newly formed Nordic Society for Combating Scientific Animal Cruelty. In this capacity he dedicated his life to, among other things, the fight against animal vivisection.[61]

Had he lived to see them, Schopenhauer would no doubt have applauded Nordvall's achievements (and possibly taken partial credit). Already in his lifetime, he admired the work of the various animal protection societies that were emerging around the world, from Perner's Munich Society for the Protection of Animals, to the Animals Friends Society in Philadelphia, and the Society for the Prevention of Cruelty to Animals in London, later to become the RSPCA.[62] English courts, especially, were leading the way in animal rights by handing down fines and other penalties for animal abuse. Schopenhauer welcomed the news, reported in the *Birmingham Journal* in December 1839, that a group of eighty-four dog-fighters were publicly marched to the local police station in handcuffs, its two ring leaders fined one pound and eight and a half shillings and sentenced to fourteen days' hard labor in case of nonpayment.[63] He also firmly sided with animals when they took matters into their own hands—or rather their teeth. Of the practice of chaining up dogs, he wrote:

> I can never look at such a dog without heartfelt compassion for it and deep indignation for its master, and with gratification I think of the case reported a few years ago by *The Times*, of a certain Lord who kept a large dog on a chain. Once, strolling through his yard, he could not resist the urge to pet the dog, whereupon it immediately tore open his arm from top to bottom—justifiably! It was trying to say: "You are not my master, but my devil, who makes my brief existence into a hell." May this happen to all who keep dogs on a chain.[64]

Much of Schopenhauer's sympathy for animals and disgust at animal cruelty no doubt came from his hours of observing his own beloved dogs. Occasionally, they seemed closer to humans than many tended to assume. One acquaintance recalled Schopenhauer halting mid-conversation because his dog had entered the room and started to stare intently at the unfamiliar guest: "Suddenly [Schopenhauer's] face changed while his eyes fell on the poodle, which had just run into the room and attentively fixed me as a person whom he did not really know. I said nothing, and only after a long pause did he speak again with the question: Did you see that look?"[65] The intensely inquisitive gaze of Schopenhauer's poodle suggested other humanlike capacities to him too:

> My dog leapt up in alarm when it accidentally caught a glimpse of the sun for the first time. Among the most intelligent and trained animals there appears the first feeble trace of a disinterested apprehension of their environment: dogs convey this by staring; they can be seen in the window attentively gazing at everything going on before them; sometimes apes look around as if they were trying to make sense of their environment.[66]

His observations were not limited to his dogs, as this passage shows. Almost every day of the 1854 autumn fair in Frankfurt, for example, he visited a live orangutan and encouraged everyone he knew to do the same. Its gaze betrayed no animal demeanor, he said, leading him to speculate that the ape was the "probable progenitor of our race."[67]

Schopenhauer interpreted the international animal protection movement as a social awakening of compassion, as well as further confirmation of his ethics. Compared to Buddhism, other moral systems from Judeo-Christianity to Kant had either ignored or fudged the issue of animal ethics. At most, they treated kindness toward animals as practice for compassion toward human beings, who alone truly deserved it; but rarely did they ever think that animals were of direct moral concern. Ultimately they treated animals as objects at our disposal, as though this were our God-given right. Schopenhauer loathed this position: "I find such propositions outrageous and revolting."[68] There was no reason, to his mind, why compassion should not extend to nonhuman animals too. "Compassion for animals," he wrote, "goes together with goodness of character so precisely that we can confidently assert that anyone who is cruel to animals cannot be a good human being."[69]

:::

Schopenhauer also applied his ethical and political theories to an immeasurably greater moral catastrophe. Nothing appalled him more than what he knew of the Atlantic slave trade, which he regarded as "one of the most severe indictments against humanity." After reading a report jointly written by the British and North American Anti-Slavery Societies, he wrote:

> No one will set it aside without horror, few without tears. For whatever the reader of this book may have ever heard . . . about the unfortunate condition of the slaves, indeed, about human harshness and cruelty, will seem trivial to him when he reads how those devils in human form . . . treat their innocent black

brothers, who by injustice and force have ended up in their infernal claws.[70]

Schopenhauer interpreted anti-enslavement abolitionism as yet another compassionate humanitarian intervention, rather than a Christian one. Here too he believed that such cruelty was, if anything, a stain on Christianity, since these moral crimes were not only being committed in supposedly Christian lands but often in Christianity's name. In this respect, indeed, Christianity had an even longer list of offenses to answer for:

> the long catalogue of inhuman cruelties that have accompanied Christianity, in the numerous religious wars, the irresponsible crusades, the extermination of a large part of the native inhabitants of America and the population of that part of the world with negro slaves dragged there out of Africa, without right, or any semblance of right, torn away from their families, their fatherland, their part of the world and condemned to endless convict labour, in the unremitting persecutions of heretics and inquisition courts that cry out to the heavens . . . would sooner assure a verdict to the detriment of Christianity.[71]

Similarly, when in 1833 "the great-hearted British nation" bought the freedom of the slaves in all its colonies for 20 million pounds, Schopenhauer regarded it as the (belated) triumph of compassion, not of Christian virtue. To anyone who would defend Christianity on this point, he replied first that "in the whole of the New Testament no word is spoken against slavery," and second that "even in 1860 in North America, one man appealed in debates about slavery to the fact that Abraham and Jacob also kept slaves."[72]

Enslavement in the United States was, furthermore, confirmation to Schopenhauer of his political principles. American political values ought to have attracted Schopenhauer: small government, for example, with strong protections for property and privacy. In theory, it ruled with pure and abstract principles of justice, rather than the arbitrary foundation of a God-given ruler; and in practice, it provided material prosperity for many. But, in the end, America was a republic born of a revolution that broke away from a hereditary monarchy, and its success, to him, was ultimately "not attractive." Even worse than its "ignorance . . . stupid Anglican bigotry, foolish conceit, and brutal viciousness" was the "Negro slavery that cries to heaven, combined with the most extreme cruelty towards the slaves, the most unjust oppression of the free blacks, [and] lynch-law."[73] The "North American Free States," he wrote, should really be called the "Slavery States."[74] America was thus not an example of a successful democratic republic, primarily because it was a democracy in name only. In reality, it was an "ever-increasing ochlocracy"—that is, mob rule.[75]

If America only happened to be a slaveholding republic, then it would not have been an argument against the very idea of republics, but rather a cautionary tale for how, or how not, to implement one. History up until Schopenhauer's day, however, provided little to no examples of long-lasting, stable republics, and none that were not propped up by an enslaved underclass. Every successful republic, in short, was a slaveholding republic. This, Schopenhauer pointed out, went all the way back to the ancients: "namely the small Greek republics, the Roman and the Carthaginian, which were all conditioned by the fact that five-sixths or perhaps seven-eighths of their population consisted of slaves."[76] Likewise in the year 1840, Schopenhauer noted, of the United States' sixteen million inhabitants, three million were enslaved. And in many ways the modern American republic was even worse than its ancient predecessors. Ancient slaves, Schopenhauer said (not quite accurately), were "born in the master's house, a contented race faithfully devoted to their master."[77] Slaves in America, by contrast, were "dragged there out of Africa, without right, or any semblance of right."[78] The two were "as different . . . as are their respective colours"—a pointed reminder that American slavery spanned not only oceans, but also races.[79]

The issue of slavery was another way for Schopenhauer to mount his argument about the best, or least worst, form of government. Even though monarchy always risked becoming despotism, compared to republics it still had a greater likelihood of providing stability, order, and protection for all subjects (so his argument went). With its material prosperity, minimal state interference, and strong protections at least for the dominant scion of society, the United States appeared to disprove Schopenhauer's view. In reality, however, America had merely masked its descent into lawlessness: it was anarchy in disguise. At the very least, then, republicanism faced a dilemma. If, on the one hand, a republic is genuinely free, then it can only provide the lowest level of political stability. Citizens must accept their hard-won liberty on the condition of social fragility and insecurity, which, to some, will be a fair price to pay for slipping the monarchical yoke. But if, on the other, it is a slaveholding republic, then its manifest security and prosperity—for some, not all—is purchased at the highest moral cost. Since the latter is not a bargain that anyone can accept in good conscience, it depends instead upon the corrosion of private morality, with human hearts becoming increasingly hardened to one another. This was, of course, a dilemma over which America was shortly to go to war with itself.

∴

With his support for humane societies against various forms of cruelty, Schopenhauer was, if not ahead of his time, then certainly moving along with it. It would be misleading, however, to portray him as wholly enlightened even on these issues.

Animal rights and welfare would obviously seem to encourage vegetarianism, for example, and Schopenhauer was even aware that in much of the world, including the parts where his favored religions of Buddhism and Hinduism were to be found, human beings easily sustained themselves without meat. Nevertheless, he exempted himself along with his fellow northern Europeans on the somewhat shaky grounds that in cold climates, "one cannot exist at all without eating meat." "I have been told," he continued, "that even in Copenhagen a six-week criminal sentence to bread and water . . . is regarded as life threatening."[80] On the other hand, he still maintained that animal deaths should be quick, unforeseen, and even assisted by chloroform to anesthetize any pain. Similarly, he was not opposed to animal labor altogether, but only when excessive strain made it cruel. On the use of animals, then, Schopenhauer's principles favored amelioration over abolition.[81]

Furthermore, even as he supported righteous moral causes, he occasionally revealed attitudes that were stuck in their time, or even lagging behind it in a deeply repellent way. For example: "That the negroes were enslaved more than other races, and on a large scale," he once wrote, "is evidently a result of their being, in contrast to other races, inferior in intelligence—which, however, does not justify such slavery."[82] Similarly, because he believed that the Christian attitude toward animals was a remnant of the Old Testament, in which Adam is entrusted with naming and thereby ruling over the animals, his pro-animal statements were often accompanied by anti-Semitic slurs: "Europe . . . is so permeated by the Jewish stench that the obvious simple truth 'an animal is essentially the same as a human being' is an offensive paradox."[83]

These instances of racism are all the more surprising in the light of Schopenhauer's wider views on race, which in some ways would seem to undermine the basis of white supremacism. In short, he didn't even believe in whiteness. He believed, instead, that "human beings do not naturally have white skin, and that by nature they have black or brown skin . . . and so there is no white race."[84] Accordingly, "the Adam of our race would have to be thought of as black . . . and it is ridiculous when painters represent this first human being as white." Moreover, since God supposedly made the first man in his own image, "he too should be depicted as black."[85] It seems, in fact, that Schopenhauer altogether dismissed racial distinctions drawn along color lines: "to speak of such and to divide people, childishly, into white, yellow and black races, as still happens in all the books, is evidence of great prejudice and lack of reflection."[86] Such distinctions fall away the further back we go in human history, including even those distinctions drawn between different species. At the risk, perhaps, of problematically presenting them as more primitive than white Europeans, Schopenhauer credited nonwhite human beings as staying closer in kin to nonhuman animals: "here in the West," he said, "which has made them pale and white, and where the ancient, true, profound, original religions of their homeland could not follow, humans no longer recognize animals as their brothers."[87]

Abolishing prejudices and specious distinctions in some places but reinscribing them in others, Schopenhauer's views on race were therefore not admirable in every respect. It is clear enough, however, that none of these distinctions, across neither race nor species, mattered to his moral philosophy. His ethics, indeed, following from his metaphysics, was a solvent of all such distinctions. Any being that suffers—which, in the end, is any being that feels—was to him a possible object of cruelty and therefore a fitting object for compassion.

CHAPTER 9

Portrait of the Philosopher as an Old Man
How Schopenhauer Found Fame

One afternoon in early February 1858, at around three o'clock, a young Frankfurt photographer named Carl Friedrich Mylius was carrying out a delicate assignment. He was about to call on Schopenhauer at home, unannounced, in the hope of taking his picture. When he knocked on the door of Schöne Aussicht 17, like every other visitor, he was met with Schopenhauer's housekeeper. The master usually had a nap at around this time of day, she informed him, so she would have to go and see. He begged her not to disturb Schopenhauer, as he could always come back later. But it was already too late; she had disappeared back inside. From behind closed doors, Mylius heard what sounded like arguing, followed by a loud bang and elongated cries of "Damn it!"[1]

Eventually, Mylius was led inside and presented to Schopenhauer. The philosopher stood in a large room with his back to the window, one hand tucked into his chest like Napoleon, the other drumming impatiently on the pane of glass behind him. "What do you want from me?" he demanded. By way of an explanation, with profuse apologies, Mylius produced a letter from the *Leipziger Illustrirte Zeitung*, Germany's first illustrated magazine. He had been commissioned to take Schopenhauer's picture; it would be the basis for a woodcut illustration to feature alongside an article on the philosopher. The letter only added to Schopenhauer's agitation. He took to the nearest mirror, running his hands backward through his hair until it stood on end, repeating to himself: "The damned public want to see me. The . . . public!" It wouldn't be his first photograph—far from it—but it was a novelty to be approached by a national paper.

Having learned from past mistakes, Schopenhauer proceeded to advise Mylius about how to capture his best features. "Look here," he insisted, as he laid out examples of earlier imperfect pictures on the windowsill for Mylius to inspect. "What do you say about these eyes?" Mylius didn't follow, and so, pointedly, Schopenhauer handed him a magnifying glass. On closer examination, Mylius saw precisely what he meant. Gesturing over to a wide-eyed stuffed owl, Schopenhauer declared: "Look, *those* are eyes."

They arranged a date and hour in March for Schopenhauer to visit Mylius's studio. In the conservatory where the picture was taken, Schopenhauer stood in front of a mirror, just as he had done at home, practicing a twisted grimace and muttering to himself once again about the dreaded public. He then laid out his pocket watch on a side table and announced, "I'll give you twenty minutes. If you're not done, then I'll leave. I haven't got time to wait any longer." It turned out, however, that even this stipulation was results dependent. The first exposures, taken on plates coated with a light-sensitive emulsion before being fed into the camera apparatus, were unsatisfactory on account of Schopenhauer's constant unrest. But when he saw that he was spoiling all the pictures, he suddenly found the time for half a dozen more shots, until Mylius was happy with at least two.

Schopenhauer worried about how the photos would come out. He had since learned that Mylius was ordinarily a landscape photographer, specializing in city scenes. Had he known in advance that the *Illustrirte Zeitung* wanted to take his picture, then he might have suggested a portraitist whom he knew and trusted from previous sittings.[2] It did not help to settle his nerves that Mylius took around two months to send him a copy. In that time, his friend and dining partner, the French painter Jules Lunteschütz, who had completed his own portrait of Schopenhauer a few years before, and was midway through a second, had tipped him off that Mylius had done a poor job. Judging by what Lunteschütz had said, he concluded that he was going to come out looking like "a disgusting brat."[3]

Thankfully, when he did receive his copy, along with yet another unreserved apology from Mylius, Schopenhauer found that it wasn't half as bad as Lunteschütz had made out. He was not completely pleased with the nose and the mouth, admittedly, but the upper parts were excellent, especially the forehead, and the eyes—the all-important eyes—were "pretty good too."[4] The woodcut based on the photograph was published on December 4, 1858.[5]

As challenging as the sitting was for both parties, no ill will lingered between them. They certainly never forgot one another. Once, when Mylius had set up in the street to photograph a town house, shrouded beneath a black cloth, someone came up behind him and yelled, "Cuckoo!" He turned around to find it was Schopenhauer.[6] In return, in late September 1860, Mylius paid Schopenhauer the unique tribute of being the first to take a picture of his gravestone at Frankfurt cemetery.[7] As a city photographer turned portraitist, whose best work required a compliant sitter, he was ideally suited to the task.

:::

In his lifetime, Schopenhauer witnessed a revolution in the history of the recorded image. On August 19, 1839 (when Schopenhauer was fifty-one years old), at a joint meeting of the French Academy of Sciences and the Académie des Beaux-Arts in Paris, a chemist and painter named Louis Daguerre (who was the same age) unveiled to the world a new method of fixing projected images onto silver-coated copper plates. In the notebook that he reserved for agreeable quotations and snippets from curious news stories, Schopenhauer inserted a postcard-sized slip of paper on which he had handwritten the precise chemical process for producing these marvelous pictures, just as one might save a good recipe.[8] On the grounds of the scientific breakthrough alone, he held that Daguerre's name deserved to go down in history: "Daguerre's discovery," he later wrote, "is a hundred times more ingenious than the much admired discovery of Le Verrier."⁹ Urbain Le Verrier, who was also championed by the French Academy, had predicted the existence and position of the planet Neptune, not through direct observation, but by using mathematics and physics alone, which was of course highly commendable. But discovering an existing body, even in outer space, was not quite as impressive in Schopenhauer's estimation as creating something entirely new. If one of their two names is better known today, then it is indeed Daguerre's, although it surely helped that he patented his new invention as the daguerreotype. Outside of France, and ultimately inside it too, Le Verrier had less luck in naming Neptune after himself.

For this reason, Schopenhauer belongs to a small set of philosophers whose early life is visually depicted exclusively by means of paintings and drawings, but whose later life was captured in photographs. Fichte and Hegel died before the invention of proper portrait photography, whereas Nietzsche and Freud were born afterward, leaving us photos of them as children. Other members of the same club as Schopenhauer include Schelling, who had a daguerreotype taken by Hermann Biow in 1848, looking every bit of his seventy-three years, and Karl Marx, of whom several iconic pictures were taken.¹⁰ Merely potential members of the club include the Danish proto-existentialist Søren Kierkegaard, who for some reason was never photographed, and the English utilitarian John Stuart Mill, of whom there are many photographs but who seems never to have been visually depicted as a youth.

In fact, a case could well be made that Schopenhauer was the first major philosopher ever to be photographed. At the very least, he was an early and enthusiastic adopter.

For the first couple of years, daguerreotypes were rarely used for portraits because the exposure took twenty to thirty minutes, far too long even for those with more time and patience to spare than Schopenhauer. In the early 1840s, however, the introduction of high-speed lenses and extrasensitive plates reduced the time to half a minute. Evidently, Arthur must have written to Adele about his desire to have his picture taken as soon as the opportunity arose, because on November 25, 1841, she wrote back with a special request: "Please allow your dog to have a portrait too! Send me a copy as a gift."¹¹

The first studios appeared in Paris and London, but in the fall of 1842 news began to circulate of traveling photographers passing through Frankfurt. Schopenhauer leaped at the chance, and his first daguerreotype was taken on September 3, 1842, by a photographer now unknown.[12] Due to improper care, the original image turned completely blank by the 1930s, but a copy taken beforehand shows Schopenhauer as young as he was ever photographically depicted, not long after his clash with the Royal Danish Society, with his immaculately back-groomed gray hair and side-whiskers, and a determined expression angled defiantly away from the camera.[13] As requested, he duly sent a copy to Adele—with no evidence of a poodle portrait, sadly. In her reply on November 3, 1842, she said that daguerreotypes made him look twenty years older, neatly glossing over the fact that it had been about that long since she had last laid eyes on him.[14]

On April 7, 1846, a French photographer named Christian Louis Leblanc set up a studio in Frankfurt for six months. There Schopenhauer had two daguerreotypes taken on May 16, 1846. As he did with many of his pictures, Schopenhauer eventually gifted them away. The one he considered the best so far, he gave to Sibylle Mertens-Schaaffhausen, the woman who had cared for Adele in her dying years, and thus to whom, he admitted, he owed an enormous obligation. He also trusted that, with her being a collector of fine art and antiquities, the picture would one day find its way into a worthy public collection. Sure enough, she later bequeathed it to the Goethe National Museum in Weimar.[15] The second best one, he gave away to Julius Frauenstädt on October 30, 1851, with the instructions to "honor it: for I will never be daguerreotyped so young again."[16]

Schopenhauer usually gave his pictures away as a token of his gratitude toward the recipient, rather than a sign that he was fully happy with the image. In fact, on reflection, in these ones from Leblanc's studio, he thought he looked rather indignant, as though he had just finished writing his furious essay on university philosophy. And for a long time after this sitting, he wasn't even close to being satisfied with any subsequent pictures of himself: the French daguerreotypists, he thought, were naturally unsurpassable. A newer form of photography had already become dominant by the early 1850s, based on the English photographer Henry Fox Talbot's 1844 method of creating paper negatives from which multiple prints could be made.[17] In August 1850, Schopenhauer experimented with having a talbotype, better known as a calotype, taken of himself at the newly opened studio of Friedrich Hermann Hartmann. But he was disappointed with the results, which had to be touched up by hand, as was so often the case with this form of photography, and so he palmed his copy off on his housekeeper.[18] Hartmann himself, after moving to Basel, went on to capture an iconic image of Friedrich Nietzsche in 1875.

Dissatisfied with these newer methods, Schopenhauer reverted back to the trusty daguerreotype, which in his view created sharper, if one-off, images. He did so at the hands of Jacob Seib, who had since taken over Leblanc's studio, and conveniently offered either paper photographs or daguerreotypes. Schopenhauer had sat for Seib before, and did not take kindly to him at first: he was, in Schopenhauer's words, "such an unbearable, indescribably disgusting lump . . . that his very presence puts a scowl on my face."[19] But Seib had since established himself as the foremost photographer in Frankfurt after taking portrait pictures of sixty members of the ill-fated National Assembly in 1848. On September 3, 1852, Seib captured a defining image of Schopenhauer, impatiently propped up on one elbow, signature scowl across his face and several large veins bulging from his forehead. He had Seib take two more pictures on June 4, 1853, and twice again on May 18, 1855.

In total, thirty-one pictures were taken of Schopenhauer in the two decades or so that it was possible in his lifetime: eleven paper photographs and twenty daguerreotypes.[20]

:::

Such a technological revolution as the daguerreotype also opened up new horizons for philosophical reflection. Schopenhauer had been interested in vision and optics ever since one of his earliest works, *On Vision and Colors*, which was first published in 1816 after his collaboration with Goethe on color theory, and revised for a new edition in 1854. In these revisions, Schopenhauer used the

Figure 6. Schopenhauer (September 3, 1852) by Jacob Seib. Courtesy of Schopenhauer-Archiv der Stadt- und Universitätsbibliothek Frankfurt am Main.

daguerreotype as a source of confirmation for some of his claims about visual perception. First, he noted, the daguerreotype was further proof of his view that color is a subjective phenomenon, or more precisely: "that it is a function of the eye itself and consequently pertains immediately to the eye and only secondarily and mediately to objects."[21] He was already convinced about this by the fact that many people are not color-sighted, but the daguerreotype now allowed every sighted person to see an objective reproduction of the world captured only in gradations of light and dark.

Figure 7. Schopenhauer (May 18, 1855) by Jacob Seib. Courtesy of Schopenhauer-Archiv der Stadt- und Universitätsbibliothek Frankfurt am Main.

The daguerreotype also supported a more complex thesis about visual perception. Photographic images had made it possible, in turn, to create stereoscopic ones: two pictures of the same thing from ever so slightly different angles, which, when viewed separately but simultaneously through a pair of tubes, produced the appearance of a three-dimensional object. The stereoscope effectively replicated—and indeed depended on—the binocular vision of human beings and other animals. To Schopenhauer, it was striking proof of "the intellectual nature of intuition," or in other words, that vision involved not only sensation but also the cognition required to combine a pair of flat images into one seamless object.[22]

These thoughts were not all that revolutionary for the time—though they were by no means agreed upon either—as even in the absence of ways to fix an image, scientists and artists had long been drawing various lessons about human vision from the study of optics. But Schopenhauer's observations about the birth of photography were not limited to their impact on our best theories of visual perception. He also showed some awareness of how the photographic image might revolutionize our visual culture. "Just as every human being has a physiognomy by which he is provisionally judged," he wrote, "so does every age."[23] The objectivity of the photograph, however, had ramifications for how one culture could represent itself to the next. Before the photograph, every image that a culture projected of itself was of necessity a thoroughly artistic confection, and often a highly managed one at that. Even a building designed to last for countless generations could be clad in a facade that borrowed from bygone ages: "With what reverence will posterity regard our palaces and country houses produced in the most wretched rococo style of the age of Louis XIV!" "But," Schopenhauer continued, "it will have a hard time knowing what to do with the portraits and daguerreotypes depicting bootblack physiognomies with their Socratic beards, and fops in the costume of the peddling Jews of my youth."[24] After the photograph, in other words, it was harder for certain features of a culture to be concealed, forgotten, or erased. It was not that photography admitted no artistry or subterfuge at all; Schopenhauer was as sensitive as anyone, if not more so, to how a photograph could fail to record things as they are, or rather as we would have them be seen. Nevertheless, in the end, a photograph is a mechanical process with objective results: it could only document what is there, more or less. Hence, an unflattering photographic portrait, as compared to a painted one, was all the more embarrassing and painful to the sitter, and it was harder—but still not impossible—to lay the blame on the photographer.

On the other hand, if photographic truth offended human vanity, then it also served our curiosity like never before. Each of us, Schopenhauer observed, yearns to see what a person of distinction really looks like. This desire, he thought, is rooted in our steadfast assumption of the basic (yet specious) physiognomic principle that the exterior of a human being graphically reproduces their interior;

and that the face, in particular, manifests one's inner essence. Before photography, the best ways to know what a person looked like were "the rush to those places where he is expected to be, and . . . the efforts of the daily newspapers, especially in England, to describe him minutely and strikingly." "Daguerre's invention," however, "so highly valued for precisely this reason, satisfies our need most perfectly."[25] With this, Schopenhauer was just a thought or two away from predicting the paparazzi.

:::

"The world wants to know what your devoted servant Arthur Schopenhauer actually looks like": so Schopenhauer signed off a letter to his long-suffering publisher F. A. Brockhaus on October 10, 1859, in the midst of last-minute corrections to the third and final edition of *The World as Will and Representation*.[26]

By then, his last and possibly best photograph had already been taken. Earlier that year, Schopenhauer had received a request for his picture from Heinrich Gustav Brecht, a court assessor in Berlin and soon-to-be mayor of Quedlinburg in Harz, Saxony-Anhalt. The request was apparently prompted by the article on Schopenhauer in the *Illustrirte Zeitung*, complete with the woodcut illustration copied from Mylius's picture. On February 8, 1859, Schopenhauer wrote a cordial reply that he was most pleased by Brecht's interest in his philosophy and his person. He added, however, that Mylius's photograph had been made "ten times worse" by the woodcutter: "the eyes squint, the mouth is twisted: there is scarcely even a remote resemblance left . . . I am often photographed for all kinds of strangers, but always inadequately."[27] Schopenhauer saw an opportunity. He had been keen to give another chance to a local photographer named Johann Schäfer, for whom he had first sat, with unremarkable results, on January 16, 1856, but who since then was said to have acquired state of the art equipment, capable of producing exquisite portraits. With Brecht's assent, Schopenhauer arranged for Schäfer to take the new picture.

When in late February Schopenhauer still hadn't had his new photo taken, he worried that Schäfer had mistakenly sent Brecht

Figure 8. Schopenhauer (1859) by Johann Schäfer.

a copy from the earlier, unsatisfactory sitting. But in March 1859, Schäfer took three new photographs, exquisite as promised. They still featured Schopenhauer's by-now completely colorless sidewhiskers and trademark tufts of back-combed hair; he was still dressed in the black frock coat and white cravat of his youth, with his pince-nez held in one hand and the other resting on his lap near to his watch chain. But unlike in his first daguerreotype, though just as defiantly, he stared directly into Schäfer's lens, somehow appearing both wearied by life and smoldering with vitality.

For once, Schopenhauer was satisfied with the results. He was sufficiently happy to allow Schäfer to make more copies for other private buyers, which Schäfer duly did in both large and small formats, as well as oval-shaped bust portraits, one of which was acquired by Elisabet Ney.[28] There was, however, later a rift between Schopenhauer and Schäfer. Schopenhauer had inscribed a special copy of the photograph with his autograph and the Latin motto *Quidquid fit necessario fit*, "Whatever happens, necessarily happens," one of the main claims of his prizewinning essay on free will. It was intended for Brecht, as the original requester, but, according to Lunteschütz, Schäfer had the temerity instead to submit it for an exhibition in Paris without Schopenhauer's authorization. Rather than be flattered at the prospect of being internationally exhibited, Schopenhauer thought it was doubly dishonorable of Schäfer not only to desert his obligation to Brecht but also to distribute this unique copy illicitly when he had already given his permission to have other copies made and sold. In an apologetic letter, Schopenhauer informed Brecht that he was now refusing Schäfer's requests to inscribe further copies. He wanted so little to do with the photographer, in fact, that he instructed Brecht, in order finally to get his signed copy, to acquire a blank one first and then send it to him to be returned inscribed.[29]

Aside from the sour ending, Schopenhauer's session with Schäfer was a success. But it was only part of what he meant when he boasted to his publisher that the world suddenly wanted to see him. In fact, it wasn't even primarily photographic depictions that he had in mind. The week before, Elisabet Ney had come to stay with him to sculpt his bust, and at the same time a highly distinguished local painter named Angilbert Göbel was just finishing a copper engraving based on an oil painting that he had made, at his own expense, between the years 1857 and 1859. It happened to be Schopenhauer's favorite.

Another painter, named Julius Hamel, made several portraits of Schopenhauer, both before and after his death. One that was painted in the spring and summer of 1856 was, by all accounts,

Figure 9. Schopenhauer (1856) by Julius Hamel. Hamel's portrait featured in a set of postage stamps issued by the Free City of Danzig in 1938 to commemorate the 150th anniversary of Schopenhauer's birth, along with Ruhl's 1815 portrait and Schäfer's 1859 photograph. Courtesy of Schopenhauer-Archiv der Stadt- und Universitätsbibliothek Frankfurt am Main.

quite the ordeal. Although Schopenhauer acknowledged it was a finely painted picture, the portrait itself, he thought, was poorly done: "The young man has talent," he said of Hamel, who was in his early twenties at the time, "but it's not a likeness; I look like a village mayor."[30] Tactless as ever, Schopenhauer made his opinions known to Hamel's face before the painting was even finished. In one sitting, as Hamel later recalled, things had started out well, as he quietly listened to Schopenhauer with his head bowed toward the canvas, until the sitter suddenly got up to take a look at the work in progress and started chastising the painter like a schoolboy.

In anger, he picked the painting up and threw it into the corner of the room. But then, after a few moments of staring at Hamel, Schopenhauer slowly walked over to the picture, picked it up, and gently placed it back on the easel. "My dear Herr Hamel," he said by way of explanation, "I didn't mean it in a bad way, and you mustn't forget that the picture represents me after all." Following the outburst, Schopenhauer calmly went back to dispensing wisdom, including not only how much money Hamel should ask for the picture, but also the advice—perhaps addressed to himself—that one must always respect one's portrait, even when it is imperfect.[31]

:::

As with photography, Schopenhauer had his own ideas about what makes for a good painted portrait. There was, to his mind, one overarching golden rule and then some more specific rules pertaining to subjects like himself.

The golden rule, which he took from the celebrated German archaeologist Johann Joachim Winckelmann, was that a good portrait represents "the ideal of the individual."[32] This deceptively simple two-part proposal made portraiture both similar and different from other artistic disciplines. To start with the differences, other arts in Schopenhauer's view aimed not at individuality but rather universality: the usual purpose of art is to display the timeless quintessence of its subject matter, albeit in and through one well-wrought exemplar. The portrait, by contrast, when done well, reveals the sitter's unique character.

On this view, even sculpture or historical painting, though they both depict human forms, do not quite match portraiture's level of specificity. Sculpture presents the exterior body, which is, at best, a physiognomic clue to the model's inner character; but more often than not a sculpture stands for an abstract and anonymous ideal of the human physique. Historical painting, similarly, reveals ubiquitous qualities of humanity, although generally moral rather than bodily ones, as, for example, the endless depiction of war that epitomize our valor, pride, and bravery—or, indeed, our rapacity, folly, and cruelty.

All artistic depictions, however, including portraits, aim for an ideal presentation of their subject matter. These two sides of artistic representation in fact work together: only by some degree of idealization, on the one hand, can art can reveal the essence of an individual being or a universal truth, on the other. To perceive and depict these ideals requires of artists, not only supreme technical abilities, but also extraordinary powers of intellectual vision. This partly explains why Schopenhauer's respect and admiration for great artists was almost boundless. So long, of course, as they did as their job right.

When the golden rule of portraiture is applied to subject matter like Schopenhauer, it produces some more specific subsidiary rules. First, if a good portrait captures the ideal of the individual, and if the individual in question is a great thinker, then it must somehow make an image of the extraordinary intellectual powers of its subject matter too. This, as Schopenhauer had claimed in the first edition of *The World as Will and Representation*, is made evident in the thinker's pensive gaze: "Both lively and steadfast, it bears the character of thoughtfulness, of contemplation, as we can see in the portraits of the few faces belonging to the geniuses that nature now and then brings forth among the untold millions."[33] In the 1844 second edition, he expanded on this thought by adding that the expression of genius should be characterized by pure contemplation, as distinct from the ordinary faces—such as that, for example, of a village mayor—which look far from contemplative but rather are visibly dominated by the will to life.[34]

Moreover, by the time everyone wanted to see his picture, Schopenhauer was not only a recognized man of genius, but an old one at that. Though he may have feared the effects and outcome of old age, he did not demur from the look. In fact, in his view, it was impossible to depict a truly wise sage without including some visible signs of aging:

> precisely that slow formative process of the enduring facial expression through countless transitory, characteristic contractions of the features is the reason why intelligent faces develop only gradually and even achieve their elevated expression only in old

age, whereas portraits from their youth show only the earliest traces of it.³⁵

As a subject matter for portraiture, Schopenhauer therefore fell into the category of men belatedly made famous by their works, who are naturally depicted as gray and wrinkled. "But from a eudaemonological perspective, this is as it should be," Schopenhauer added. "Fame and youth all at the same time are too much for a mortal."³⁶

∷∷

Schopenhauer's remark about premature fame was a considered one. Fame, according to him, had a role to play in his vision of the good life—suspending, for the time being, the many question marks that he had spent his career raising over the very idea of a good life—but it had its pitfalls too.

Insofar as he had a formula for a good life, he divided its main ingredients into three:

(1) What one *is*: that is, personality in the widest sense. Hence this includes health, strength, beauty, temperament, moral character, and intelligence and its cultivation.
(2) What one *has*: that is, property and possessions in every sense.
(3) What one *represents*: By this expression we usually mean what someone is in the eyes of others, thus how he is represented by them. Hence it consists in their opinion of him and is divided into honour, rank, and fame.³⁷

The first category, what one *is*, includes all of our intrinsic qualities, that is, those that we possesses regardless of our relation to other people or things. The other two, by contrast, are defined by relationships such as ownership over external goods (what one *has*) and how we are viewed by other people (what one *represents*). Partly for this reason, what a person is, in Schopenhauer's view, takes precedence over everything else. Thus, although fame is included in the general formula, it notably comes at the very end, indicating its contribution, on the one hand, but also its low priority, on the other.

Fame, indeed, was not even top of the representational goods for Schopenhauer: he gave that distinction to honor. "Honour," he said, "is external conscience and conscience is internal honour"—or, in case this elegant formulation should appear "more of a polished than a clear and thorough explanation," he clarified: "Honour is, objectively, other people's opinion of our value and, subjectively, our fear of this opinion."[38]

To his mind, there were many important differences between fame and honor. The main one was that "everyone must strive for honour, i.e. a good name . . . and only very few aspire to fame."[39] Honor, that is, is a quality that can be shared by all, and happily so; it is feasible, and indeed desirable, that everyone should strive to be honorable.[40] Fame, by contrast, cannot be shared around in the same way for a couple of reasons. First, fame is not simply a matter of being well known but rather being better known by comparison to others. It is therefore, of necessity, differentially distributed. Furthermore, the right kind of fame is due to extraordinarily great achievements, which, also by definition, are not ordinarily expected of everyone. Thus, our default position in life is honor and obscurity: fame is acquired, whereas honor is lost.[41] And while the right kind of fame can contribute to the good life, it cannot be an essential requirement; by contrast, one can hardly call good a life that is dishonorable.

Not only was fame secondary to honor, according to Schopenhauer, it was also secondary, of course, to what one is actually famous for. This, he wrote, was true of all the representational goods, such as honor, splendor, rank, and fame:

> it will contribute to our happiness if we achieve in good time the simple insight that we all primarily and actually live in our own skin, not in the opinions of others, and that, accordingly, our actual and personal state, as it is determined by health, temperament, abilities, income, wife, child, friends, place of residence, and so forth, is a hundred times more important for our hap-

piness than what it pleases others to make of us. The opposite delusion makes us unhappy.[42]

Even though Schopenhauer's lifestyle conspicuously lacked some of these essential goods, most notably a wife and child, there was still some consolation to be had in the principle. Throughout his life so far in obscurity, it was nevertheless always the case that "whoever just *deserves* the fame without actually receiving it possesses by far the most important thing, which can console him about the fame he lacks."[43] This much was evident to him in our esteem toward great people of the past: what made their lives so great was not the mere fact that we remember them now but that in life they had the opportunity to enjoy whatever it was that made them so memorable. "Value lies not in fame itself," he wrote, "but in what secures the fame." "And pleasure," he added, thinking of lasting works of genius, "is to be found in begetting immortal children."[44]

The divide between fame and value opens up the possibility of two kinds of injustice: overrated hacks and unappreciated geniuses. As Lessing put it, and Schopenhauer agreed: "Some people are famous and others deserve to be."[45] Naturally, whenever Schopenhauer discussed undeserving fame, his usual targets were not far behind: "The entire history of literature, of ancient and modern times," he wrote, "has produced no example of false fame on a par with that of Hegelian philosophy."[46] A downside of such false fame, according to Schopenhauer, is that it never lasts long. The right kind of fame is carried forward by real and recognized achievements, whereas false fame is founded on something more specious and ephemeral: "unjust praise, good friends, bribed critics, hints from above and collusion from below."[47] The hints from above come from a shameless and dishonest press; the collusion below from a gullible, insecure, and undiscriminating public.[48] Schopenhauer misapplied this point to Hegel, whose later fame and favor, like his own, fluctuated over time without ever completely fizzling out. But a true example from history of flash-in-the-pan fame is always hard to find because, by nature, it has now been mostly forgotten.

Genuine fame, according to Schopenhauer, was always a slow burn. Even the fame of the truly great philosophers who were known within their lifetime paled in comparison to the esteem and admiration that grew around them after their deaths, sometimes long after.[49] The list, for Schopenhauer, included Aristotle, whose fame spread far and wide outside of Greece, dipping almost into oblivion in the Western world, only to be revived again centuries later. It included Epicurus, who in life, according to Seneca, was virtually unknown outside of Athens. It also included heretical thinkers, who were not not-famous but rather positively infamous, such as the excommunicated Jewish-Dutch philosopher Baruch Spinoza or the persecuted Italian cosmologist Giordano Bruno. Even Kant only became properly well known, like Schopenhauer, in his sixties. And then, above all, there was David Hume, who was not only in his fifties by the time anyone paid attention to his luminous and lucid works, but continued to be hated by Anglican preachers right down to the present day. "I can think of no greater token of his fame," said Schopenhauer, himself no admirer of the English clergy.[50] For this reason, he wished that someone someday would compile a definitive list of neglected geniuses into "a tragic literary history [of] how the different nations, each of which after all takes the greatest possible pride in the great writers and artists it has to show for itself, actually treated them during the course of their lives."[51]

Suffice to say, then, that Schopenhauer did not consider adulation to be worth chasing for its own sake, especially if disapprobation could be as good a sign of one's actual worth as any esteem. Those who thirsted for fame after death, as distinct from the worthwhile things that bring fame, were in his view "clinging to life" by striving for a posthumous existence.[52] The taste of fame, when sought from such a motive, creates a dangerous cycle, because it "resembles sea water; the more we drink of it, the thirstier we become."[53]

But if fame was really so bogus, then why did Schopenhauer ever want it for himself? Why did it even feature at all in his picture of the good life? A possible answer is that fame is, or can be, a form of validation for one's own achievements. "Fame," Schopenhauer remarked, "affects the person who is praised mainly as an external symptom, by means of which he receives the confirmation of his own high opinion about himself. Therefore, we might say that just as light is not visible unless it is reflected by a body, every excellence becomes completely certain of itself only through its reputation."[54] Even on these grounds, however, contemporary fame can still be called into question because, evidently, its light shines as much on the mediocre (or worse) as the truly exceptional.

For an alternative reason why fame, despite everything, still contributed to the good life, Schopenhauer produced a motto from a scarcely quoted enslaved Roman-Syrian writer named Publilius Syrus: "Powerless is all virtue," wrote Publilius, "if its fame does not extend widely."[55] On this view, by the same power that makes it an ideal accelerant of dubious notions and nefarious individuals, fame—when placed in the right hands—can be used to disseminate thoughts and ideas that are really worth spreading.

∴

It wasn't the article in the *Leipziger Illustrirte Zeitung* that made Schopenhauer famous. Not so long before, in fact, he wanted to avoid precisely that sort of attention. On October 15, 1853, he wrote to Frauenstädt with strict instructions on the matter: "I hope that you, my dear apostle, will not think of arranging an illustration for me in the *Illustrirte Zeitung! Di meliora!* I do not want to serve the idle reading public with my person for amusement."[56] Only dead authors, in his view, should ever appear in portraits appended to their works.

By the 1850s, Frauenstädt was the primary member of a small circle of admirers who had gathered around Schopenhauer since his move to Frankfurt. He referred to them affectionately—and one hopes a touch ironically—as his apostles.

Before Frauenstädt, there was Johann August Becker, a lawyer in Alzey and later judge in Mainz. On July 31, 1844, Becker initiated a correspondence with Schopenhauer by sending him a polite request to provide some comments and questions about his work. Through a series of lengthy missives, over the course of several years, together they combed through the finer details of Schopenhauer's philosophy. Undoubtedly, Becker was Schopenhauer's most prized philosophical correspondent precisely because, while he was unfailingly cordial, he was also the least fawning. As Schopenhauer wrote to him on May 5, 1852: "Of all my apostles, you are the one who understands me most correctly—all said without flattery. But unfortunately," he lamented, "you have a stubborn fear of printer's ink! That's why, out of four apostles, I have only two evangelists."[57]

Schopenhauer's two "evangelists," also referred to as his "active apostles," were those who had gone to the trouble of publishing their expositions and defenses of his work. One of them was, of course, Frauenstädt, who evangelized in numerous ways. He not only drew on Schopenhauer's philosophy for his 1848 work *On the True Relation of Reason to Revelation*, but even dedicated the book to him. Then, in 1854, after a few more publications on Schopenhauer, Frauenstädt published a general introduction to his work titled *Letters on the Schopenhauerian Philosophy*. After Schopenhauer's death, Frauenstädt produced several other scholarly landmarks, including the first collected works and a lexicon of key terms.[58] Schopenhauer's second evangelist, and the earliest of all his apostles, was Friedrich Ludwig Dorguth, with whom he had corresponded since the end of 1836. Another lawyer but based in Magdeburg, Dorguth published a pamphlet on Schopenhauer in July 1845. To Schopenhauer's delight, Dorguth characterized him as German philosophy's Kaspar Hauser, the boy whose story was adopted as folklore by the public when he appeared out of the blue one day in the town of Nuremberg, claiming to have grown up isolated in a dark dudgeon, and rumored to be a royal heir by birthright.[59]

As for the last of the four apostles, Schopenhauer had high hopes that he too would become an evangelist like Frauenstädt and Dorguth; but instead, like Becker, he proved to be ink-shy. Adam Ludwig von Doß, whom Schopenhauer referred to as "John the Apostle" on account of his young age, was a legal trainee who had happened upon *The World as Will and Representation* in a Passau bookstore in 1846.[60] He visited Frankfurt three years later, prompting Schopenhauer to sing his praises to Frauenstädt at the end of 1849: "His zeal is indescribable and gives me great pleasure. He stayed for fourteen days just to visit me every other day. Unfortunately he hasn't released anything to press yet; he's only twenty-six years old. But he is a writing apostle, writing letters to people he doesn't even know. . . . I tell you, a fanatic!"[61] In the light of Doß's epistolic campaign, it's a wonder that Schopenhauer didn't christen him as his Saint Paul. Doß died in 1873 as a retired district court counselor in Munich, meaning that three out of Schopenhauer's first four apostles were jurists rather than philosophers.[62] On the plus side, he was never short of legal advice.

Later there came more followers. There was, for example, David Asher, who became another regular correspondent after his visit to Schopenhauer in August 1854. Dressed in a yellow linen morning suit, Schopenhauer greeted Asher frostily at first, because not only had Asher disturbed him during his usual working hours, but he had the temerity to arrive with his own manuscript for Schopenhauer to read and comment on. When Asher properly introduced himself, however, Schopenhauer recognized his name from a letter he received long ago, and his whole manner instantly changed to one of friendliness: "And finally," as Asher later recollected, "sitting on the sofa next to him, I had the opportunity to look face-to-face at the man whose spirit had had such a powerful effect on me."[63]

Last but far from least, in the same year as Asher's visit, Schopenhauer met Wilhelm Gwinner, a Frankfurt native who was, yet again, a lawyer by training. Gwinner recalled first hearing the sound of Schopenhauer's voice in 1847, when they were seated near to one another at dinner. Schopenhauer, in Gwinner's words, was happily discussing logical laws while "making a face as if he were talking to his beloved."[64] They got to know one another properly from April 1854 onward, but unlike with the other apostles, who were scattered across Germany, theirs was not merely an epistolary friendship. Instead, Gwinner became a frequent visitor to Schöne Aussicht, and therefore an acquaintance of his dog Atma too. This, combined with his fanatical search for every story, saying, and anecdote of the philosopher's life, later made him Schopenhauer's first biographer and a major source on which all subsequent biographies were bound to draw.[65] Helen Zimmern, for example, paid due homage to Gwinner in the preface to her own biography of Schopenhauer, passages of which were virtual translations from Gwinner's German into English, by rightly describing his memoir as "a model of condensation, good taste, and graphic power."[66]

With a devoted and capable entourage in place, the aging Schopenhauer now had a plentiful supply of youthful energy, and tireless legwork, to fuel his rise to fame.

∴

"My philosophy has just set foot in England," Schopenhauer wrote to another apostle, Ernst Otto Lindner, on April 27, 1853. He had discovered his newfound international fame in a remarkably roundabout way. Yet another apostle, who was yet another lawyer, by the name of Dr. Martin Emden, was casually browsing through a stack of English magazines laid out in a Frankfurt club, when to his surprise he spotted Schopenhauer's name in *The Economist*. It appeared in a summary of the latest issue of a different periodical, the *Westminster Review*, the third article of which was entirely devoted to Schopenhauer and his work:

> In the third article we learn that Arthur Schopenhauer, who has been attempting to make a metaphysical reputation for himself for almost forty years, has at length succeeded by his caustic attacks in attracting some attention. The present notice of his works is, we believe, the only one that has appeared in our language. As one of the curiosities of literature, the man and his writings are deservedly made known to us, otherwise he is not worth much notice. Whatever effects he may have on his own countrymen, his theory of the world being all will—which revives the Darwin theory, and might lead, were it well founded, to the growth of wings on the human body, as well as to making of any kind of morality kings and slaveholders might wish—is not likely to have much effect out of Germany. Mr Schopenhauer, is, however, not popular even in Germany, and if he ever get [*sic*] a widely extended reputation, it is more likely to begin abroad than at home.[67]

Schopenhauer knew that these fourteen lines in *The Economist* were not entirely favorable, and that they even contained some "extremely absurd stuff," referring presumably to the misconception that on his account reality is governed by our whims and wishes.

But he also recognized, first, that it was still twice as much as anyone else had discussed him outside of Germany, and, second, that this did not entail that the review itself was written in the same manner. To see for himself, he immediately ordered a copy of the *Westminster Review*.[68]

It was not by chance that Schopenhauer chose Lindner to share this piece of news. Lindner just so happened to be the editor of the *Vossische Zeitung*, a Berlin-based national newspaper with similar liberal leanings to the *Westminster Review*. Sensing before even seeing it that the article might be favorable to him, Schopenhauer was thus laying the groundwork to have it translated and published in Germany. Lindner duly leaped into action: he acquired and shared a copy of the article in question before the one that Schopenhauer had ordered for himself had even arrived. On May 9, Schopenhauer replied to Lindner with his flattered first—or rather third—impressions:

> I really enjoyed the article and read it three times. The man's warmth is striking, and you can see that he is trying to dampen it for fear of appearing to be a partisan of such a heretic, atheist, and diabolist.... The translated passages are very good.... He seems to have understood Kant's philosophy as a whole.... The presentation of my system is, of course, very inadequate, especially in the ethical part.... The best thing, as you say, is the beginning, namely the description of my relationship with the professors.... I would be all the more pleased if you, excellent apostle, found ways and means to inform the Germans in detail about this.[69]

With Schopenhauer's seal of approval, in June 1853, Lindner published a German translation of the article, composed, in fact, by his wife, who was a British émigré. Schopenhauer's one stipulation, made in a postscript, was to find a way to avoid reproducing the article's use of the term "misanthropic," which in his view "evil tongues" were already overusing to describe his "withdrawn way of life." Even this request he later retracted, however, on the grounds that "one must translate faithfully and honestly."[70]

At times like these, Schopenhauer did not take the acts of his apostles for granted. He was positively grateful for them. "It is a real strengthening of the heart in old age," he declared to Lindner, "when the friends of our youth have almost all died away, that we now find new and young friends who surpass our former ones in participation and zeal: and it is doubly so if we do not make these new friends by chance, or common agreements, but due to the best and noblest part of ourselves. I am so happy to have acquired such young friends."[71] He regarded his apostles as his friends, who appreciated him for his better self and whom he appreciated back. Schopenhauer was happy, for once.

At the time of his discovery, he knew nothing about the production of the article that awarded him such high praise. Not coincidentally, it would seem, it was published in the extraordinary two-year period that the *Westminster Review* was effectively edited by the soon-to-be acclaimed novelist Mary Ann Evans, better known as George Eliot. Officially, Eliot was an assistant to the editor and owner John Chapman; but, as herself a translator of heretical post-Hegelian philosophy, such as David Friedrich Strauss's *The Life of Jesus* and Ludwig Feuerbach's *The Essence of Christianity*, under Eliot's influence the magazine had significantly expanded its coverage of German intellectual culture. As she wrote to a friend on April 4, 1853: "Pray read the article on Schopenhauer next—I think it one of our best."[72]

Because anonymous authorship was common at the time, it took Schopenhauer a good few years and his growing network of contacts just to find out the author's identity. In June 1855, he was visited in Frankfurt by "an intelligent, well-bred Yankee" named Edward Young, the son of a Boston minister and recent graduate of Harvard Divinity School, who was on a four-year trip around Germany to study the latest developments in the field of theology.[73] Later, on March 21, 1856, Young sent Schopenhauer a letter correctly identifying the author of the article as John Oxenford.[74] Aside from writing for the *Westminster Review*, Oxenford was the theater critic for *The Times*, the author of several dramas and librettos, and, like Schopenhauer, a skilled multilinguist, having already translated works by Goethe into English, as well as Calderón and Molière.

Oxenford's superbly titled "Iconoclasm in German Philosophy" drew a sharp line between what it did and did not agree with in Schopenhauer. "Few, indeed," it began, "we venture to assert, will be those of our English readers who are familiar with the name Arthur Schopenhauer. Fewer still will there be who are aware that the mysterious being owning that name has been working for something like forty years to subvert the whole system of German philosophy."[75] From here, Oxenford regaled his readers with the legend of "this misanthropic sage of Frankfort,"[76] almost exactly as Schopenhauer would have styled it himself—perhaps, one presumes, because Oxenford based the major plot points on Schopenhauer's own telling through the multiple prefaces to his major works, each of which found new ways to declaim and denounce the alleged academic conspiracy against him. Oxenford even found a way to echo the ending of *The World as Will and Representation* on the word "nothing," by repeatedly saying that this had been Germany's soundless response to Schopenhauer's decades of philosophical labor. Hence why Schopenhauer liked the first few pages best.

More specifically, Oxenford recommended Schopenhauer's style: the English reader would find Schopenhauer, above all, *readable*. By this, Oxenford meant not only that Schopenhauer could write in any number of entertaining modes, from grand theorizing and garrulous storytelling to sarcastic wit and scathing diatribe. Rather, Schopenhauer aimed, successfully, at making himself understood. "The general fault of German metaphysicians is that they do not even afford you a fair ground of attack," opined Oxenford. "Now Schopenhauer gives you a comprehensible system, clearly worded; and you may know, beyond the possibility of a doubt, what you are accepting, and what you are rejecting."[77] To Oxenford, this itself was a source of evidence that Schopenhauer's account of his own distinction from the German philosophical establishment, and treatment at their hands, was largely correct rather than a matter of sour grapes. Oxenford, who like George Eliot was no slouch when it came to German letters, could see for himself that "too many philosophical works of modern Germany encourage the suspicion that the animadversions of Schopenhauer are not altogether unfounded."[78] The story, to Oxenford's ears, rang true.

A downside of Schopenhauer's readability, however, was that

Oxenford saw clearly and immediately what he could never accept of his philosophy. Schopenhauer's pessimism was frankly at odds with a cherished doctrine of Victorian liberalism: namely, boundless social progress. The *Westminster Review*, after all, had been an organon of radical liberal thinking since its inception by the paradigmatically utilitarian philosopher Jeremy Bentham in 1823 and then under the editorship of Bentham's most famous protégé, John Stuart Mill. What the English reader really wanted from Germany, Oxenford concluded, was "a writer of equal power, comprehensiveness, ingenuity and erudition, ranged on a side more in harmony with our own feelings and convictions."[79] Until such time, Schopenhauer would do.

Schopenhauer kept track of his other appearances in the *Westminster Review* after Oxenford's article. In fact, he learned that he had made his first appearance precisely one year before in a subsection of the April 1852 issue titled "Contemporary Literature of Germany," and then briefly again in the same subsection in January 1853. Unlike "Iconoclasm in German Philosophy," these articles did not exclusively focus on Schopenhauer, although they already presented him as the aging enfant terrible of German philosophy. He was offended by an appearance in the October 1856 issue, which did him the great dishonor of suggesting that the main ideas of his philosophy derived from Hegel. "The *Westminster Review*'s twaddle really annoyed me," he immediately wrote to Frauenstädt. "I don't think Oxenford wrote that; [if he did, then] he must have forgotten everything he said about me, or else he was drunk."[80] These slights notwithstanding, Schopenhauer always recommended Oxenford as the model of style for any future translator. When he wrote to David Asher on October 22, 1857, about the idea of Asher translating his work, he said of Oxenford: "I was *quite amazed*," using the English words. "Not just the meaning, but the style, my manners and gestures, to my astonishment: as if in a mirror!"[81] In being seen, Schopenhauer saw himself.

: : :

Oxenford pardoned Schopenhauer's pessimism as the price of enjoying an otherwise digestible German. But there were other, indeed opposite, possible explanations for why Schopenhauer caught on at precisely this moment. In Germany at least, if not yet in England, the spirit of progress, as eulogized by liberal Oxenford, had stalled since the failed revolutions of just a few years before. Pessimism was, perhaps, the order of the day.

On the other hand, Schopenhauer himself always rejected the suggestion that his pessimism emerged from dark times in Germany. According to the formerly Hegelian philosopher Kuno Fischer, who in 1854 embarked on a multivolume history of modern philosophy, if Schopenhauer had been born in the right place and time earlier in the 1700s, then he would have been an optimist like Leibniz. "That's how crazy Hegelianism makes you," Schopenhauer wrote about Fischer to Frauenstädt. Apart from being irrelevant—for even if these were the origins of his pessimism, it wouldn't make him wrong—it was also, in his view, untrue. The philosophical formation of his pessimism occurred between 1814 and 1818, he testified, a time of liberation for Germany after the Napoleonic Wars.[82]

Had he lived to see it, Schopenhauer would have welcomed the arc of Fischer's nine-volume history, which culminated with the life and works of Schopenhauer himself. By that time, the write-up of Fischer's mammoth edifice in the *Westminster Review*, in January 1895, could end its opening paragraph with the pleasing line, "Hegel is hardly read at all; only students read Kant; but Schopenhauer's works sell by the thousands."[83]

Either way, all of a sudden, the times were finally catching up with Schopenhauer: the outsider had moved into the mainstream.[84] Lindner, who along with his unsung wife had played such an indispensable role in importing Schopenhauer's English fame back into Germany, paid close attention to how this turn of events affected him:

> He took great, immediate joy in the gradual growth of his fame and, as he often expressed to me, wished to live a long time to see the complete downfall of professorial philosophy with his own eyes. "My opponents think I'm old and will die soon," he said, "then it would be over for me. Well, they can no longer keep quiet about me, and I can live to be ninety years old." Only

the fear of gradually losing his hearing completely, this thought of old age embittered him; and at one point he was literally horrified at the idea that, as a result of all the mental work, he could end up like Kant in the last years of his life.[85]

With fame came happiness, then, but also worry. The philosopher who had made his name by arguing that a short life is a better life—or, better still, no life at all—now anxiously hoped for a couple more decent decades to see his project through. If in these final years Schopenhauer was even more impatient than usual ("I'll give you twenty minutes, I haven't got time to wait any longer"), perhaps it was only because he had been patient long enough.

CHAPTER 10

You Are Not Nothing

How Schopenhauer Survived Death

On July 1, 1859, Schopenhauer moved house—but not by much, and not for long. He moved one over: from Schöne Aussicht 17 to Schöne Aussicht 16. A family on the first floor of number 16, the Schneiders, had recently vacated one-half of the ground floor, where previously they had run a store. As there was still time left on the rental contract, Herr Schneider agreed to sublet the rooms to Schopenhauer, who was having trouble with his own landlord and seeking an apartment large enough to accommodate his library.[1]

Frau Schneider was not best pleased. She had heard all about this monstrous old man, their next-door neighbor Schopenhauer: that he was an angry, unkind, violent soul, and so utterly intolerant of noise that he once thrashed a women who dared loiter outside his door. "He beat a woman and he will beat our children too," she warned, referring to their wild brood of five, but principally their daughter Lucia and her two older brothers, who were prone to outbreaks of raucous horseplay. "Right," Herr Schneider replied: "Perhaps they'll be better behaved." And true enough, for a short time, the mere thought of Schopenhauer downstairs scared the Schneider children straight, little Lucia above all.[2]

One day Lucia and her brothers were playing circus, climbing over chairs and tables and making a tremendous racket. (Luckily for them, Schopenhauer hadn't moved in yet.) Their English governess, Miss Bessie, tried in vain to regain control with cries of "naughty boys!" and "naughty girl!" Their father entered the room: "Are you crazy? What's going on here?" Miss Bessie explained that the children were disobeying her orders. "Very well," he said. "I'll fetch Schopenhauer right away. . . . Good thing he's moving in downstairs." At this, the first time that Lucia ever heard the name Schopenhauer, there fell a deathly silence. The children crept over to beg their father's forgiveness. Who was this Schopenhauer, they inquired? A little, gray, grumpy old man, he explained, with a big wooden stick. He warned them never to disturb Schopenhauer, who had no patience for little boys and girls. After Herr Schneider had left, the children conferred about this frightening revelation. One of Lucia's brothers bravely vowed to protect her with the whip he was cracking moments ago as the ringmaster of their make-believe circus. The other guessed that he was probably called Schopenhauer because he drank too much—*Schoppen*, with a double *P*, being another word for bottle—and made the universal gesture for glugging. Nevertheless, they were terrified of their new neighbor, whom they were still yet to meet. From then on, the slightest naughtiness was met with the threat: "Get Schopenhauer up here!"

Lucia's first real encounter with Schopenhauer seemed to confirm all her worst fears. She was about to be taken on a walk when Miss Bessie remembered that she had forgotten something upstairs, leaving Lucia in the downstairs hallway alone. It must have been winter by then, or at least the fall, as she was bundled up in a white fur coat with a hat and muff—a little polar bear, her father would say. She heard loud barking from outside the front door and suddenly a large brown dog burst in. He put his paws up on her shoulders, and she felt the heat of his tongue on her face. Closely following the dog came Schopenhauer, a small gray man as described. He cursed and waved his dreaded stick, not at Lucia, she realized, but to discourage the dog from jumping up any more at the terrified girl. When Miss Bessie came running back downstairs, alerted by Lucia's cries, Schopenhauer apologized to her in the purest English. Then he tore into his apartment, slamming the door behind him.

The next day, Lucia came home from school to a nicer surprise. Schopenhauer's housekeeper, Margarete, had called by to leave a little doll for her, along with the pledge of a peacemaking paw from his poorly behaved poodle. But now, according to her parents, Lucia was obliged to go back downstairs to say thank you. She replied that she would rather not have the doll; but it was no use resisting, she had to obey.

Lucia and Miss Bessie knocked on Schopenhauer's front door several times because, as Margarete explained when she finally answered, they were both going profoundly deaf. Outside ears sometimes heard their loud exchanges as heated arguments, not always inaccurately. For the same reason, she advised the visitors to speak up with Schopenhauer, but despite their best efforts he failed to notice them as they entered his study. When eventually he swung around from his desk, startled and irritable, Lucia braced herself for another fright. Nervously she stuck out a hand and thanked him in words rehearsed upstairs. Up close he was no less terrifying to her, despite the smile that now broke across his lips: with his wide nose, bushy eyebrows, pinched mouth, and tangled white hair, she found him repulsive. (He made a much better impression on English Miss Bessie, who raved about him afterward: "Oh, Schopenhauer is a gentleman!") Instead it was Atma, her erstwhile assailant, who instantly won Lucia's heart. As promised, he gallantly gave her his paw, and even performed a few tricks. On her exit, Lucia noticed that the kitchen was filled with boxes of books and writings, never unpacked. It went unused because Schopenhauer ate out in the evenings and light at home, while Margarete kept a little stove in her room.

Later on Lucia's brothers were treated to Atma's tricks too. For one of their favorites, Schopenhauer placed a lump of sugar on top of Atma's nose and began slowly to recite the alphabet. At the letter *S*, Atma flicked the lump into the air and devoured it. Not once did he let it drop to the floor, at least according to Lucia's memory. The children would often bring sugar lumps downstairs for precisely this purpose, although Schopenhauer only very occasionally obliged. If they tried to get Atma to perform the trick for themselves, he would shake the sugar lump off out of loyalty to his master.

They also borrowed books from Schopenhauer's library, exclusively preferring the ones with pictures. He was pleased to find that Lucia's brothers could translate the captions of a book filled with illustrations of English cities and castles. Lucia's own translation skills were not yet so well honed. Once, she recited to him the English hymn "Gentle Jesus":

> Gentle Jesus, meek and mild,
> Look upon a little child;
> Pity my simplicity,
> Suffer me to come to thee . . .

He asked her if she knew what it meant in German. "No," Lucia replied. "God can speak English." Schopenhauer was amused.

Over time the children got bolder with Schopenhauer, although they were never totally fearless. Lucia sometimes took a shortcut into his apartment by climbing through the study window. The first time, she did so with great caution because, as she swung her legs into the room, Schopenhauer was laid out on his cot reading. He briefly looked up from his book but said nothing, so she continued to lower herself inside. She usually settled on the windowsill because the chairs, table, and sofa were all covered with books and papers. In the brief period that Lucia knew Schopenhauer, she almost always saw him at his writing table, furiously at work. She and Atma sat and observed as he gesticulated wildly, ran his hands through his hair, banged on the tabletop, ground his teeth, and chewed his pen. If his audience of two started playing loudly among themselves, he would order them to leave. Atma relented at once, but Lucia protested that she was no dog: "I'll stay!" Exasperated, he replied, "But then, get down!" pointing back over to the seat that was the windowsill. This command she was willing to obey, wanting to show him that she too could be well behaved, so she settled down with Atma in her arms, quiet as a mouse, and promptly fell asleep.

The more Lucia got to know Schopenhauer, the more curious about him she became. "Where is your wife, Herr Schopenhauer?" she once plucked up the courage to ask. At home she had overheard her parents use the name Johanna Schopenhauer. His first reply was evasive. "She's at the back of the room," referring to Margarete. "Oh no," Lucia clarified, "I don't mean her, I mean your real wife." He confessed he never had one, and told her not to bring it up again. Lucia was not the only one to be curious about Schopenhauer either. Her teachers at school often asked how he was and what he talked about with her and her brothers, which gave her a feeling of great importance.

Even though her parents had instructed her to refer to him as Doctor Schopenhauer, Lucia noticed that at the building entrance he was simply listed as "Arthur Schopenhauer." She took her cues from Margarete instead, who only ever addressed him as Herr. The rest of the Schneider family also wondered why he did not advertise his doctorate, as he was quite entitled to do. With neighborly pride Herr Schneider answered, "His name is enough for him, he knows that no title in the world can equal the name Arthur Schopenhauer!" To tease Lucia, or so she suspected, and perhaps to keep some distance, Schopenhauer never quite said her own name correctly, always overpronouncing it as "Ludschia."

In September 1860, Schopenhauer had a horrible cough. Sometimes, he dozed off at his desk, nodding his head with his pen still in hand. One day, when Lucia too was plagued by a cough, she offered him a special sweet to suck on. When she told him that they were called *Schillerträne*, he surprised her with a laugh she never heard before or again: "What, my friend Schiller cried such sweet tears?" (Later her parents had to explain the reference.) "Where do you get them from?" She proudly told him the exact location of the little shop that sold them and offered to buy him his own bag. He gave her the money, and a little while later she returned to pour out the blue and red candy stones on his desk. He took one for himself and pushed the rest back over to her, despite her stubborn protests that he should keep them. "The only thing that helps me is tea," he explained. "Sweets are for little girls."

There came a time when Lucia was seldom allowed to visit Schopenhauer anymore, except sometimes to keep Atma company. On one occasion that she was taken through to see him, she noticed how Atma, at the foot of his bed, never took his gaze off his master, as though he were his personal physician. When Schopenhauer convulsed with a coughing fit, Lucia fled the room terrified. Eventually even Atma was not allowed to come too close.

The last time that Lucia ever saw Schopenhauer alive, she was playing with Atma in the deserted living room and heard him calling. When she entered his bedroom, it was filled with a smokey mist and smelled of a mixture of tea and soot. She called for Margarete, who argued with Schopenhauer as she refilled his burned-out oil lamp and opened the windows.

Whenever Lucia came home from school, she always inquired about Schopenhauer. One day, tearful Margarete led her by the hand into his bedroom. There he sat quite upright in bed, but his head drooped forward on to his neatly folded hands. Atma restlessly paced the floor. "For us children," Lucia recalled, many decades later, "since my dear father also died soon, it was the end of a happy childhood, because now the struggle with life began."[3]

Knowing how much his children adored Schopenhauer's poodle, Herr Schneider had hoped, before he died too, that the family could rehome him. But Schopenhauer had already legally entrusted Atma's care with Margarete, who soon moved to Heidelberg. The children were instead bought a little white bichon named Chéri. Lazy, gluttonous, and stupid—in Lucia's opinion—Chéri was no substitute for loyal, affectionate, intelligent Atma. Perhaps it was Atma, she later wondered, upon whom Schopenhauer's dying gaze had fallen.

:::

Death shouldn't trouble a pessimist. Schopenhauer, for one, was relentless in making this point. "Death," he wrote, "is the great opportunity not to be I any longer."[4] It is a return to "the lost paradise of non-being."[5] We ought therefore to go gratefully to our graves: "If we were to knock on gravestones and ask the dead whether they would like to rise again they would shake their heads."[6] Thus: "It often even appears as a good, something we desire, as Friend Death."[7] These laments—or consolations?—Schopenhauer wrote in a chapter on death that he added to the second edition of *The World as Will and Representation*, published in March 1844. In the same spirit, to its third and final edition, published a few months after moving into Schöne Aussicht 16, he added the following advice: "One could say to the dying man: 'you are ceasing to be something that it would have been better for you never to have become.'"[8]

What is more puzzling to a pessimist, but to almost no one else, is the fear of death. If death is preferable from a pessimist's perspective, then what is there to fear in it? Nobody can deny that death is frightening, and Schopenhauer was personally just as susceptible to this fear as anyone else. His answer, however, was that the very stubbornness of the fear of death, despite the obvious truth of pessimism, is evidence that this fear's origins are not in knowledge and reflection. "Fear of death," he wrote, "is independent of all cognition."[9] If we did managed to view death in the cold light of truth, we would see that there is nothing to fear. But instead, the fear is rooted in our blind desire to exist: or rather, more precisely, it is "only the converse of the will to life, which we in fact all are."[10] From this perspective, it is indeed true that "the greatest of evils, the worst thing that could ever be threatened, is death."[11] Another way to appreciate this point is through the same fear as found in other animals. Very few, if any, nonhuman animals have an abstract, reflective fear of death. Nevertheless, almost all animals, including most humans, have a visceral aversion to any potentially deadly situation.

Like many before him, Schopenhauer saw the origins of philosophy in two places: the wonder of life and the fear of death. As he well knew, both thoughts went all the way back to Socrates. In Plato's dialogue *Theaetetus*, Socrates famously taught that "philosophy begins in wonder"; while in *Phaedo*, the scene of Socrates's own dying moments, he defined philosophy as the "preparation for death."[12] Schopenhauer put his own spin on these ideas, and even found a connection. His interpretation of the wonder in which all philosophy begins was, naturally, something closer to existential horror than idle curiosity or admiring awe. Not only that the world miraculously exists, but also that it is so miserable, was to him a cause for metaphysical speculation. Were it not so full of pains, ills, and finally death, then we might not stop to wonder why.[13] Such as it is, we do. The problem of evil, of which the problem of death is only a principal example, therefore lies at the root of all philosophy.

Part of the point of religious and philosophical systems, then, is to provide not only understanding of life but also consolation for death. One popular strategy is simply to deny death: to claim that we are, in some way or part, immortal. Another would be to take some solace in the very idea of total annihilation. The pessimist's proposal, which prefers nonbeing to being, is a version of this strategy; but it need not go so far. A more famous version, indeed perhaps the best known, was proposed by the ancient Greek hedonist Epicurus: "Death," said Epicurus, "is nothing to us."[14] When we are, it is not; and when it is, we are not. Death is not something that happens to us, but rather the end of all our happenings.

Schopenhauer was only partially satisfied by the Epicurean argument. If death really were our annihilation, then perhaps it ought to cause no more anxiety than the infinite state of nonbeing that precedes birth—which is to say no anxiety at all. But he questioned the premise that death is, in every way and at bottom, complete annihilation. Equally, however, he rejected the assumption that the only other alternative to annihilation would be personal immortality: "it cannot be denied that at least in Europe, people's opinions . . . very often vacillate between the view of death as an absolute annihilation and the assumption that we are immortal, flesh, blood and all. Both are equally false."[15] Viewed from a "higher perspective," he argued, death is neither total annihilation nor personal immorality.[16]

What, then, is death to us? To elevate us to a higher perspective on it, Schopenhauer distinguished between a few different standpoints. First, there are the subjective and the objective points of view. Subjectively, death is as unimaginable as it is terrifying: we literally cannot picture the world without us. "Try to imagine vividly a time not far from now when you are dead," Schopenhauer suggested as a thought experiment: "You are thinking yourself away while letting the world continue on: but you will soon find, to your amazement, that you were nevertheless still there. . . . The result is really this: the time in which I do not exist will come objectively: but it can never come subjectively."[17] From the objective standpoint, by contrast, death is not only imaginable but all too real. There is no shortage of evidence that a dead person is fully extinguished: "The sight of a corpse shows me that sensibility, irritability, circulation of blood, reproduction, etc. have come to an end here. From this I can conclude with certainty that whatever actuated them, although wholly unknown to me, does not do so anymore."[18] If, according to the Epicurean idea, we do not experience our own death, then it is certainly experienced outwardly by those around us.

Our partial previews of the subjective standpoint on death can nevertheless be comforting. A dreamless sleep or general anesthetic tells us that it is a completely painless nonexperience. The glimpses we get of the objective perspective on death, by contrast, are often more disturbing. "People of advanced old age totter about or rest in a corner, only shadows, ghosts of their former being. What is left in them for death to destroy?" Schopenhauer sorrowfully asked.[19] (Recall little Lucia's frightened witness to Schopenhauer's own final days.) Even if to a pessimist the end of life is not especially regrettable, but perhaps welcome, or to the Epicurean it is nothing at all, it remains perfectly rational on either view to fear our own steady destruction through age and illness.[20]

Higher above the subjective and the objective standpoints on death, Schopenhauer distinguished between the empirical and the metaphysical points of view. The empirical standpoint concerns how death appears—or doesn't—in our experience. To the empirical subject, death is indeed no more than an eternal sleep, whereas to outside observers it is the more or less rapid disappearance of any vital signs. Things are quite different from a metaphysical perspective. Instead of individual lives, which undoubtedly come into and go out of existence, the metaphysical standpoint concerns what is, was, and always will be. To help illustrate his point, Schopenhauer proposed an analogy:

> No thoughtful and well-governed mind will think that, because the powerful arm that bent the bow of Odysseus three thousand years ago no longer exists, the force that worked so energetically in the bow is completely annihilated as well; but, after further

consideration, neither would they assume that the force that bends the bow today only comes into existence with this arm.[21]

There is, on the one hand, the epic hero Odysseus as he draws force into his bowstring. The force itself, on the other hand, did not come into and out of being in this moment, but was merely temporarily concentrated there. Likewise, on the matter of death: "It is more accurate to claim that the force actuating an earlier, now extinguished, life is the same force active in a now blooming life."[22] Death may totally annihilate the individual being, but it does not, in Schopenhauer's view, annihilate the animating principle of life. Empirically, we naturally identify with the time-bound span of our conscious existence; we are, as it were, the momentary twang of Odysseus's bow. But we are also "the life force [that] remains entirely untouched by the changes of form and state."[23] This life force is what, in other places, Schopenhauer names the will to life. If we accept that the will to life is our true essence, then "the imperishability of our true essence can certainly be proven."[24]

To most, though, this will not provide much comfort. When other philosophical or religious systems attempt to offer consolation for death, it is usually the subjective, empirical part of ourselves that they try to argue is immortal. What we really seem to want is some reassurance that the side of ourselves with which we most strongly identify in life—the thinking, feeling, formerly breathing part—somehow survives death. Schopenhauer denied that it does. "But still it is something," he added with a shred of hope.[25] With an open mind, we might see that there is something noble and even marvelous about the basic stuff of life from whence we came and to which we shall return. A deep appreciation of this fact might even supersede our natural desire to be fixed forever in our current form.

The matter of finding solace in death, then, turns on the question of what of us dies and what survives. "The word 'I' contains a huge equivocation," Schopenhauer observed: "Depending on how I understand this word, I can say: 'death is my total end,' but also: 'my personal appearance is just as small a part of my true being as I am an infinitely small part of the world.'"[26] The side of us that seemed to come from nothing, the side that we secretly or openly hope will go on forever, indeed goes back to nothing. The side of us that came before, however, will go on after us, indeed will outlast us as indefinitely as it preceded us. "Accordingly," advised Schopenhauer, "instead of telling people: 'you arose with birth but are immortal'; we should say: 'you are not nothing.'"[27] If immortality is what we seek, then there is a kind of immortality in this, indeed the only defensible kind: "We can only think of ourselves as *immortal* to the extent that we think of ourselves as *unborn*."[28]

There is, however, a final step, one that we cannot say with any confidence that even Schopenhauer himself took. For it is one thing to obtain a higher vantage point on life and death, but it is quite another to live one's life and die one's death from that standpoint. The required transformation is not simply of our consciousness, but of our very being. "We would not be made happy by simply being transported to a 'better world,'" Schopenhauer argued: "We would also need to be fundamentally altered so that we would no longer be what we are and would instead become what we are not."[29] The person most reconciled to death is, unsurprisingly, the one least attached to life in the first place: "To die willingly, gladly, joyfully, is the prerogative of someone who is resigned," concluded Schopenhauer. "For he alone wills to die *actually*, not merely *apparently*."[30]

In case this ultimate form of consolation should seem out of reach for most people—because it is—there are some other sources of solace on the road to the higher perspective.

First, Schopenhauer reminds us that while every individual human being inevitably dies, humankind in general lives on. This is just as well, in his view, because "the individuality of most people is so miserable and worthless that they really do not lose anything," whereas humankind itself "might still have some value."[31] Of course, when people die, they and those who are left behind really do lose something, indeed some lose everything, and the dead are missed as individuals, not as abstract human beings. Nevertheless, when we think and talk about our lost loved ones, alongside their unique quirks and traits, and sometimes through them, we call to mind the universal moral qualities that they embodied: their courage, their kindness, their compassion, in a word their humanity.

In a similar sort of mood, Schopenhauer also wrote the following uncharacteristically uplifting line: "The spirit of love that would lead someone to spare his enemy or someone else to risk his life to befriend a person he has never seen, can never pass away and come to nothing."[32] One side of humanity that survives the death of every human being—the side that "might still have some value"—is the justice and kindness that Schopenhauer called compassion. We might like to think that our individual personality can, in fact, survive in the personal qualities that each of us imparts to the next generation. Perhaps a fragment of Schopenhauer's personality survived in Lucia Schneider, not only in her memories but also, for example, in the affection for poodles that he passed on to her. But if our immortality were in our personal qualities, then it would be no more than an "endless series of short, troubled, and mutually incoherent dreams," since even these qualities too are ephemeral despite their transferability.[33] True immortality, it seems, runs even deeper than that.

: : :

In 1913, Lucia Franz (née Schneider), now aged sixty-one, lived at Elkenbachstrasse 18, situated about half the distance between the childhood home that she had briefly shared with Schopenhauer and the cemetery where he was finally laid to rest. That year, she gathered her reminiscences in a series of letters to Paul Deussen, founding president of Germany's Schopenhauer Society and editor of its journal, *Jahrbuch der Schopenhauer-Gesellschaft*, who combined and published them verbatim in its third issue. If after half a century she was nonetheless correct to recall seeing Schopenhauer laid out on his deathbed, his arms neatly folded across his chest, then someone must have moved his body while she had been at school that day.

According to his friend and first biographer Wilhelm Gwinner, when Schopenhauer was discovered dead by his doctor, he was not in bed at all but slumped in the corner of his sofa.[34] By all accounts, however, Lucia was right to recall that Schopenhauer suffered from persistent breathing difficulties in the last few months of his life, and probably died of a cardiovascular illness, such as a pulmonary embolism. Up until then, he was robust for a man of his age; well into his late sixties, he regularly swam in the chilly waters of the River Main.[35] But one day in April 1860, as he briskly walked home from lunch, he began to have palpitations and found himself struggling for air. At the time his doctor could find no organic cause, but still recommended rest and a lighter diet. (Gwinner also tried in vain to get him to give up his cold baths.) His symptoms recurred throughout the summer, culminating in a serious attack in August that drained all the color from his face and almost suffocated him. On September 9, after yet another suffocating episode, Schopenhauer was diagnosed with pneumonia. At this point, feeling gravely ill, he began to foresee his death; but he recovered quickly enough to get himself out of bed and receive some final visitors in the next few days. The last time that Gwinner ever spoke with Schopenhauer, on September 18, he had recently suffered another attack. Although he continued to complain of palpitations while they sat together on the sofa, and despite all his breathing difficulties, his voice lacked none of its usual vigor. He told Gwinner that to attain absolute nothingness would be a blessing, but added that death offered no such hope, as indeed nothing could.[36]

On the morning of September 20, Schopenhauer dropped to the floor with severe chest cramps, injuring his forehead. He felt better later that day and made it through the night, even getting up early the next morning for a cold wash and breakfast as normal. Margarete opened his bedroom window to let in some fresh air and then left him alone. When she came back with his doctor, at around quarter past eight on September 21, he was dead. He appeared to have gone peacefully, so far as could be told, just as he had always wanted.

He left two versions of his will.[37] The first, drafted on June 26, 1852, allocated a large portion of his fortune to a fund set up in Berlin to support Prussian soldiers wounded in the battles to defend legal order in Germany against the riots and rebellions of 1818 and 1848, as well as the surviving dependents of the soldiers who lost their lives. He also left a legacy to some distant relatives in Danzig, including his remaining share of the family estate in Ohra, which he had once shared with Johanna and Adele. Using the initials FSB, he marked the backs of a selection of daguerreotypes to be donated to the Frankfurt City Library. He appointed Frauenstädt as his literary executor, as his most philosophically minded follower, including ownership of his manuscripts, copies of his works, and their publishing rights. Having befriended so many lawyers, he had his pick of legal executors, but in the end chose Martin Emden, the friend who accidentally discovered his rise to fame in English literary culture. Emden was also allotted the remainder of Schopenhauer's belongings including his library, musical instruments, and pictures. Atma was left to Margarete along with a sum of money to keep him well-fed. At the end of his original will, Schopenhauer laid out strict and detailed instructions for the careful search of all the compartments, drawers, and nooks and crannies of his desk, to make sure that it was fully stripped and emptied of all its writings and fragile documents, including all his debts.

By February 4, 1859, Schopenhauer's will required some revisions. In 1856, he sold off his share in the family estate, so this could no longer be redistributed to his remaining relatives. In 1858, Emden died, and so Gwinner was appointed as Schopenhauer's legal executor instead, as well as the recipient of his personal library. A few more of the other disciples were also left some small souvenirs: to Ernst Lindner, the editor who published his wife's German translation of the Oxenford article, Schopenhauer left the gold chain of his pocket watch; to David Asher, his golden spectacles; and to his dining partner, the gossipy French painter Jules Lunteschütz, an ivory bust of his great-grandfather and a pastel portrait of his mother. It was in this amendment that Schopenhauer also included the generous sum of money for Caroline "Ida" Richter, his Berlin beloved who, in his mind at least, came the closest of any woman to being his wife.

In accordance with his wishes, no autopsy was performed on Schopenhauer's body. When Gwinner had asked him about the prospect of being dissected, he hesitated for a moment before replying, "If they didn't know anything before, then they shouldn't know anything afterwards either." Gwinner did, however, have a plaster cast made of the top half of Schopenhauer's head by the sculptor Johann Nepomuk Zwerger, measurements from which he submitted to the phrenologist Gustav Scheve for a detailed character analysis.[38] Asked where he would like to be buried, Schopenhauer confidently replied, "It doesn't matter, they will find me."[39] He was more particular about the length of time between death and burial: no fewer than five days. His reluctance to have a postmortem, despite his freedom from all superstition and his admiration for anatomical science, might well have had the same source as his fear of a premature burial. For these five days he lay in the mortuary at the cemetery in a heavy oak coffin, his head adorned with a crown of laurels. On Wednesday, September 26, 1860, by which time the odor of decay was proof of death even to the nonspecialist, it was officially recorded in the Frankfurt church register.[40] The entry made two errors. Although it correctly recorded Danzig as his place of birth, it nevertheless described him as being "from Berlin in the Kingdom of Prussia," which, given his feelings about his woeful Berlin years, was an association he would have strenuously downplayed. His name was also incorrectly spelled: "Schoppenhauer" with a double *P*.[41]

On the same day that his death was registered, Schopenhauer was finally committed back to the earth. A handful of assorted mourners attended, only a few close friends and no close relatives since there were none left. Gwinner's eulogy began:

> The coffin of this rare man, who dwelt in our midst for a generation and yet remained a stranger, evokes unusual reflections. None who stand here are bound to him by the sweet ties of blood; alone as he lived, he died. And yet in the presence of this dead man something tells us that he found compensation for his loneliness. When we see friend or foe descend, forsaken, into the night of death, our eyes search for a joy that may endure, and every other feeling is stilled in a burning desire to know the sources of life. This ardent yearning after the knowledge of the eternal, which comes to most men only in sight of death, rarely, and evanescent as a dream, was to him the constant companion of a long life. A sincere lover of Truth, who took life seriously, he shunned mere appearances from his very youth, regardless

that this might isolate him from all relations human and social. This profound, thoughtful man, in whose breast a warm heart pulsated, ran through a whole lifetime like a child angered at play—solitary, misunderstood, but true to himself. Born and educated in competence, his genius was unhampered by the burdens of this world. He was ever grateful for this great boon; his one desire was to merit it, and he was ready to renounce all that delights the heart of other men for the sake of his lofty calling. His earthly goal was long veiled to him; the laurel that now crowns his brow was only bestowed in the evening of life, but firm as a rock was rooted in his soul belief in his mission. During long years of undeserved obscurity he never swerved an inch from his solitary lofty way; he waxed grey in the hard service of the coy beloved he had chosen, mindful of the saying written in the Book of Ezra: "Great is truth, and mighty above all things."[42]

Schopenhauer himself had used the quotation from the Book of Ezra as the epigraph to the second edition of *The Two Fundamental Problems of Ethics*, which he managed to publish just weeks before his death.[43] Along with his many intellectual virtues, Gwinner lauded Schopenhauer's concealed moral qualities: "Ordinary people saw the misanthrope in him. But, however little he thought of people, he felt for them; he was full of compassion."[44]

The gravestone was pointedly understated: a large rectangular slab of black Belgian granite, laid flat on the ground rather than reaching up to the sky, and inscribed with no personal details beyond the words "Arthur Schopenhauer."[45] "Nothing more, no date, nor year, nothing at all, not a syllable," he requested. His name was enough.

POSTSCRIPT

Silhouettes

On a Thursday evening in Weimar, in early December 1806, Johanna Schopenhauer was preparing to host her usual salon. A special drawing table had been set up for its most distinguished guest, Johann Wolfgang von Goethe. On the table, as an offering to Goethe, Johanna left a handmade cut-out silhouette of a blossoming chestnut branch entwined with fuchsia. She had been inspired by his high praise of an artist from Hamburg by the name of Philipp Otto Runge, who had taken the paper-cut artform out of drawing rooms and into the realms of high culture. As chance would have it, Goethe came with his own gift for Johanna: a small bunch of flowers crafted by none other than Runge himself. Compared to Runge's exquisitely miniature bouquet, Johanna immediately noticed the deficiencies of her own life-sized first attempt. But, to her surprise, when her other guests arrived, they apparently failed to distinguish between her work and Runge's. After each one had finished admiring the chestnut branch, Goethe burst out with childlike glee: "No, the woman, the little woman has done that! She does such tricks. Just look, just look how pretty it is." Later on, as the others drifted into the next room for a piano recital, Johanna spent all evening at the drawing table working with Goethe. She jubilantly relayed this story in a letter to Arthur, advising him to seek out Runge in Hamburg. There he still wallowed in the tedium of his apprenticeship.[1]

If any member of the Schopenhauer family could rightfully claim to have mastered the art of the silhouette, however, it was Adele. Like her mother, some of Adele's best work was inspired by Goethe. In 1820, she created a sublimely intricate illustration of Goethe's 1804 ballad "Hochzeitlied" (or "Wedding Song"). It depicted a raucous wedding party attended by dwarves and elves, including over seventy individually impish figures, eight horses, one donkey, and a three-dimensional four-poster bed.[2] Goethe was sufficiently impressed by Adele's cut-outs that, in the same year, he sent one as a gift to the Frankfurt actress and poet Marianne von Willemer. The dramatist Karl Immermann wanted to publish a collection of Adele's works in 1837, which might have been an opportunity for Adele to break free from the private environs of the salon and its gift-based cultural economy; but the project came to nothing.[3] Given the chance, in fact, Adele would have chosen to train as a fine artist, and she recognized her own ability to do so. In one of her diary entries, she records the time she showed some examples of her work to a woman in Karlsbad named Madame Lutherod. "When she saw my cut-outs," Adele wrote, "she said: 'If you were a man, you would have become a sculptor.' I liked that, because it's true."[4] Adele even visited the Berlin studio of Christian Daniel Rauch in 1819, the same sculptor who decades later successfully championed Elisabet Ney. Disappointingly, Rauch joined the ranks of men who contrasted the delicacy of Adele's art and mind, on the one hand, with her physical appearance, on the other, by deeming her "horrifyingly ugly."[5]

Often during the writing of this book, the general image of a silhouette has come to mind, and not just because it was an artform favored by Johanna and Adele. A silhouette is the ideal symbol for lives that were (almost) not to be. It is a presence defined by absence, both there and not there. Its existence, moreover, is highly precarious, whether as a paper cut-out or merely a shadow. I introduced Schopenhauer's life with the counterfactual proposal that we wouldn't still be talking about him had his father not died. And, of course, his famous philosophical pessimism rests on one of the oldest counterfactuals in written history: that it would be better for us not to exist. But—as must be inevitable for any sort of life-writing—the more that I have written about Schopenhauer as we know him, the more junctures I have found at which he might never have been.

Naturally, Schopenhauer's possible lives were strongly bound up with his mother's. Johanna's own fate changed when a kindly Scottish chaplain, uniquely ready and able to take her intellect seriously, happened to move in next door to her childhood home. It laid the foundations for the cultivated cosmopolitan that she was to become, which, in turn, made her an appealing marriage prospect to the worldly Heinrich Floris. Without that match, in the strongest possible sense, there would be no Arthur Schopenhauer. And when Heinrich Floris died, who can estimate the likelihood that Arthur would ever have left Hamburg, had Johanna's long-suppressed ambitions not driven her to do so first and with barely a moment's hesitation, not to mention her personal network of elite artists and intellectuals? Even Adele's shadow selves were in some way bound up with Arthur's. Once he finally left his apprenticeship, Arthur saw it as his goal, and his alone, to keep the Schopenhauer family name alive with his reputation as a thinker instead. But if Madame Lutherod spoke the truth when she claimed that Schopenhauer's sister would have been a sculptor if only she were born a man, then perhaps today we would associate their name, like those of Schlegel, Humboldt, and Grimm, with a talented pair of brothers.

Once we start tugging at threads like these, fairly soon the whole tapestry begins to unravel. What if Schopenhauer had successfully toppled Hegel's philosophical supremacy in Berlin? Would he have stayed, and like Hegel perished? And when he did leave, what if his beloved Ida had followed him to Frankfurt? Would he have committed to a married life like his oldest friend Anthime? What if the collapse of Muhl's bank had wiped out his entire inheritance, as it effectively did for Johanna and Adele? Could his career have survived, or even got started, if he had to work for a living? And what if he had followed Adele's advice of helping to raise even one of his two illegitimate children? We could go on.

If, on the other hand, we hold the threads in place, then contingent twists of fate can instead seem like inevitabilities. With an upbringing like his, for example, *of course* Schopenhauer turned out the way he did. Badgered and bribed into accepting an education for business, rather than the academic one to which he was so evidently suited, but still treated to all the cultural delights and natural splendors that Europe could offer, and thereby also inadvertently exposed to the darkest sites of pain and misery—*of course* Schopenhauer was always going to stand at a distance from the inner sanctum of academic philosophy, and be worldly wise despite his world-wearily withdrawn way of living. Raised with foreign languages as if they were his native tongue, *of course* Schopenhauer's horizon of reference points, as well as his models for good prose style, were so much wider and more diverse than those of his German peers. Disapproved of, nevertheless, by both his parents, either on the grounds of his social skills or his vocational skills, *of course* Schopenhauer was always going to present himself to the world as a man with something to prove.

Another very tempting "of course" of Schopenhauer's life is *of course* Schopenhauer fixated on the question of whether life is worth living, given that, at such a formative age, his own father died by suicide. And *of course* he firmly concluded that it is not worth living, given the bitter and traumatic toll that this loss must have taken on him. Writing this book, however, has frequently shown me a different, and opposite, inevitability. Rather than leading him to his life-denying conclusions, if anything, the death of Schopenhauer's father only seemed to intensify his own personal drive to live. He was, after all, given a literal and metaphorical change of fortune: the wealth that he inherited, his "consecrated treasure," represented both new liberties and new responsibilities. After so much soul-searching, when he finally resolved to invest his inheritance in himself, Schopenhauer only subjected himself even further to his father's judgment—an especially risky psychological burden to inflict on oneself once the person in question is long dead. Failure to succeed would have been utterly devastating, as well as another possible way that we would not be talking about Schopenhauer today. Now we have the benefit of hindsight; we can only associate

Schopenhauer's name with an influential and canonical philosopher. But his parents' worries about him, along with his sister's, and even his own, can only be fully understood from the perspective of an unknown and highly uncertain future. And if this is even partly what was driving Schopenhauer through life, then all of it is to say, once more, that a strong will to live is not always accompanied by pleasant feelings, but often quite the opposite.

There is a point in his own written work where Schopenhauer reflects on his ambition as a philosopher. Just before the very last book of *The World as Will and Representation*, which deals with the overall ethical significance of his philosophy, he refers his reader to his other treatments of ethics, such as his prize essays for the two Scandinavian academies as compiled in *The Two Fundamental Problems of Ethics*. He takes it as an opportunity to remind his reader of the importance of reading all his works in full:

> In general I require that anyone who wants to be acquainted with my philosophy must read every line I have written. I am not prolific, I do not strive to earn honoraria, nor am I in the business of churning out compendia. My goal is not to meet with ministerial approval—in short, I am not the sort of person whose pen is swayed by personal ambition: I strive only for truth, and I write as the ancients wrote, with the sole intention of preserving my thoughts so that they can someday benefit those who understand how to think about them and to value them. This is why I have not written very much, but this little with care and over long intervals.[6]

Much of this rings true, at least when seen in the right light. The claim that he was not so prolific may seem false in view of the literally thousands of pages to his name. But still, he was moderate insofar as he only ever printed what he believed was truly worth reading, as opposed to what might earn him public adulation or a good living. Compare this with the bloated bulk of work by his peers, made up of frequent and fragmentary appearances in journals, periodicals, and other ephemera, whereas barely a word of Schopenhauer's fell outside of fully considered book-length treatments published several years apart. Hovering here in the background, once again, are the material conditions for such a relaxed attitude toward publishing: only someone with Schopenhauer's healthy finances could so easily afford to pick and choose all their writing assignments.

The further claim that he was never swayed by personal ambition may also seem untrue given all that has been said so far about his desire to prove himself and thereby save his endangered family name, not to mention his unconcealed resentment at spending so much of his life in complete obscurity. But, on a second look, Schopenhauer's claim is not that he *lacked* all ambition. If anything, his mission statement is extremely ambitious: to illuminate nothing other than the pure, profound, eternal truths. His real achievement, then, was to stop his personal ambitions—which clearly he had—from tainting and twisting his philosophical ones. It must have been tempting, after all, to bend his philosophy or his style to suit the tastes of his peers and the public. If it took a certain kind of courage for Schopenhauer to invest in himself in the first place, despite his father's disapproval from beyond the grave, then it also took immense patience and integrity to hold his nerve for quite so long. It was a rare cost of living that paid off in the end.

Acknowledgments

I thank all of the following people for their indispensable support: my agent Kat Aitken and editor Kyle Wagner, without whom this book would not exist; Nigel Warburton for introducing me to Kat and for his advice and guidance about developing the proposal; Kyle's colleagues at the University of Chicago Press, especially Kristin Rawlings for help with preparing the manuscript for production, Mark Reschke for keen-eyed copyediting, Nathan Petrie for a comprehensive marketing strategy, and the multiple anonymous reviewers, who gave such positive and constructive feedback on the initial proposal and the first full manuscript; Guy Longworth and Fabienne Peter, two successive heads of the Department of Philosophy at the University of Warwick, for their unfailing support for my work and a generous period of study leave; my colleagues David James and Tobias Keiling for their help with some finer historical and linguistic details, respectively; Oliver Kleppel, Matthias Jehn, and Stephen Roeper at the Schopenhauer archive in Frankfurt for sourcing several images and granting permission to use them; and last but not least, the Document Supply team at the University of Warwick Library, Jude Acton, Mary Jones, Sara Potter, Sue Pudge, and Linda Simmonds, for tracking down books, papers, and other obscure documents, and generously extending all my loans, no questions asked. Countless biographical details in this book were available to me through the work of previous biographers, scholars, and chroniclers of Schopenhauer, including especially David E. Cartwright, Ludger Lütkehaus, Patrick Bridgwater, Arthur Hübscher, Helen Zimmern, and Wilhelm Gwinner. I thank the following translators of Schopenhauer's works into English, especially my former PhD supervisor Christopher Janaway as the general editor of the excellent Cambridge Editions of the Works of Schopenhauer: David E. Cartwright, Adrian Del Caro, Edward E. Erdmann, Sabine Roehr, Judith Norman, and Alistair Welchman; and E. F. J. Payne for his English translations of Schopenhauer's manuscript remains.

I thank my parents, Margaret and Philip Woods, for constantly encouraging me to follow my interests and believing in everything I do. This book is dedicated to my dad, who died of cancer halfway through the writing process. You were always so proud of me, and I am so proud of you. Above all, I send my love to my wife, Tilly—my lifeboat, my lighthouse—whom I can never thank enough.

Chronology

1788	February 22	Birth of Arthur Schopenhauer in Danzig to parents Heinrich Floris and Johanna (née Trosiener)
1793	Late March	Family relocates to Hamburg
1797	June 12	Birth of sister and only sibling, Adele Schopenhauer
	July	Two years in Le Havre with family of father's business associate; meets childhood best friend, Anthime Grégoire
1799	Summer	Enrolls at Dr. Runge's school
1800	July 16–October 17	Trip with parents through Hannover and Weimar to Karlsbad, Prague, and Dresden
1803	May 3	Start of grand tour with parents; journey through the Netherlands and then to England via boat from Calais to Dover
	May 25	Arrival in London
	June 30–September 20	Boards at Reverend Lancaster's school in Wimbledon; parents explore England and Scotland
	October	Remainder of stay in London
	November 5	Journey through Rotterdam and Brussels to Paris
	November 27	Arrival in Paris
	December 17–25	Schopenhauer family visit Grégoire family in Le Havre
	December 26	Return to Paris
1804	January 27	Long journey through southern France, Switzerland, and southern Germany to Braunau (June 30), Vienna (July 27), and Dresden (August 12)

	April 8	Visits the Bagne of Toulon to witness the infamous "galley slaves"
	August 25	Ends grand tour in Berlin
	September	Visits Danzig with family except father; apprenticeship with Jakob Kabrun
	December	Returns to Hamburg
1805	January	Starts apprenticeship with senator Martin Johann Jänisch
	April 20	Death of father, Heinrich Floris Schopenhauer (family privately suspect suicide)
1806	September 21	Mother and sister leave for Weimar, arriving September 28
1807	Early May	Travels to Gotha via Weimar, enrolls at Gotha gymnasium
	December 23	Returns to Weimar after being effectively expelled from Gotha gymnasium
1809	February	Inherits share of father's estate
	October 9	Matriculates as medical student at Göttingen; learns of South and East Asian culture from lectures on ethnography by Arnold Heeren, and of animal suffering in comparative anatomy with Johann Friedrich Blumenbach
1810	Summer semester	Attends philosophy lectures; introduced to the works of Plato and Kant by Gottlob Ernst Schulze
1811	April	Vacation in Weimar; commits to studying philosophy
	September	Moves to Berlin, enrolls at university
	Winter semester	Attends lectures of Johann Gottlieb Fichte
1812	September–October	Vacation via Dresden to Teplitz
	Winter semester	Begins to visit patients on psychiatric wing of Berlin Charité hospital
1813	May	Leaves Berlin via Dresden (May 22) to Weimar (July) and then via Jena to Rudolstadt
	October 3	Awarded doctorate in absentia from Jena with dissertation, *On the Fourfold Root of the Principle of Sufficient Reason*
	Early November	Returns to Weimar
	November 23	First of several visits to Johann Wolfgang von Goethe to work on color theory
1814	March 26	Begins to read the *Oupnek'hat*, a Latinate version of the *Upanishads*
	April–May	Final rift with mother, leaves Weimar

	May 24	Arrives in Dresden
1815	July	Completes manuscript of *On Vision and Colors*
1816	Early May	Publication of *On Vision and Colors*
	Summer	Trip on horseback to Teplitz
1817	March	Begins transcribing *The World as Will and Representation*
	Summer	Trip to Saxon Switzerland Mountains
1818	March	Completes manuscript of *The World as Will and Representation*
	September 23	First trip to Italy
	Late October–Early November	Venice
	Mid-November	Bologna
	Late November	Florence
	December	Rome
		Publication of *The World as Will and Representation*
1819	March–April	Naples
	April	Rome
	Spring	First daughter born to a housemaid in Dresden; she does not survive infancy
	June	Milan
	Beginning of July	Collapse of Muhl bank causes financial trouble for Schopenhauer family; return journey to Germany, starting with Heidelberg
	August 19–20	Weimar; visits Goethe for the last time
	August 25	Dresden
	Winter	Enquires about academic jobs at Heidelberg, Göttingen, and Berlin
	December 31	Submits application for *Privatdozent* (unsalaried lecturer) post at Berlin
1820	March 13	Returns to Berlin for test lecture
	March 23	Passes test lecture at Berlin University; engages in a dispute with Hegel
1821		Meets dancer Caroline "Ida" Richter and starts relationship that lasts until flight from Berlin cholera epidemic; begins to consider marriage

	August 12	Altercation with neighbor, the seamstress Caroline Louise Marquet; start of protracted legal battle
1822	May 27	Leaves for second trip to Italy
	June 6–8	Nuremberg
	August 17	Milan
	September 11	Florence
1823	May 3	Journey from Florence via Trento to Munich
	May 27	Munich, blighted by several illnesses
1824	May 25–June 22	Spa therapy in Gastein
	June 27	Leaves Munich for Mannheim via Stuttgart and Heidelberg
	July 7–August 28	Mannheim
	August 29	Travels to Frankfurt and later Dresden (September 13) via Leipzig
	Winter	Dresden
1825	May	Berlin
1827	May 4	Loses legal battle with Marquet, ordered to pay annual alimony and legal costs
	September	Enquires about job in Würzberg
1828	February	Enquires about job in Heidelberg
1829	March–June	Works on Latin version of *On Vision and Colors* (published June 1830)
1831	August 25	Flees Berlin during cholera epidemic; ends relationship with Ida Richter
	August 28	Arrives in Frankfurt
1832	January–February	Self-imposed isolation in new Frankfurt apartment
	July 15	Experiments with living in Mannheim
1833	Summer	Decisive return to Frankfurt
1835		Second daughter born; she also does not survive infancy
1836	March	Publication of *On the Will in Nature*
	November 17	Correspondence with Friedrich Dorguth, first of Schopenhauer's four main "apostles"
	December 10	Reestablishes contact with childhood French pen pal, Anthime Grégoire
1838	April 17	Death of mother, Johanna Schopenhauer

1839	January 26	Awarded a prize by Norwegian Royal Society of Sciences for essay "On the Freedom of the Will"
1840	January 30	*Not* awarded a prize by Danish Royal Society of Sciences for essay "On the Basis of Morals," despite being the competition's only entrant
	September	Publication of two competition essays as *The Two Fundamental Problems of Ethics*
1842		Death of Marquet, absolving him of annual alimony
	September 3	First daguerreotype taken
1844	March	Second edition of *The World as Will and Representation* with new second volume
	July 31	Starts correspondence with Johann August Becker
1845	July	Starts work on final book, *Parerga and Paralipomena*
		Dorguth publishes pamphlet on Schopenhauer's philosophy
		Disappointing final meeting with Anthime and daughter in Frankfurt
1846	July	First of several visits from Julius Frauenstädt, later to become literary executor of Schopenhauer's estate
1847	December	Second and revised edition of the *Fourfold Root*
1848		Frauenstädt dedicates a book to Schopenhauer
	September 18	Street fighting breaks out in Frankfurt over insurrection of the National Assembly; briefly intervenes by allowing counterrevolutionary Austrian soldiers to take cover in his apartment
1849		Adam Ludwig von Doß stays in Frankfurt for two weeks to pay frequent visits to Schopenhauer
	March	Last meeting with sister in Frankfurt
	August 25	Death of sister, Adele Schopenhauer
	December	Death of white poodle, Atma; replaced by brown poodle, also Atma
1851	Late November	Publication of *Parerga and Paralipomena*
1852	June 26	Writes first will and testament
1853	April	Anonymous publication of John Oxenford's article "Iconoclasm in German Philosophy" in the *Westminster Review*
1853	April–June	Successfully enquires with Ernst Otto Lindner about publishing German translation of Oxenford article in the *Vossische Zeitung*

1854		Frauenstädt publishes *Letters on the Schopenhauerian Philosophy*
	April	Begins friendship with Wilhelm Gwinner later to become legal executor of Schopenhauer's estate
	August	David Asher visits Schopenhauer
	Late September	Second edition of *On the Will in Nature*
	December	Second edition of *On Vision and Colors*
		Richard Wagner sends Schopenhauer an early draft from *The Ring Cycle*
1855	October	Philosophy faculty at Leipzig hold essay competition on Schopenhauer's philosophy
	December	First translation of Schopenhauer in French is published
1856	Spring–Summer	Sits for portrait by painter Julius Hamel
1858	February	Photograph solicited by Carl Friedrich Mylius for *Leipziger Illustrirte Zeitung*
	December 4	Article on Schopenhauer appears in the *Illustrirte Zeitung* with woodcut based on Mylius photograph
1859		Meeting in Frankfurt with future translator of his works, Jessie Taylor (aka, Jessie Laussot, aka Mrs. Karl Hillebrand)
	February 4	Writes second will and testament with additional codicil
	March	Last photographs by Johann Schäfer
	July 1	Moves next-door (from 17 to 16 Schöne Aussicht in Frankfurt)
	October 1–early November	Sits for bust by sculptor Elisabet Ney
	November	Third edition of *The World as Will and Representation*
	Fall–Winter	Becomes acquainted with Lucia Schneider (latterly Franz) and family
1860	September	Second edition of *The Two Fundamental Problems of Ethics*
	September 21	Death of Arthur Schopenhauer in Frankfurt

Notes

Preface

1. A recent exemplar of the genre—and one of my personal favorites—is Sarah Bakewell, *How to Live: A Life of Montaigne in One Question and Twenty Attempts at an Answer* (Chatto & Windus, 2010).
2. Samuel Beckett to Thomas McGreevy, ca. July 18 to 25, 1930, *The Letters of Samuel Beckett*, vol. 1, *1929–1940*, ed. Martha Dow Fehsenfeld and Lois More Overbeck (Cambridge University Press, 2009), 33.
3. *WWR* 1:84; see also *MR* 3:186. Schopenhauer elaborates on his theory of the comical at length in *WWR* 2:98–109.
4. *WWR* 2:595.
5. *MR* 1:437.
6. BM 204.
7. *MR* 4:130.
8. *PP* 2:273.
9. David Cartwright, *Schopenhauer: A Biography* (Cambridge University Press, 2010), 528–29; see also Helen Zimmern, *Arthur Schopenhauer: His Life and His Philosophy* (Longmans, Green, and Co., 1876), 52; and Ludger Lütkehaus, *Die Schopenhauers: Der Familien-Briefwechsel von Adele, Arthur, Heinrich Floris und Johanna Schopenhauer* (Haffmans Verlag, 1991), 39.

Introduction

1. *MR* 4:503.
2. *MR* 4:503.
3. Paul Bishop, "Schopenhauer's Impact on European Literature," in *A Companion to Schopenhauer*, ed. Bart Vandenabeele (Wiley-Blackwell, 2012), 333.

4. Thomas Mann, *Freud, Goethe, Wagner* (Knopf, 1942), 17. See also Paul Bishop, "Thomas Mann on Schopenhauer: A Philosopher of the Future?," in *The Schopenhauerian Mind*, ed. David Bather Woods and Timothy Stoll (Routledge, 2023), 496–513.

5. André Gide, *If It Die*, trans. Dorothy Bussy (Penguin, 1957), 166.

6. Quoted in Christine Battersby, "Schopenhauer's Metaphysics and Ethics: Mapping Influences and Congruities with Feminist Philosophers," in *The Palgrave Handbook of German Idealism and Feminist Philosophy*, ed. Susanne Lettow and Tuija Pulkinnen (Palgrave Macmillan, 2023), 420–25.

7. Iris Murdoch, *Metaphysics as a Guide to Morals* (Vintage, 1992), 58.

8. Murdoch, *Metaphysics as a Guide to Morals*, 79.

9. For more of Schopenhauer's views on death and immortality, see chapter 10.

10. *WWR* 1:310, emphasis added.

11. Friedrich Nietzsche, *Beyond Good and Evil*, trans. Judith Norman (Cambridge University Press, 2002), 76.

12. Albert Camus, *The Myth of Sisyphus*, trans. Justin O'Brien (Vintage, 1983), 7.

13. For more of Schopenhauer's view on suicide, see chapter 3.

14. Georg Lukács, *The Theory of the Novel*, trans. Anna Bostock (Merlin, 1980), 243.

15. *GB* 401; see Cartwright, *Schopenhauer*, 533, 540.

16. Cartwright, *Schopenhauer*, 344–46.

17. Georg Lukács, *The Destruction of Reason*, trans. Peter Palmer (Humanities Press, 1978), 22.

18. Theodor W. Adorno, *Negative Dialectics*, trans. E. B. Ashton (Routledge, 1973), 364. See also Brian O'Connor, "Melancholy and Pessimism: Adorno's Critique of Schopenhauer," in *The Schopenhauerian Mind*, ed. David Bather Woods and Timothy Stoll (Routledge, 2023).

19. Jean Améry, *On Suicide: A Discourse on Voluntary Death*, trans. John D. Barlow (Indiana University Press, 1999), 151.

20. Max Horkheimer, *Critique of Instrumental Reason*, trans. Matthew J. O'Connell et al. (Verso, 2012).

21. Horkheimer, *Critique of Instrumental Reason*, 83.

22. Bryan Magee, *The Philosophy of Schopenhauer* (Oxford University Press, 1997), 413.

23. See the chronology of Schopenhauer's life at the back of the book.

Chapter One

1. Hegel's doctors attributed his death to cholera, but this is disputed by scholars. See Terry Pinkard, *Hegel: A Biography* (Cambridge University Press, 2002), 659.

2. Cartwright, *Schopenhauer*, 129–30.

3. Wilhelm Gwinner, *Schopenhauers Leben: Zweite, Umgearbeitete und Vielfach Vermehrte Auflage der Schrift* (F. A. Brockhaus, 1878), 620.

4. March 10, 1832, in Lütkehaus, *Die Schopenhauers*, 455.

5. Cartwright, *Schopenhauer*, 453–55.

6. From Goethe's Kophtische Lieder ("Coptic Song"): "habet die Narren eben zum Narren wie sichs gebührt." See Lütkehaus, *Die Schopenhauers*, 187.

7. *GB* 242, quoted in Christopher Janaway, introduction to *PP* 2:xiv.

8. Quoted in *PP* 1:273 and often mistakenly attributed to Schopenhauer himself.

9. Zimmern, *Arthur Schopenhauer*, 173; *MR* 4:498.

10. Aristotle, *Eudemian Ethics* 7, 2; Cicero, *Paradoxa Stoicorum*, II, 17.

11. Cartwright, *Schopenhauer*, 12; *MR* 1:75.

12. *PP* 1:374. See also *BM* 118 and *WWR* 1:428.

13. David Vincent, *A History of Solitude* (Polity, 2020), 1–18.

14. Cartwright, *Schopenhauer*, 12n.

15. While the first English translation of Zimmermann's *Über die Einsamkeit* translates the key word as "solitude," when it is cited in the most recent translation of Schopenhauer's work, the translators waver between *On Solitude* (*PP* 1:374) and *On Loneliness* (*BM* 118 and *WWR* 1:428).

16. *PP* 1:370 and 376, respectively.

17. *PP* 2:584–85.

18. Zimmern, *Arthur Schopenhauer*, 159.

19. *PP* 1:369.

20. *PP* 1:369.

21. *PP* 2:501.

22. *PP* 1:369.

23. *PP* 1:377.

24. *PP* 1:378.

25. *PP* 1:378.

26. *PP* 2:563.

27. Charles Darwin, *Evolutionary Writings*, ed. James A Secord (Oxford University Press, 2008), 3.

28. *PP* 2:563.

29. *PP* 2:446.

30. *PP* 2:443.

31. *PP* 2:443.

32. *PP* 2:441.

33. *PP* 1:369.

34. *PP* 2:443.

35. *PP* 2:500.

36. *PP* 2:445.

37. *PP* 2:497.

38. *PP* 2:501.

39. *WWR* 1:9–10.

40. *WWR* 1:10.
41. *WWR* 1:10.
42. *WWR* 1:20.
43. *WWR* 1:21.
44. *WWR* 1:22.

Chapter Two

1. *WWR* 1:217.
2. Cartwright, *Schopenhauer*, 75–76.
3. Cartwright, *Schopenhauer*, 75–76.
4. *MR* 4:119.
5. Patrick Bridgwater, *Arthur Schopenhauer's English Schooling* (Routledge, 1988), 101; Cartwright, *Schopenhauer*, 72–73.
6. Bridgwater, *English Schooling*, 238.
7. Bridgwater, *English Schooling*, 101.
8. See *WWR* 2:647–48.
9. Cartwright, *Schopenhauer*, 12.
10. Cartwright, *Schopenhauer*, 27–28.
11. Cartwright, *Schopenhauer*, 31–32.
12. Lütkehaus, *Die Schopenhauers*, 32; cf. Cartwright, *Schopenhauer*, 121.
13. Cartwright, *Schopenhauer*, 18–27, for a full account of Schopenhauer's glorious two years in Le Havre, including his friendship with Anthime in later life. As Cartwright says, "In the greater context of his life, [Anthime] may have been the most intimate friend Schopenhauer ever had, if one bears in mind that he lived a life with few truly intimate friends" (20).
14. Bridgwater, *English Schooling*, 97.
15. For many more details of Schopenhauer's visit to London, see "Arthur Schopenhauer's English Diary," in Bridgwater, *English Schooling*, 97–139.
16. Bridgwater, *English Schooling*, 110.
17. Ruth Michaelis-Jena and Willy Merson, introduction to *A Lady Travels: The Diaries of Johanna Schopenhauer* (Routledge, 1988), xi.
18. Michaelis-Jena and Merson, *A Lady Travels*, xii.
19. Patrick Bridgwater (*English Schooling*, 83n) wonders whether Schopenhauer's copy of John Locke's *An Essay Concerning Human Understanding* is the same copy that Richard Jameson purchased in Edinburgh in 1761. See Bridgwater, *English Schooling*, 29–94, for an extraordinarily detailed profile of Jameson, from which everything in this paragraph derives.
20. Bridgwater, *English Schooling*, 78.
21. Bridgwater, *English Schooling*, 88.
22. Johanna Schopenhauer, *A Lady Travels: Diaries of Johanna Schopenhauer*, trans. Ruth Michaelis-Jena and Willy Merson (Routledge, 1988), 55.
23. J. Schopenhauer, *A Lady Travels*, 97.
24. J. Schopenhauer, *A Lady Travels*, 104.

25. J. Schopenhauer, *A Lady Travels*, 199.
26. J. Schopenhauer, *A Lady Travels*, 200.
27. J. Schopenhauer, *A Lady Travels*, 200.
28. J. Schopenhauer, *A Lady Travels*, 200.
29. *WWR* 1:340.
30. *PP* 1:18n.
31. Bridgwater, *English Schooling*, 243; see also Cartwright, *Schopenhauer*, 42–51. For the letters from this period in the original German, see Lütkehaus, *Die Schopenhauers*, 52–63.
32. Bridgwater, *English Schooling*, 243.
33. Cartwright, *Schopenhauer*, 69–70.
34. *WWR* 1:339–40.
35. *WWR* 1:338.
36. *WWR* 1:340.
37. Quoted in Marianna Thomas, ed., *Eastern State Penitentiary Historic Structures Report* (Philadelphia Historical Commission, 1994), 38. See this source for a thorough and comprehensive history of the Eastern State Penitentiary, which is available on its website (www.easternstate.org). For its architectural history, see Nicholas Pevsner, *A History of Building Types* (Thames & Hudson, 1976), 159–69. For its penological history, see Thorsten Sellin, "The Origin of the 'Pennsylvania System of Prison Discipline,'" *The Prison Journal* 50 (1970): 13–21; and Sharon Shalev, *Supermax: Controlling Risk Through Solitary Confinement* (Routledge, 2009), 12–27. For philosophical perspectives, see Michel Foucault, *Discipline and Punish: The Birth of the Prison*, trans. Alan Sheridan (Penguin, 1991), 123–31 and 236–39; and Lisa Guenther, *Solitary Confinement: Social Death and Its Afterlives* (Minneapolis: University of Minnesota Press, 2013), 3–61. For further analysis of Schopenhauer's remarks on the Pennsylvania system, see David Woods, "Seriously Bored: Schopenhauer on Solitary Confinement," *British Journal for the History of Philosophy* 27, no. 5 (2019): 959–78.
38. "Overview," Eastern State Penitentiary, accessed May 4, 2023, https://www.easternstate.org/research/history-eastern-state/biographies.
39. Pentonville Prison turned out to be "perhaps the most thorough and purest example of the separate and solitary system in Europe" (Thomas, *Eastern State Penitentiary*, 65).
40. Thomas, *Eastern State Penitentiary*, 66. See also "The Separate System," *The Times*, no. 19520, Saturday, April 10, 1847, 7, which discusses the congress and favorably mentions Pittsburgh's Western State Penitentiary.
41. Thomas, *Eastern State Penitentiary*, 197–98.
42. Charles Dickens, *American Notes* (Penguin, 2000), 111–12.
43. *The Times*, Tuesday, October 25, 1842.
44. Quoted in Pevsner, *Building Types*, 168.
45. See Guenther, *Solitary Confinement*, 9.
46. *WWR* 1:375.
47. *WWR* 2:612–13.

48. For a critique of the supermax prison, as well as its historical relation to the Pennsylvania system, see Sharon Shalev, *Supermax*.

49. *WWR* 1:220.

50. *WWR* 1:351.

51. *WWR* 2:592.

52. *WWR* 2:596, translation modified. The same remarks are found at *MR* 3:66, suggesting that Schopenhauer acknowledged the response to the hellishness of his philosophy from 1820 at the latest, not two years after *The World as Will and Representation* first appeared.

53. *PP* 2:272.

54. This style of objection is often leveled, not at pessimists, but at optimists who attempt to account for the pervasive suffering in life by thinking of it as a sort of punishment. See Mara van der Lugt, *Dark Matters: Pessimism and the Problem of Suffering* (Princeton University Press, 2021), 371n.

55. *PP* 2:309, emphasis added.

56. *MR* 4:119, translation modified. See Cartwright, *Schopenhauer*, 78.

Chapter Three

1. Cartwright, *Schopenhauer*, 15.
2. Cartwright, *Schopenhauer*, 94.
3. Zimmern, *Arthur Schopenhauer*, 21; Gwinner, *Schopenhauers Leben*, 34.
4. Rudiger Safranski, *Schopenhauer and the Wild Years of Philosophy*, trans. Ewald Osers (Harvard University Press, 1991), 53–54; see also Cartwright, *Schopenhauer*, 87.
5. Cartwright, *Schopenhauer*, 87.
6. Safranski, *Schopenhauer*, 55; Cartwright, *Schopenhauer*, 455.
7. See *WWR* 1:441–565 for Schopenhauer's general critique of Kant's philosophy. See BM 123–180 for Schopenhauer's specific critique of Kant's ethics, especially 131–32 on the matter of suicide.
8. Immanuel Kant, *Groundwork for the Metaphysics of Morals*, trans. Allen W. Wood (Harvard University Press, 2018), 35, 42. However, for a persuasive Kantian defense of a possible moral justification for suicide in specific and limited circumstances, see J. David Velleman, "A Right of Self-Termination?," *Ethics* 109, no. 3 (1999): 606–28.
9. David Hume, *Essays: Moral, Political, and Literary* (Liberty Fund, 1985), 588. See Cartwright, *Schopenhauer*, 93–94.
10. *PP* 2:218.
11. Safranski, *Schopenhauer*, 55; see also Cartwright, *Schopenhauer*, 88.
12. *PP* 2:218.
13. *BM* 221.
14. Hume, *Essays*, 577n.
15. *PP* 2:279.

16. *PP* 2:278.
17. *PP* 2:279.
18. *PP* 2:276.
19. Al Alvarez, *The Savage God: A Study in Suicide* (Bloomsbury, 2002), 64.
20. *WWR* 1:393.
21. For recent scholarly debate, see David Hamlyn, *Schopenhauer: The Arguments of Philosophers* (Routledge, 1999); Dale Jacquette, "Schopenhauer on the Ethics of Suicide," *Continental Philosophy Review* 33 (2000): 43–58; Sandra Shapshay, "Review of *The Philosophy of Schopenhauer* by Dale Jacquette and *Schopenhauer* by Robert Wicks," *Mind* 119, no. 475 (2010): 804; Michal Masny, "Schopenhauer on Suicide and Negation of the Will," *British Journal for the History of Philosophy* 29, no. 3 (2021): 494–516; and Colin Marshall, "Schopenhauer on the Futility of Suicide." *Mind* 134, no. 533 (2025): 171–90.
22. *PP* 2:279.
23. A possible exception is the philosopher Philipp Mainländer (1841–76), who developed an interpretation of Schopenhauer's pessimism that recommended suicide, and then sadly followed that recommendation. See Frederick C. Beiser, *Weltschmerz: Pessimism in German Philosophy, 1860–1900* (Oxford University Press, 2016), chapter 9.
24. *PP* 2:279.
25. *WWR* 1:427.
26. *WWR* 1:428.
27. *PP* 2:279.
28. *WWR* 1:117.
29. *PP* 2:280; see also *WWR* 1:326 and *WWR* 1:343.
30. E.g., *MR* 1:33, 76, 183, 207, 433, 448, 531; see also *MR* 3:411–15.
31. *WWR* 1:404.
32. *WWR* 1:403.
33. *PP* 2:152.
34. *WWR* 1:403.
35. *WWR* 1:404.
36. *WWR* 2:607; see also *MR* 4:452.
37. *WWR* 1:403.
38. *WWR* 1:404.
39. *WWR* 1:404.
40. *WWR* 1:404.
41. *MR* 3:413–14.
42. Cartwright, *Schopenhauer*, 85–86.
43. Bridgwater, *English Schooling*, 257n.
44. Bridgwater, *English Schooling*, 257, translation modified; see Lütkehaus, *Die Schopenhauers*, 64.
45. Lütkehaus, *Die Schopenhauers*, 64.
46. Lütkehaus, *Die Schopenhauers*, 65; cf. Cartwright, *Schopenhauer*, 44–45.

47. Lütkehaus, *Die Schopenhauers*, 66; cf. Cartwright, *Schopenhauer*, 86.
48. *MR* 3:415; also *MR* 3:586. See Cartwright, *Schopenhauer*, 90–91.

Chapter Four

1. Zimmern, *Arthur Schopenhauer*, 247; Cartwright, *Schopenhauer*, 547.
2. Cartwright, *Schopenhauer*, 88.
3. Cartwright, *Schopenhauer*, 136.
4. Safranski, *Schopenhauer*, 105.
5. *MR* 4:503.
6. *MR* 4:503.
7. Cartwright, *Schopenhauer*, 107; cf. Lütkehaus, *Die Schopenhauers*, 115.
8. See Cartwright, *Schopenhauer*, 108.
9. Johanna to Arthur, April 28, 1807, in Lütkehaus, *Die Schopenhauers*, 163.
10. Cartwright, *Schopenhauer*, 123.
11. *MR* 2:3–5; *PP* 2:336; see Cartwright, *Schopenhauer*, 141–42.
12. *MR* 1:467; see Cartwright, *Schopenhauer*, 144–58.
13. Cartwright, *Schopenhauer*, 149.
14. For a biographical sketch of Fichte's encounter with Kant, see Allen W. Wood, *Fichte's Ethical Thought* (Oxford University Press, 2016), 6–7.
15. Quoted in George di Giovanni, translator's introduction to *Religion Within the Boundaries of Mere Reason*, trans. and ed. Allen W. Wood and George di Giovanni (Cambridge University Press, 1996), 47.
16. Immanuel Kant, "Über den Verfasser des Versuchs einer Kritik aller Offenbarung" [On the author of the *Attempt at a Critique of All Revelation*], *Allgemeine Literatur-Zeitung*, August 22, 1792, quoted in Michael Rosen, "Fichte's Way," *The Nation*, August 13, 2013, https://www.thenation.com/article/archive/fichtes-way/.
17. Immanuel Kant, "Erklärung in Beziehung auf Fichte's Wissenschaftslehre" [Declaration regarding Fichte's *Wissenschaftslehre*], *Allgemeine Literatur-Zeitung*, August 28, 1799; translated in Immanuel Kant, *Correspondence*, ed. Arnulf Zweig (Cambridge University Press, 1999), 559–60.
18. *MR* 2:xiv.
19. *MR* 2:260.
20. Gwinner, *Schopenhauers Leben*, 260.
21. See *MR* 2:17–20.
22. *MR* 2:18.
23. *MR* 2:18.
24. *MR* 2:20.
25. *MR* 2:18.
26. *MR* 2:18–19.
27. *MR* 2:18–19.
28. Cartwright, *Schopenhauer*, 177–78.

29. Roy Porter, *Madness: A Brief History* (Oxford University Press, 2003), 140.
30. *MR* 1:95.
31. *WWR* 1:44.
32. *MR* 1:201.
33. *WWR* 1:44.
34. *FR* 75; see also *MR* 1:21.
35. *MR* 1:19–20.
36. *MR* 1:169–70.
37. *WWR* 1:216.
38. *MR* 1:95.
39. *MR* 1:468.
40. *WWR* 2:416.
41. *WWR* 2:417.
42. *WWR* 2:417.
43. *WWR* 2:416; see also *MR* 3:228, which reveals that Schopenhauer made this claim as early as 1825.
44. *WWR* 2:417.
45. *WWR* 2:419.
46. Translated from Marcel Zentner, *Die Flucht ins Vergessen: Die Anfänge der Psychoanalyse Freuds bei Schopenhauer* (Wissenschaftliche Buchgesellschaft, 1995), 28, in Stephan Atzert, "Schopenhauer and Freud," in *A Companion to Schopenhauer*, ed. Bart Vandenabeele (Wiley-Blackwell, 2012), 348.
47. *WWR* 2:571.
48. *WWR* 2:417–18.
49. Sigmund Freud, "On the History of the Psycho-Analytic Movement," in *The Standard Edition of the Complete Psychological Works of Sigmund Freud*, ed. and trans. James Strachey (Hogarth Press, 1914), 15. Quoted in Andrew Brook and Chris Young, "Schopenhauer and Freud," in *The Oxford Handbook of Philosophy and Psychoanalysis*, ed. Richard Gipps and Michael Lacewing (Oxford, 2018), 75.
50. Porter, *Madness*, 127.
51. *WWR* 2:418–19.
52. *MR* 3:413; see also 407–8.
53. *WWR* 2:537.
54. Porter, *Madness*, 188–89.
55. See Asti Hustvedt, *Medical Muses: Hysteria in Nineteenth Century Paris* (Bloomsbury, 2011).
56. *MR* 2:53.
57. *MR* 2:53.
58. *WWR* 1:214.
59. Cartwright, *Schopenhauer*, 178n.
60. Translated from Zentner, *Die Flucht ins Vergessen*, 23, in Atzert, "Schopenhauer and Freud," 347.

Chapter Five

1. *FR* 49; *GB* 61.
2. Dialogue quoted in Cartwright, *Schopenhauer*, 363; see also Pinkard, *Hegel*, 464; and Gwinner, *Schopenhauers Leben*, 266.
3. Cartwright, *Schopenhauer*, 361.
4. For full details of Schopenhauer's habilitation, see Arthur Hübscher, "Schopenhauer als Hochschullehrer," *Jahrbuch der Schopenhauer-Gesellschaft*, 1958, 172–75.
5. Hübscher, "Schopenhauer als Hochschullehrer," 187.
6. Hübscher, "Schopenhauer als Hochschullehrer," 188.
7. Hübscher, "Schopenhauer als Hochschullehrer," 232.
8. Hübscher, "Schopenhauer als Hochschullehrer," 236.
9. Hübscher, "Schopenhauer als Hochschullehrer," 237.
10. Hübscher, "Schopenhauer als Hochschullehrer," 24, 236.
11. Hübscher, "Schopenhauer als Hochschullehrer," 237–38.
12. Hübscher, "Schopenhauer als Hochschullehrer," 136.
13. Hübscher, "Schopenhauer als Hochschullehrer," 352; cf. Lütkehaus, *Die Schopenhauers*, 289. Due to lack of extant letters from Arthur to his family in this period, Arthur's remark (as well as his offer to share his inheritance) is only known via a fragment from a letter to Adele written in July 1819, which is quoted verbatim in a letter from Adele to Ottilie von Goethe, dated July 28, 1819. Arthur's original letter would appear to be the same one in which he suggested that Johanna's behavior had contributed to Heinrich Floris's death, which in turn prompted Johanna finally to tell Adele the truth, which she had always suspected, about the nature of Heinrich Floris's demise (see chapter 3).
14. *PP* 1:22.
15. *MR* 2:459–60.
16. Cartwright, *Schopenhauer*, 239, 266–67.
17. Christopher Janaway, "Schopenhauer's 'Indian' Ethics," in *Schopenhauer's Moral Philosophy*, ed. Patrick Hassan (Routledge: 2022), 173–74.
18. Cartwright, *Schopenhauer*, 283.
19. For Schopenhauer's personal and philosophical relationship with the *Oupnek'hat*, along with a detailed history and analysis of the text, see Urs App, "Required Reading: Schopenhauer's Favorite Book," *Schopenhauer Jahrbuch* 93 (2012): 65–86. See also Urs App, "Notes and Excerpts by Schopenhauer Related to Volumes 1–9 of the Asiatik Researches," *Jahrbuch der Schopenhauer-Gesellschaft*, 1998, 11–34; Urs App, "Schopenhauer's India Notes of 1811," *Jahrbuch der Schopenhauer-Gesellschaft*, 2006, 15–34; and Urs App, "Schopenhauer's Initial Encounter with Indian Thought," *Jahrbuch der Schopenhauer-Gesellschaft*, 2006, 35–76.
20. *WWR* 1:5.
21. *WWR* 1:23.
22. *WWR* 1:23.

23. *WWR* 1:24.
24. *WWR* 1:124.
25. *WWR* 1:124.
26. *WWR* 1:129.
27. *WWR* 1:149.
28. *WWR* 1:136–37. Cf. Magee, *The Philosophy of Schopenhauer*, 144.
29. *WWR* 1:219.
30. *WWR* 1:208.
31. *WWR* 1:295.
32. *WWR* 1:334.
33. *WWR* 1:419.
34. *WWR* 1:439.
35. *MR* 1:76.
36. Cartwright, *Schopenhauer*, 35; translated into an English edition as *A Lady Travels: Journeys in England and Scotland from the Diaries of Johanna Schopenhauer*, trans. Ruth Michaelis-Jena and Willy Merson (Routledge, 1988).
37. Cartwright, *Schopenhauer*, 288–89.
38. For full details of the five reviews and one critical monograph writing in immediate response to *The World as Will and Representation*, see Cartwright, *Schopenhauer*, 380–93.
39. Cartwright, *Schopenhauer*, 337.
40. Cartwright, *Schopenhauer*, 341; Gwinner, *Schopenhauers Leben*, 154.
41. *MR* 3:12–13.
42. Cartwright, *Schopenhauer*, 357.
43. Schulze's review appeared in *Göttingische Gelehrte Anzeigen*, no. 70, April 30, 1814; see also Cartwright, *Schopenhauer* 359–62.
44. Gwinner, *Schopenhauers Leben*, 229.
45. Gwinner, *Schopenhauers Leben*, 247–64.
46. Gwinner, *Schopenhauers Leben*, 254.
47. Gwinner, *Schopenhauers Leben*, 252.
48. Gwinner, *Schopenhauers Leben*, 249.
49. Pinkard, *Hegel*, 464.
50. Cartwright, *Schopenhauer*, 365, 429–30. Schopenhauer's Berlin lectures are unavailable in English translation, but a recent German edition has renewed scholarly interest in their relevance to the development and Schopenhauer's philosophy. See Arthur Schopenhauer, *Vorlesung über Die gesamte Philosophie oder die Lehre vom Wesen der Welt und dem menschlichen Geiste*, vols. 1–4, ed. Daniel Schubbe (Meiner, 2022).
51. Lütkehaus, *Die Schopenhauers*, 315–16.
52. Cartwright, *Schopenhauer*, 195n.
53. Cartwright, *Schopenhauer*, 366.
54. *MR* 3:396–97.
55. Cartwright, *Schopenhauer*, 430.
56. *WWR* 1:456.

57. *PP* 1: 174–75.
58. WN 318.
59. See the essay "On Language and Words," *PP* 2:506–19. As a lifelong polyglot, Schopenhauer was deeply sensitive and insightful about the use and abuse of language. On the substance of Schopenhauer's insults toward university philosophers, see Michel-Antoine Xhignesse, "Schopenhauer's Perceptive Invective," in *Language, Logic, and Mathematics in Schopenhauer*, ed. Jens Lemanski (Birkhäuser, 2020), 95–107.
60. *PP* 1:145.
61. *PP* 1:147.
62. *PP* 1:133; see also *WWR* 1:19, *WWR* 2:598, and *PP* 2: 298.
63. *PP* 1:127.
64. *PP* 1:173.

Chapter Six

1. François de La Rochefoucauld, *The Maxims*, trans. F. G. Stevens (Humphrey Milford, 1940), 27; quoted by Schopenhauer at *WWR* 2:547.
2. Gwinner, *Schopenhauer Leben*, 263–64; see Cartwright, *Schopenhauer*, 350.
3. *MR* 3:11.
4. *WWR* 2:607; see Cartwright, *Schopenhauer*, 350.
5. *MR* 3:4.
6. *MR* 3:7; see Cartwright, *Schopenhauer*, 349–50.
7. *MR* 3:11.
8. Lütkehaus, *Die Schopenhauers*, 286.
9. Arthur Hübscher, "Adele an Arthur Schopenhauer: Unbekannte Briefe I," *Jahrbuch der Schopenhauer-Gesellschaft*, 1977, 133–87.
10. *G* 220; see Cartwright, *Schopenhauer*, 344.
11. Quoted in Safranksi, *Schopenhauer*, 245; see Anacleto Verrecchia, "Schopenhauer e la vispa Teresa," *Jahrbuch der Schopenhauer-Gesellschaft*, 1975, 187–99.
12. Safranksi, *Schopenhauer*, 244; Cartwright, *Schopenhauer*, 346–47.
13. Letter dated March 22, 1819, in Lütkehaus, *Die Schopenhauers*, 284.
14. *G* 197n.
15. Cartwright, *Schopenhauer*, 342.
16. Safranski, *Schopenhauer*, 246.
17. May 12, 1819; Cartwright, *Schopenhauer*, 343.
18. Cartwright, *Schopenhauer*, 344.
19. Lütkehaus, *Die Schopenhauers*, 285.
20. Cartwright, *Schopenhauer*, 345.
21. Lütkehaus, *Die Schopenhauers*, 380–81; Cartwright, *Schopenhauer*, 303.
22. Lütkehaus, *Die Schopenhauers*, 320.
23. Cartwright, *Schopenhauer*, 235.
24. Cartwright (*Schopenhauer*, 234) suggests that this remark refers to the

chemistry professor Gottfried Wilhelm Osann, with whom Adele became close enough that Louis Stromeyer erroneously thought that they were in fact engaged at some point. In truth, Osann's family disapproved, and in 1827 he married a servant girl instead.

25. Lütkehaus, *Die Schopenhauers*, 319.
26. *WWR* 2:549.
27. *MR* 3:15, translation modified.
28. *WWR* 2:595.
29. *MR* 3:17, translation modified.
30. *WWR* 2:576.
31. *WWR* 2:554.
32. *WWR* 2:574; see also *MR* 3:641.
33. *WWR* 2:574.
34. *MR* 3:288–92.
35. *MR* 3:292; *MR* 4:457; *WWR* 2:541.
36. *WWR* 2:540; the biography was Friedrich Wilhelm Schubert's *Immanuel Kants Biographie* (1842).
37. *WWR* 2:540; *MR* 4:457.
38. *WWR* 2:540.
39. *MR* 3:290 and 292; the source was Friedrich Fischer's *Naturlehre der Seele* [Natural science of the soul] (1834).
40. *WWR* 2:534.
41. *WWR* 2:584; an almost identical remark is found in *PP* 2:560.
42. *WWR* 2:558.
43. *WWR* 2:577.
44. For example, Bryan Magee (*The Philosophy of Schopenhauer*, 346–49) says that Schopenhauer's addendum is "about male homosexuality" in general, rather than pederasty in particular. Magee also speculates on Schopenhauer's own sexuality, suggesting the addendum contains "internal evidence." Although Schopenhauer had one or two intimate male relationships (e.g., Anthime), there is no evidence of a sexual relationship with another man in Schopenhauer's biography. Equally, of course, at the time, such evidence would not have been the kind of thing to record, and the primary biographical sources for Schopenhauer are admittedly fragmentary (e.g., his family were prone to destroy his letters, and his executor Wilhelm von Gwinner claimed to have destroyed many autobiographical writings after using them as materials for the first biography of Schopenhauer; see Arthur Hübscher's introductory comments at *MR* 4:358).
45. *WWR* 2:582.
46. BM 132n5.
47. BM 132.
48. BM 132n5.
49. BM 132.
50. *WWR* 1:407.

51. *PP* 2:285.
52. See Arthur Hübscher, "Ein Lebensbericht für Anthime Grégoire," *Jahrbuch der Schopenhauer-Gesellschaft*, 1970, 41–49.
53. Arthur Hübscher, "Anthime Grégoire," 42.
54. *PP* 2:138.
55. Gwinner, *Schopenhauers Leben*, 441.
56. Cartwright, *Schopenhauer*, 21.
57. Cartwright, *Schopenhauer*, 21.
58. Hübscher, "Anthime Grégoire," 45.
59. Hübscher, "Anthime Grégoire," 45. For more evidence that Schopenhauer seriously considered marriage during his Berlin years, see *MR* 4:483, 493, and 502–6.
60. The painter Jules Lunteschütz claimed that Schopenhauer also pledged to take care of Caroline Richter's child Carl (*G* 193), though this is doubtful.
61. Cartwright, *Schopenhauer*, 403–4.
62. *GB* 222.
63. *G* 15–16.
64. Cartwright, *Schopenhauer*, 26.

Chapter Seven

1. *PP* 2:575.
2. *PP* 2:577.
3. According to the *Bulletin of the Munich Animal Protection Society* of December 1858; see *PP* 2:577.
4. *MR* 3:64; *PP* 1:422.
5. Details from *G* 50–51; *GB* 74–78, 79–82; Gwinner, *Schopenhauer Leben*, 305–9; Cartwright, *Schopenhauer*, 408–9.
6. Cartwright, *Schopenhauer*, 411.
7. Lütkehaus, *Die Schopenhauers*, 442; Cartwright, *Schopenhauer*, 461.
8. Cartwright, *Schopenhauer*, 460.
9. Adele Schopenhauer, *Tagebuch einer Einsamen*, ed. H. H. Houben (Matthes & Seitz, 1985), 52; Cartwright, *Schopenhauer*, 462.
10. *G* 66–67.
11. Lütkehaus, *Die Schopenhauers*, 490–91; see Cartwright, *Schopenhauer*, 462.
12. Cartwright, *Schopenhauer*, 462.
13. Although Arthur initially gave his immediate approval of Adele's last will and testament, as well as Sibylle's general management of it (*GB* 238), within a year of Adele's death he contested an item concerning the Schopenhauer family's estate in Ohra, Danzig. In January 1849, Arthur had given Adele his consent for her to sell her 3/9 share of the property to Sibylle for 3,700 thalers. His consent was required as the sole presumptive heir of her share in the event of her death, which by then was imminent. However, it later emerged that Adele had not sold her share for this cash capital sum, but rather a lifetime annuity, which ex-

pired along with her. Arthur was within his rights to claim that this invalidated his original consent and thus the sale. He had one of his many lawyer friends, Martin Emden, draw up a settlement (*GB* 257). Sibylle complied, but she was often slow to respond to his instructions and requests, mainly due to her own ill health, resulting in repeated and persistent letters over several years. See Carol Diethe, *Towards Emancipation: German Women Writers of the Nineteenth Century* (Berghahn Books, 1998), 61.

14. Cartwright, *Schopenhauer*, 457.
15. Gwinner, *Schopenhauers Leben*, 300.
16. Lütkehaus, *Die Schopenhauers*, 392.
17. Lütkehaus, *Die Schopenhauers*, 396.
18. Lütkehaus, *Die Schopenhauers*, 445–46.
19. *PP* 2:556.
20. *PP* 2:550.
21. *PP* 2:557.
22. *PP* 2:558.
23. *PP* 2:558. See Thomas Grimwood, "The Limits of Misogyny: Schopenhauer, 'On Women,'" *Kritike* 2, no. 2 (December 2008): 141–43; and S. Pearl Brilmyer, "Schopenhauer and British Literary Feminism," in *The Palgrave Schopenhauer Handbook*, ed. Sandra Shapshay (Palgrave-Macmillan, 2017), 414. For other critical reappraisals of Schopenhauer on women, see also Angelika Hübscher, "Schopenhauer und 'die Weiber,'" *Jahrbuch der Schopenhauer-Gesellschaft*, 1977, 187–203; Christine Battersby, "Schopenhauer's Metaphysics and Ethics: Mapping Influences and Congruities with Feminist Philosophers," in *The Palgrave Handbook of German Idealism and Feminist Philosophy*, ed. Susanne Lettow and Tuija Pulkkinen (Palgrave-Macmillan, 2022), 411–29; and Judith Norman, "Pushing Back: Reading *The World as Will and Representation* as a Woman," in *Schopenhauer's "The World as Will and Representation": A Critical Guide*, ed. Judith Norman and Alistair Welchman (Cambridge University Press, 2022): 245–63. My discussion owes a great deal to these sources.
24. *PP* 2:560.
25. *PP* 2:560.
26. Lütkehaus, *Die Schopenhauers*, 390–91.
27. *PP* 2:559.
28. See Cartwright, *Schopenhauer*, 404–6.
29. *MR* 3:177–79.
30. *MR* 4:144.
31. *MR* 3:178.
32. *PP* 2:558.
33. *PP* 1:321–22; see also *MR* 3:180.
34. *PP* 1:323.
35. *PP* 1:324.
36. *PP* 1:323.
37. *PP* 2:558.

38. *PP* 2:559.

39. C. A. Creffield, "Zimmern, Helen (1846–1934)," in *Oxford Dictionary of National Biography* (Oxford University Press, 2004). Accessed July 31, 2023, from www.oxforddnb.com/view/article/55284.

40. "Helen Zimmern Dies at 87 in Florence," *The New York Times*, January 13, 1934, 13.

41. See Helen Zimmern, "Calcio, or Football in Italy," *The Leisure Hour* (March 1900): 439–42.

42. T. E. Jessop, "*Schopenhauer: His Life and Philosophy*. (Revised edition.) By Helen Zimmern," *Philosophy* 11, no. 28 (October 1932): 489–90.

43. Carol Diethe, *Nietzsche's Women: Beyond the Whip* (De Gruyter, 1996), 99.

44. Helen Zimmern, "Nietzsche Erinnerungen," *Frankfurter Generalanzeiger*, November 16, 1926. For an English rendering, see "Memories of Nietzsche," *The Living Age* 331 (1926): 272.

45. Katheryn Bachelor, *Translations and Paratexts* (Routledge, 2018), 94n9; Diethe, *Nietzsche's Women*, 99.

46. Quoted in Bachelor, *Translations and Paratexts*, 86.

47. Zimmern, "Memories of Nietzsche," 272.

48. Bachelor, *Translations and Paratexts*, 86; Diethe, *Nietzsche's Women*, 84; C. A. Creffield, "Zimmern, Helen."

49. Zimmern, "Memories of Nietzsche," 272.

50. Zimmern, *Arthur Schopenhauer*, 228–29; quoted and discussed in Brilmyer, "Schopenhauer and British Literary Feminism," 403.

51. Quoted in Ruth Michaelis-Jena and Willy Merson, *A Lady Travels*, xi.

52. "Wagner," *The New Statesman*, April 3, 1926.

53. Raymond Furness, *Richard Wagner* (Reaktion, 2013), 82.

54. Furness, *Richard Wagner*, 82–83.

55. *G* 368; translated in Cartwright, *Schopenhauer*, 430n.

56. Brilmyer, "Schopenhauer and British Literary Feminism," 404.

57. This was despite the fact that even Dircks's translation was a little prudish: for example, she translated Schopenhauer's essay as "The Metaphysics of Love," thereby omitting the word "sexual" from its title. Mitzi M. Brunsdale, "The Effect of Mrs. Rudolf Dircks' Translation of Schopenhauer's 'The Metaphysics of Love' on D. H. Lawrence's Early Fiction," *Rocky Mountain Review of Language and Literature* 32, no. 2 (Spring 1978): 120–29.

58. Charles Darwin, *The Descent of Man, and Selections in Relation to Sex* (D. Appleton and Company, 1889), 586; Havelock Ellis, *Man and Woman: Study of Human Secondary Sexual Characters* (Walter Scott Publishing Company, 1894), 214. For an excellent discussion, see Brilmyer, "Schopenhauer and British Literary Feminism," 404–7.

59. Cartwright, *Schopenhauer*, 430n.

60. Zimmern, *Arthur Schopenhauer*, 242.

61. Bride Neill Taylor, *Elisabet Ney, Sculptor* (Devin-Adair Co., 1916), 10.

62. Taylor, *Elisabet Ney*, 24–26.

63. Henry B. Dielmann, "Elisabet Ney, Sculptor," *The Southwestern Historical Quarterly* 65, no. 2 (October 1961), 163–64.
64. Dielmann, "Elisabet Ney, Sculptor," 165.
65. *G* 350–51; see also Bride Neill Taylor, *Elisabet Ney*, 27–29.
66. Dielmann, "Elisabet Ney, Sculptor," 165.
67. *G* 224–25, translated in Dielmann, "Elisabet Ney, Sculptor," 165.
68. Letter to Adam von Doss, March 1, 1860 (*GB* 470).
69. *G* 351.
70. Sandra Salser Long, "Arthur Schopenhauer and Elisabet Ney," *Southwest Review* 69, no. 2 (Spring 1984): 139–40.
71. Dielmann, "Elisabet Ney, Sculptor," 164, suggests this as a possibility.
72. Long, "Arthur Schopenhauer and Elisabet Ney," 139.
73. Long, "Arthur Schopenhauer and Elisabet Ney," 146. See this source for a detailed and insightful account of Schopenhauer and Ney.

Chapter Eight

1. *MR* 3:155; Gwinner, *Schopenhauers Leben*, 295; Cartwright, *Schopenhauer*, 411.
2. *GB* 87–88.
3. *MR* 4:489; for more of Schopenhauer on the Italian national character, see *MR* 4:184.
4. Cartwright, *Schopenhauer*, 414.
5. Gwinner, *Schopenhauers Leben*, 297.
6. Gwinner, *Schopenhauers Leben*, 296.
7. Cartwright, *Schopenhauer*, 430.
8. Cartwright, *Schopenhauer*, 432.
9. Cartwright, *Schopenhauer*, xxii, 417; *GB* 97, 117–23, 131.
10. *MR* 3:199.
11. *MR* 4:483.
12. Gwinner, *Schopenhauers Leben*, 303.
13. *WWR* 1:329–34. For a full discussion, see Sean Murphy, "Acquired Character," in *The Schopenhauerian Mind*, ed. David Bather Woods and Timothy Stoll (Routledge, 2023).
14. *WWR* 1:330.
15. *MR* 4:488.
16. *MR* 4:487.
17. *MR* 4:63.
18. *MR* 4:64.
19. Gwinner, *Schopenhauers Leben*, 391.
20. Gwinner, *Schopenhauers Leben*, 546.
21. The friend was Eduard Crüger, who Schopenhauer wrote to thank on November 29, 1856: "The Buddha waves down from his console and bestows his blessings on you because you rescued him from more than one hundred

years of captivity in the hands of unbelievers, and brought him to where worship and gildings awaited him" (*GB* 406). For a full investigation of the origins of Schopenhauer's Buddha statue, see Robert Wicks, "Arthur Schopenhauer's Bronze Buddha: Neither Tibetan nor Thai, but Shan," *Jahrbuch der Schopenhauer-Gesellschaft*, 2010, 307–16.

22. Gwinner, *Schopenhauers Leben*, 547.

23. *GB* 233.

24. *GB* 240.

25. *G* 100.

26. *GB* 250; Gwinner, *Schopenhauers Leben*, 525.

27. Christopher Clark, *Revolutionary Spring: Fighting for a New World, 1848–1849* (Allen Lane, 2023), 546.

28. *GB* 234–35; *G* 223; Cartwright, *Schopenhauer*, 514.

29. Christopher Clark, "Why Should We Think About the Revolutions of 1848 Now?," *London Review of Books* 41, no. 5 (March 7, 2019). See this article online to watch Clark sing the "Song of the Death of Robert Blum" in the original German.

30. *G* 223 for the first version of the story; *G* 266 for the second.

31. *G* 222–23; Cartwright, *Schopenhauer*, 515.

32. *WWR* 1:330.

33. *WWR* 1:359.

34. *WWR* 1:370.

35. *WWR* 1:374–75.

36. *WWR* 1:375–76; *WWR* 2:613.

37. *WWR* 2:613.

38. Clark, *Revolutionary Spring*, 546–47.

39. BM 232; see *WWR* 2:600, however, for Schopenhauer's preference for Voltaire over Rousseau.

40. BM 223.

41. *PP* 2:208.

42. *PP* 2:219.

43. *GB* 185.

44. BM 258.

45. *G* 276.

46. *G* 385; see Cartwright, *Schopenhauer*, 485.

47. Martin Pasgaard-Westerman, "Strictly Incognito? Schopenhauer's Prize Essay on Morals and the Royal Danish Academy," *Schopenhauer Jahrbuch*, 2020, 22; see also Patrick Stokes, "'Either Shudder or Laugh': Kierkegaard on Schopenhauer," in *The Schopenhauerian Mind*, ed. David Bather Woods and Timothy Stoll (Routledge, 2023), 469.

48. Quoted in Pasgaard-Westerman, "Strictly Incognito," 34.

49. Quoted in Pasgaard-Westerman, "Strictly Incognito," 35. See this source for a forensic investigation of the Danish Royal Society's judgment of Schopenhauer's essay.

50. *PE* 1.
51. BM 258.
52. BM 11.
53. BM 197.
54. BM 245.
55. BM 249.
56. *WWR* 2:616.
57. Pasgaard-Westerman, "Strictly Incognito," 36.
58. *PE* 28.
59. *GB* 247.
60. *PP* 2:337; *GB* 281.
61. *G* 276–77.
62. For Schopenhauer on animal rights, see Stephen Puryear, "Schopenhauer on the Rights of Animals," *European Journal of Philosophy* 25, no. 2 (2017): 250–69.
63. BM 230.
64. *PP* 2:267.
65. Gwinner, *Schopenhauers Leben*, 536.
66. *FR* 383–84.
67. Gwinner, *Schopenhauers Leben*, 536; see also Zimmern, *Arthur Schopenhauer*, 243.
68. BM 161.
69. BM 229.
70. *PP* 2:193.
71. BM 222.
72. BM 218–19.
73. *PP* 2:228.
74. *PP* 2:320.
75. *PP* 2:228.
76. *PP* 2:231.
77. *PP* 2:315.
78. BM 222.
79. *PP* 2:315.
80. *PP* 2:144.
81. BM 231.
82. *FR* 364.
83. *PP* 2:335; see also *PP* 1:69. See Yitzhak Y. Melamed, "Schopenhauer on Spinoza: Animals, Jews, and Evil," in *The Schopenhauerian Mind*, ed. David Bather Woods and Timothy Stoll (Routledge, 2023), 391–95; and Christopher Janaway, "Schopenhauer, Europe, and Eurocentrism," in *The Schopenhauerian Mind*, ed. David Bather Woods and Timothy Stoll (Routledge, 2023), 352–54.
84. *WWR* 2:563.
85. *PP* 2:143.

86. *PP* 2:142.
87. *FR* 93.

Chapter Nine

1. *G* 321–23. These are, notably, Mylius's own recollections from decades later. Schopenhauer did not leave his own full account of their first meeting, except for brief mentions in letters to friends in February and March of 1858. This chapter is heavily indebted to the following sources: Arthur Hübscher, *Schopenhauer-Bildnisse: Eine Ikonographie* (Verlag von Waldemar Kramer, 1968); Eberhard Mayer-Wegelin, "'Ich gebe Ihnen 20 Minuten Zeit...': Schopenhauers Verhältnis zur frühen Photographie," *Jahrbuch der Schopenhauer-Gesellschaft*, 2011, 271–80; and Jochen Stollberg, "Der Philosoph und die Eitelkeit: Arthur Schopenhauer und sein Bildnis," *Jahrbuch der Schopenhauer-Gesellschaft*, 2011, 281–99. For information about the heroic work to gather, preserve, restore, and catalog photographs of Schopenhauer, see Jochen Stollberg, "Die Restaurierung der Daguerreotypien aus dem Schopenhauer-Archiv," *Jahrbuch der Schopenhauer-Gesellschaft*, 2004, 299–307.
2. Letter to David Asher, February 25, 1858 (*GB* 422).
3. Letter to David Asher, April 13, 1858 (*GB* 427).
4. Letter to David Asher, June 24, 1858 (*GB* 429).
5. Mayer-Wegelin, "Schopenhauers Verhältnis zur frühen Photographie," 276. The originals and the glass negatives from Mylius's shoot are sadly now lost.
6. *G* 323.
7. Mayer-Wegelin, "Schopenhauers Verhältnis zur frühen Photographie," 276.
8. Stollberg, "Die Restaurierung der Daguerreotypien", 300–301.
9. *PP* 2:116.
10. For this reason, both Schopenhauer and Schelling are mentioned in the critical theorist Walter Benjamin's delightful essay "Little History of Photography." See *Walter Benjamin: Selected Writings*, vol. 2, *Part 2: 1931–1934*, trans. Rodney Livingstone et al.; ed. Michael W. Jennings, Howard Eiland, and Gary Smith (Belknap/Harvard University Press, 2005), 507–30.
11. Lütkehaus, *Die Schopenhauers*, 437.
12. Mayer-Wegelin, "Schopenhauers Verhältnis zur frühen Photographie," 272.
13. Stollberg, "Der Philosoph und die Eitelkeit," 286.
14. Lütkehaus, *Die Schopenhauers*, 443.
15. Hübscher, *Schopenhauer-Bildnisse*, 137.
16. Letter to Julius Frauenstädt, October 30, 1851 (*GB* 268). See Stollberg, "Die Restaurierung der Daguerreotypien," 307.
17. Mayer-Wegelin, "Schopenhauers Verhältnis zur frühen Photographie," 273.
18. Hübscher, *Schopenhauer-Bildnisse*, 145. See also "Hartmann, Hermann,"

Frankfurter Personenlexikon, accessed September 22, 2023, at https://frankfurter-personenlexikon.de/node/3503.

19. Letter to Julius Frauenstädt, October 30, 1851 (*GB* 268). See Mayer-Wegelin, "Schopenhauers Verhältnis zur frühen Photographie," 274.

20. Mayer-Wegelin, "Schopenhauers Verhältnis zur frühen Photographie," 271.

21. *VC* 262.
22. *VC* 220.
23. *PP* 2:403.
24. *PP* 2:404.
25. *PP* 2:568.
26. *GB* 458.
27. *GB* 445.
28. Hübscher, *Schopenhauer-Bildnisse*, 153. At the time of writing, it is also the main photo on Schopenhauer's Wikipedia page.
29. *GB* 461.
30. Hübscher, *Schopenhauer-Bildnisse*, 115.
31. Hübscher, *Schopenhauer-Bildnisse*, 115–16.
32. *WWR* 1:250; *WWR* 1:273.
33. *WWR* 1:211.
34. *WWR* 1:211n12.
35. *PP* 2:570.
36. *PP* 1:352.
37. *PP* 1:275.
38. *PP* 1:317.
39. *PP* 1:281.
40. *PP* 1:347.
41. *PP* 1:319.
42. *PP* 1:310–11.
43. *PP* 1:350.
44. *WWR* 2:403; see also *WWR* 2:409 and *PP* 1:348.
45. *PP* 1:349.
46. *PP* 2:420.
47. *PP* 2:420.
48. *WWR* 2:96–97.
49. *PP* 1:142.
50. *WWR* 2:353.
51. *PP* 2:504.
52. *PP* 2:523.
53. *PP* 1:304.
54. *PP* 1:349.
55. *PP* 1:145.
56. *GB* 324.
57. *GB* 280.

58. Beiser, *Weltschmerz*, 67 and 75. See this source for a detailed account of Frauenstädt as a philosopher in his own right (67–86).

59. For Schopenhauer's first letter for Dorguth, see *GB* 155–56. For Schopenhauer adoption of Dorguth's comparison of him to Kaspar Hauser, see WN 307 and *PP* 1:124.

60. *G* 142.

61. *GB* 240.

62. Gwinner, *Schopenhauers Leben*, 520n.

63. *G* 182–83.

64. *G* 380.

65. Including innumerable biographical details of the current work.

66. Zimmern, *Arthur Schopenhauer*, vi.

67. *The Economist*, 11, no. 502 (April 9, 1853): 399.

68. *GB* 309.

69. *GB* 311.

70. *GB* 312; Cartwright, *Schopenhauer*, 528–29.

71. *GB* 311.

72. Brilmyer, "Schopenhauer and British Literary Feminism," 400–401.

73. Letter to Frauenstädt, June 29, 1855 (*GB* 366). Schopenhauer mistakenly says that Young is from "Oxford University near Boston," presumably confusing Oxford and Cambridge, Massachusetts (see *G* 195n). For more on Edward Young, see William W. Fenn, "Edward James Young (1829–1906)," *Proceedings of the American Academy of Arts and Sciences* 58, no. 17 (1923): 614–16.

74. *GB* 389.

75. John Oxenford, "Iconoclasm in German Philosophy," *Westminster Review*, April 1853, 388.

76. Oxenford, "Iconoclasm in German Philosophy," 407.

77. Oxenford, "Iconoclasm in German Philosophy," 393.

78. Oxenford, "Iconoclasm in German Philosophy," 391.

79. Oxenford, "Iconoclasm in German Philosophy," 407.

80. *GB* 403.

81. *GB* 420.

82. *GB* 368.

83. Maurice Todhunter, "Arthur Schopenhauer," *Westminster Review*, January 1895, 364.

84. See R. J. Hollingdale, "The Hero as Outsider," in *The Cambridge Companion to Nietzsche*, ed. Bernd Magnus and Katheleen Higgins (Cambridge University Press, 2006), 74–78.

85. *G* 168.

Chapter Ten

1. See Gwinner, *Schopenhauers Leben*, 547, who suggests that the main difference between Schopenhauer's apartments at Schöne Aussicht 16 and 17 was

that the size of the study allowed him to set up his entire library in it. Compare Cartwright, *Schopenhauer*, 546, who suggests that Schopenhauer sought to move to a ground-floor apartment in case of fire; whereas Gwinner (547n) suggests that, for this same reason, Schopenhauer had always lived on ground-floor apartments since 1836. Gwinner's claim is consistent with Frauenstädt's account of his first meeting with Schopenhauer in July 1846, when Schopenhauer was living at Schöne Aussicht 17, which mentions standing in front of Schopenhauer's door in the hallway of the ground floor. See also Walther Rauschenberger, "Schopenhauers Wohnungen während seines Lebens: Mit 16 Abbildungen," *Jahrbuch der Schopenhauer-Gesellschaft*, 1938, 292.

2. The following account is based on the testimony of Lucia Franz (née Schneider), "Über Schopenhauers häusliches Leben," *Jahrbuch der Schopenhauer-Gesellschaft*, 1914, 74–91. See also *G* 377–80, and Walther Rauschenberger, "Schopenhauer in seinen vier Wänden: Aufzeichnungen von Lucia Franz," *Jahrbuch der Schopenhauer-Gesellschaft*, 1940, 109–11.

3. Franz, "Über Schopenhauers häusliches Leben," 89.

4. *WWR* 2:524.

5. *WWR* 2:483.

6. *WWR* 2:482.

7. *WWR* 2:486.

8. *WWR* 2:517.

9. *WWR* 2:481.

10. *WWR* 2:482.

11. *WWR* 2:482.

12. Schopenhauer quotes Plato, *Theaetetus*, 155d, quoted at *WWR* 2:180, and Plato, *Phaedo*, 81a, at *WWR* 2:480.

13. *WWR* 2:181.

14. Diogenes Laertius, *Lives of Ancient Philosophers*, X, 27, quoted at *WWR* 2:484.

15. *WWR* 2:481.

16. *WWR* 2:481.

17. *WWR* 2:502–3.

18. *WWR* 2:487.

19. *WWR* 2:486.

20. *WWR* 2:485.

21. *WWR* 2:488.

22. *WWR* 2:488.

23. *WWR* 2:488.

24. *WWR* 2:488.

25. *WWR* 2:488.

26. *WWR* 2:507.

27. *WWR* 2:506.

28. *WWR* 2:503–4.

29. *WWR* 2:508.

30. *WWR* 2:525.
31. *WWR* 2:507.
32. *WWR* 2:508–9.
33. *WWR* 2:517.
34. Gwinner, *Schopenhauers Leben*, 616.
35. Letter to Frauenstädt, March 1, 1856 (*GB* 386).
36. *G* 396.
37. Gwinner, *Schopenhauers Leben*, 622–23.
38. Gwinner, *Schopenhauers Leben*, 625.
39. *G* 393–94.
40. Cartwright, *Schopenhauer*, 547.
41. Walther Rauschenberger, "Die Eintragung von Schopenhauers Tod im Frankfurter Kirchenbuch," *Jahrbuch der Schopenhauer-Gesellschaft*, 1932, 286.
42. Gwinner, *Schopenhauers Leben*, 616–17, translated in Zimmern, *Arthur Schopenhauer*, 247–48.
43. BM 1; Cartwright, *Schopenhauer*, 548.
44. Gwinner, *Schopenhauers Leben*, 620.
45. Gwinner, *Schopenhauers Leben*, 620.

Postscript

1. Letter from Johanna Schopenhauer to Arthur Schopenhauer, December 8, 1806 (Lütkehaus, *Die Schopenhauers*, 127–28). This paragraph and the one that follows it is largely informed by Catriona MacLeod, "Cutting Up the Salon: Adele Schopenhauer's 'Zwergenhochzeit' and Goethe's *Hochzeitlied*," *Deutsche Vierteljahrsschrift für Literaturwissenschaft und Geistesgeschichte* 89 (2015): 70–87; and Catriona MacLeod, "Cut-Ups on the Edge of the Photographic Century," in *Before Photography: German Visual Culture in the Nineteenth Century*, ed. Kirsten Belgum, Vance Byrd, and John D. Benjamin (Walter de Gruyter, 202), 129–56.
2. MacLeod, "Cutting Up the Salon," 84.
3. MacLeod, "Cutting Up the Salon," 79–80.
4. MacLeod, "Cutting Up the Salon," 86n.
5. MacLeod, "Cutting Up the Salon," 85.
6. *WWR* 2:478.

Bibliography

Works by Schopenhauer

BM "Prize Essay on the Basis of Morals." In *The Two Fundamental Problems of Ethics*, translated by Christopher Janaway. Cambridge University Press, 2009.
FR *On the Fourfold Root of the Principle of Sufficient Reason and Other Writings*. Translated by David E. Cartwright, Edwards E. Erdmann, and Christopher Janaway. Cambridge University Press, 2012.
FW "Prize Essay on the Freedom of the Will." In *The Two Fundamental Problems of Ethics*. Translated by Christopher Janaway. Cambridge University Press, 2009.
G *Gespräche. Neue, stark erweiterte Ausgbe.* Edited by Arthur Hübscher. Frommann, 1971.
GB *Gesammelte Briefe. 2., verbesserte und ergänzte Auflage.* Edited by Arthur Hübscher. Bouvier Verlag, 1987.
MR 1–4 *Manuscript Remains in Four Volumes*. Translated by E. F. J. Payne. Berg, 1988.
PE *The Two Fundamental Problems of Ethics*. Translated by Christopher Janaway. Cambridge University Press, 2009.
PP 1 *Parerga and Paralipomena: Short Philosophical Essays*, vol. 1. Translated by Sabine Roehr and Christopher Janaway. Cambridge University Press, 2014.
PP 2 *Parerga and Paralipomena: Short Philosophical Essays*, vol. 2. Translated by Adrian Del Caro and Christopher Janaway. Cambridge University Press, 2015.

VC "On Vision and Colours." In *On the Fourfold Root of the Principle of Sufficient Reason and Other Writings*, translated by David E. Cartwright, Edwards E. Erdmann, and Christopher Janaway. Cambridge University Press, 2012.

WN "On the Will in Nature." In *On the Fourfold Root of the Principle of Sufficient Reason and Other Writings*, translated by David E. Cartwright, Edwards E. Erdmann, and Christopher Janaway. Cambridge University Press, 2012.

WWR 1 *The World as Will and Representation*, vol. 1. Translated by Judith Norman, Alistair Welchman, and Christopher Janaway. Cambridge University Press, 2010.

WWR 2 *The World as Will and Representation*, vol. 2. Translated by Judith Norman, Alistair Welchman, and Christopher Janaway. Cambridge University Press, 2018.

Other Works

Adorno, Theodor W. *Negative Dialectics*. Translated by E. B. Ashton. Routledge, 1973.

Alvarez, Al. *The Savage God: A Study in Suicide*. Bloomsbury, 2002.

Améry, Jean. *On Suicide: A Discourse on Voluntary Death*. Translated by John D. Barlow. Indiana University Press, 1999.

App, Urs. "Notes and Excerpts by Schopenhauer Related to Volumes 1–9 of the Asiatik Researches." *Jahrbuch der Schopenhauer-Gesellschaft*, 1998, 11–34.

App, Urs. "Required Reading: Schopenhauer's Favorite Book." *Jahrbuch der Schopenhauer-Gesellschaft* 2012, 65–86.

App, Urs. "Schopenhauer's India Notes of 1811." *Jahrbuch der Schopenhauer-Gesellschaft*, 2006, 15–34.

App, Urs. "Schopenhauer's Initial Encounter with Indian Thought." *Jahrbuch der Schopenhauer-Gesellschaft*, 2006, 35–76.

Atzert, Stephan. "Schopenhauer and Freud." In *A Companion to Schopenhauer*. Edited by Bart Vandenabeele. Wiley-Blackwell, 2012.

Bachelor, Katheryn. *Translations and Paratexts*. Routledge, 2018.

Bakewell, Sarah. *How to Live: A Life of Montaigne in One Question and Twenty Attempts at an Answer*. Chatto & Windus, 2010.

Battersby, Christine. "Schopenhauer's Metaphysics and Ethics: Mapping Influences and Congruities with Feminist Philosophers." In *The Palgrave Handbook of German Idealism and Feminist Philosophy*, edited by Susanne Lettow and Tuija Pulkinnen. Palgrave Macmillan, 2023.

Beauvoir, Simone de. *The Second Sex*. Translated by Constance Borde and Sheila Malovany-Chevallier. Vintage, 2015.

Beiser, Frederick C. *Weltschmerz: Pessimism in German Philosophy, 1860–1900*. Oxford University Press, 2016.

Benjamin, Walter. *Selected Writings*. Vol. 2, *Part 2: 1931–1934*. Translated by Rodney Livingstone et al.; edited by Michael W. Jennings, Howard Eiland, and Gary Smith. Belknap/Harvard University Press, 2005.

Bishop, Paul. "Schopenhauer's Impact on European Literature." In *A Companion to Schopenhauer*, edited by Bart Vandenabeele. Wiley-Blackwell, 2012.

Bishop, Paul. "Thomas Mann on Schopenhauer: A Philosopher of the Future?" In *The Schopenhauerian Mind*, edited by David Bather Woods and Timothy Stoll. Routledge, 2023.

Bridgwater, Patrick. *Arthur Schopenhauer's English Schooling*. Routledge, 1988.

Brilmyer, S. Pearl. "Schopenhauer and British Literary Feminism." In *The Palgrave Schopenhauer Handbook*, edited by Sandra Shapshay. Palgrave-Macmillan, 2017.

Brook, Andrew, and Chris Young. "Schopenhauer and Freud." In *The Oxford Handbook of Philosophy and Psychoanalysis*, edited by Richard Gipps and Michael Lacewing. Oxford, 2018.

Brunsdale, Mitzi M. "The Effect of Mrs. Rudolf Dircks' Translation of Schopenhauer's 'The Metaphysics of Love' on D. H. Lawrence's Early Fiction." *Rocky Mountain Review of Language and Literature* 32, no. 2 (Spring 1978): 120–29.

Camus, Albert. *The Myth of Sisyphus*. Translated by Justin O'Brien. Vintage, 1983.

Cartwright, David. *Schopenhauer: A Biography*. Cambridge University Press, 2010.

Clark, Christopher. *Revolutionary Spring: Fighting for a New World, 1848–1849*. Allen Lane, 2023.

Creffield, C. A. "Zimmern, Helen (1846–1934)." In *Oxford Dictionary of National Biography*. Oxford University Press, 2004.

Darwin, Charles. *The Descent of Man, and Selections in Relation to Sex*. D. Appleton and Company, 1889.

Darwin, Charles. *Evolutionary Writings*. Edited by James A. Secord. Oxford University Press, 2008.

Dielmann, Henry B. "Elisabet Ney, Sculptor." *The Southwestern Historical Quarterly* 65, no. 2 (October 1961): 157–83.

Diethe, Carol. *Nietzsche's Women: Beyond the Whip*. De Gruyter, 1996.

Diethe, Carol. *Towards Emancipation: German Women Writers of the Nineteenth Century*. Berghahn Books, 1998.

Ellis, Havelock. *Man and Woman: Study of Human Secondary Sexual Characters*. Walter Scott Publishing Company, 1894.

Fenn, William W. "Edward James Young (1829–1906)." *Proceedings of the American Academy of Arts and Sciences* 58, no. 17 (1923): 614–16.

Foucault, Michel. *Discipline and Punish: The Birth of the Prison*. Translated by Alan Sheridan. Penguin, 1991.

Franz (née Schneider), Lucia. "Über Schopenhauers häusliches Leben." *Jahrbuch der Schopenhauer-Gesellschaft*, 1914, 74–91.

Freud, Sigmund. *The Interpretation of Dreams*. Translated by Joyce Crick. Oxford University Press, 1999.
Freud, Sigmund. "On the History of the Psycho-Analytic Movement." In *The Standard Edition of the Complete Psychological Works of Sigmund Freud*, edited and translated by James Strachey. Hogarth Press, 1914.
Furness, Raymond. *Richard Wagner*. Reaktion, 2013.
Gide, André. *If It Die*. Translated by Dorothy Bussy. Penguin, 1957.
Grimwood, Thomas. "The Limits of Misogyny: Schopenhauer, 'On Women,'" *Kritike* 2, no. 2 (December 2008): 131–45.
Guenther, Lisa. *Solitary Confinement: Social Death and Its Afterlives*. University of Minnesota Press, 2013.
Gwinner, Wilhelm. *Schopenhauers Leben: Zweite, Umgearbeitete und Vielfach Vermehrte Auflage der Schrift*. F. A. Brockhaus, 1878.
Hamlyn, David. *Schopenhauer: The Arguments of Philosophers*. Routledge, 1999.
Hollingdale, R. J. "The Hero as Outsider." In *The Cambridge Companion to Nietzsche*, edited by Bernd Magnus and Kathleen Higgins. Cambridge University Press, 2006.
Horkheimer, Max. *Critique of Instrumental Reason*. Translated by Matthew J. O'Connell et al. Verso, 2012.
Hübscher, Angelika. "Schopenhauer und 'die Weiber.'" *Jahrbuch der Schopenhauer-Gesellschaft*, 1977, 187–203.
Hübscher, Arthur. "Adele an Arthur Schopenhauer: Unbekannte Briefe I." *Jahrbuch der Schopenhauer-Gesellschaft*, 1977, 133–87.
Hübscher, Arthur. "Ein Lebensbericht für Anthime Grégoire." *Jahrbuch der Schopenhauer-Gesellschaft*, 1970, 41–49.
Hübscher, Arthur. "Schopenhauer als Hochschullehrer." *Jahrbuch der Schopenhauer-Gesellschaft*, 1958, 172–75.
Hübscher, Arthur. *Schopenhauer-Bildnisse: Eine Ikonographie*. Verlag von Waldemar Kramer, 1968.
Hume, David. *Essays: Moral, Political, and Literary*. Liberty Fund, 1985.
Hustvedt, Asti. *Medical Muses: Hysteria in Nineteenth Century Paris*. Bloomsbury, 2011.
Jacquette, Dale. "Schopenhauer on the Ethics of Suicide." *Continental Philosophy Review* 33 (2000): 43–58.
Janaway, Christopher. "Schopenhauer, Europe, and Eurocentrism." In *The Schopenhauerian Mind*, edited by David Bather Woods and Timothy Stoll. Routledge, 2023.
Janaway, Christopher. "Schopenhauer's 'Indian' Ethics." In *Schopenhauer's Moral Philosophy*. Edited by Patrick Hassan. Routledge: 2022.
Jessop, T. E. "*Schopenhauer: His Life and Philosophy*. (Revised edition.) By Helen Zimmern." *Philosophy* 11, no. 28 (October 1932): 489–90.
Kant, Immanuel. *Correspondence*. Edited by Arnulf Zweig. Cambridge University Press, 1999.

Kant, Immanuel. "Erklärung in Beziehung auf Fichte's Wissenschaftslehre." *Allgemeine Literatur-Zeitung*, August 28, 1799.
Kant, Immanuel. *Groundwork for the Metaphysics of Morals*. Translated by Allen W. Wood. Harvard University Press, 2018.
Kant, Immanuel. *Religion Within the Boundaries of Mere Reason*. Translated and edited by Allen W. Wood and George di Giovanni. Cambridge University Press, 1996.
Kant, Immanuel "Über den Verfasser des Versuchs einer Kritik aller Offenbarung." *Allgemeine Literatur-Zeitung*, August 22, 1792.
Long, Sandra Salser. "Arthur Schopenhauer and Elisabet Ney." *Southwest Review* 69, no. 2 (Spring 1984): 130–47.
Lukács, Georg. *The Destruction of Reason*. Translated by Peter Palmer. Humanities Press, 1978.
Lukács, Georg. *The Theory of the Novel*. Translated by Anna Bostock. Merlin, 1980.
Lütkehaus, Ludger. *Die Schopenhauers: Der Familien-Briefwechsel von Adele, Arthur, Heinrich Floris und Johanna Schopenhauer*. Haffmans Verlag, 1991.
MacLeod, Catriona. "Cutting Up the Salon: Adele Schopenhauer's 'Zwergenhochzeit' and Goethe's *Hochzeitlied*." *Deutsche Vierteljahrsschrift für Literaturwissenschaft und Geistesgeschichte* 89 (2015): 70–87.
MacLeod, Catriona. "Cut-Ups on the Edge of the Photographic Century." In *Before Photography: German Visual Culture in the Nineteenth Century*, edited by Kirsten Belgum, Vance Byrd, and John D. Benjamin. Walter de Gruyter, 2021.
Magee, Bryan. *The Philosophy of Schopenhauer*. Oxford University Press, 1997.
Mann, Thomas. *Freud, Goethe, Wagner*. Knopf, 1942.
Marshall, Colin. "Schopenhauer on the Futility of Suicide." *Mind* 134, no. 533 (2025): 171–90.
Masny, Michal. "Schopenhauer on Suicide and Negation of the Will." *British Journal for the History of Philosophy* 29, no. 3 (2021): 494–516.
Mayer-Wegelin, Eberhard. "'Ich gebe Ihnen 20 Minuten Zeit . . .': Schopenhauers Verhältnis zur frühen Photographie." *Jahrbuch der Schopenhauer-Gesellschaft*, 2011, 271–80
Melamed, Yitzhak Y. "Schopenhauer on Spinoza: Animals, Jews, and Evil." In *The Schopenhauerian Mind*, edited by David Bather Woods and Timothy Stoll. Routledge, 2023.
Murdoch, Iris. *Metaphysics as a Guide to Morals*. Vintage, 1992.
Murphy, Sean. "Acquired Character." In *The Schopenhauerian Mind*, edited by David Bather Woods and Timothy Stoll. Routledge, 2023.
Nietzsche, Friedrich. *Beyond Good and Evil*. Edited by Rolf-Peter Horstmann; translated by Judith Norman. Cambridge University Press, 2002.
Nietzsche, Friedrich. *The Gay Science*. Edited by Bernard Williams; translated

by Josefine Nauckhoff and Adrian Del Caro. Cambridge University Press, 2001.

Norman, Judith. "Pushing Back: Reading *The World as Will and Representation* as a Woman." In *Schopenhauer's "The World as Will and Representation": A Critical Guide*, edited by Judith Norman and Alistair Welchman. Cambridge University Press, 2022.

O'Connor, Brian. "Melancholy and Pessimism: Adorno's Critique of Schopenhauer." In *The Schopenhauerian Mind*, edited by David Bather Woods and Timothy Stoll. Routledge, 2023.

Oxenford, John. "Iconoclasm in German Philosophy." *Westminster Review*, April 1853, 388–407.

Pasgaard-Westerman, Martin. "Strictly Incognito? Schopenhauer's Prize Essay on Morals and the Royal Danish Academy." *Jahrbuch der Schopenhauer-Gesellschaft*, 2020, 23–74.

Pevsner, Nicholas. *A History of Building Types*. Thames & Hudson, 1976.

Pinkard, Terry. *Hegel: A Biography*. Cambridge University Press, 2002.

Porter, Roy. *Madness: A Brief History*. Oxford University Press, 2003.

Puryear, Stephen. "Schopenhauer on the Rights of Animals." *European Journal of Philosophy* 25, no. 2 (2017): 250–69.

Rauschenberger, Walther. "Die Eintragung von Schopenhauers Tod im Frankfurter Kirchenbuch." *Jahrbuch der Schopenhauer-Gesellschaft*, 1932, 286–87.

Rauschenberger, Walther. "Schopenhauer in seinen vier Wänden: Aufzeichnungen von Lucia Franz." *Jahrbuch der Schopenhauer-Gesellschaft*, 1940, 130–44.

Rauschenberger, Walther. "Schopenhauers Wohnungen während seines Lebens: Mit 16 Abbildungen." *Jahrbuch der Schopenhauer-Gesellschaft*, 1938, 281–93.

Rochefoucauld, François de la. *The Maxims*. Translated by F. G. Stevens. Humphrey Milford, 1940.

Rosen, Michael. "Fichte's Way." *The Nation*, August 13, 2013.

Safranski, Rudiger. *Schopenhauer and the Wild Years of Philosophy*. Translated by Ewald Osers. Harvard University Press, 1991.

Schopenhauer, Adele. *Tagebuch einer Einsamen*. Edited by H. H. Houben. Matthes & Seitz, 1985.

Schopenhauer, Johanna. *A Lady Travels: The Diaries of Johanna Schopenhauer*. Edited by Ruth Michaelis-Jena and Willy Merson. Routledge, 1988.

Sellin, Thorsten. "The Origin of the 'Pennsylvania System of Prison Discipline.'" *The Prison Journal* 50 (1970): 13–21

Shalev Sharon. *Supermax: Controlling Risk Through Solitary Confinement*. Routledge, 2009.

Shapshay, Sandra. "Review of *The Philosophy of Schopenhauer* by Dale Jacquette and *Schopenhauer* by Robert Wicks." *Mind* 119, no. 475 (2010): 798–805.

Stokes, Patrick. "'Either Shudder or Laugh': Kierkegaard on Schopenhauer." In *The Schopenhauerian Mind*, edited by David Bather Woods and Timothy Stoll. Routledge, 2023.

Stollberg, Jochen. "Der Philosoph und die Eitelkeit: Arthur Schopenhauer und sein Bildnis." *Jahrbuch der Schopenhauer-Gesellschaft*, 2011, 281–99.

Stollberg, Jochen. "Die Restaurierung der Daguerreotypien aus dem Schopenhauer-Archiv." *Jahrbuch der Schopenhauer-Gesellschaft*, 2004, 299–307.

Taylor, Bride Neill. *Elisabet Ney, Sculptor*. Devin-Adair Co., 1916.

Thomas, Marianna, ed. *Eastern State Penitentiary Historic Structures Report*. Philadelphia Historical Commission, 1994.

Todhunter, Maurice. "Arthur Schopenhauer." *Westminster Review*, January 1895, 364.

Van der Lugt, Mara. *Dark Matters: Pessimism and the Problem of Suffering*. Princeton University Press, 2021.

Velleman, J. David. "A Right of Self-Termination?" *Ethics* 109, no. 3 (1999): 606–28.

Verrecchia, Anacleto. "Schopenhauer e la vispa Teresa." *Jahrbuch der Schopenhauer-Gesellschaft*, 1975, 187–99.

Vincent, David. *A History of Solitude*. Polity, 2020.

Wicks, Robert. "Arthur Schopenhauer's Bronze Buddha: Neither Tibetan nor Thai, but Shan." *Jahrbuch der Schopenhauer-Gesellschaft*, 2010, 307–16.

Wood, Allen W. *Fichte's Ethical Thought*. Oxford University Press, 2016.

Woods, David. "Seriously Bored: Schopenhauer on Solitary Confinement." *British Journal for the History of Philosophy* 27, no. 5 (2019): 959–78.

Xhignesse, Michel-Antoine. "Schopenhauer's Perceptive Invective." In *Language, Logic, and Mathematics in Schopenhauer*, edited by Jens Lemanski. Birkhäuser, 2020.

Zentner, Marcel. *Die Flucht ins Vergessen: Die Anfänge der Psychoanalyse Freuds bei Schopenhauer*. Wissenschaftliche Buchgesellschaft, 1995.

Zimmern, Helen. *Arthur Schopenhauer: His Life and His Philosophy*. Longmans, Green, and Co., 1876.

Zimmern, Helen. "Calcio, or Football in Italy." *The Leisure Hour*, March 1900, 439–42.

Zimmern, Helen. "Nietzsche Erinnerungen." *Frankfurter Generalanzeiger*, November 16, 1926.

Index

action, 97, 176. *See also* will
Adam, 183
Adorno, Theodor W., 10
aesthetics, 105–6, 115; aesthetic experience, 106, 178; aestheticism, 106. *See also* art
Africa, 180, 181
alienists, 91. *See also* Esquirol, Jean-Étienne Dominique; Pinel, Philippe; psychiatry
Alighieri, Dante. *See* Dante
Alps, 119, 152, 162
Alzheimer, Alois, 84
America, 47–53, 151, 158, 179–82; civil war, 182; independence, 51, 181; origins, 180–81; politics, 180–82; prison system, 47, 48–53; slavery in, 179–82
Améry, Jean, vi, 10–11
anarchy, 169, 182
Anglophilia, 2, 38, 49
animals, nonhuman, xiii, 67, 77, 83, 85–86, 97–98, 105, 140–41, 177–79, 182–83, 184, 192, 220; and abolitionism, 183; consciousness, 97–98, 192; death, 182, 220; definition, 97–98; and ethics, 177–79, 182–83, 184; functions, 97; labor, 141–42, 182; meat, 182; protection, 141, 177–78, 179; vivisection, 77, 177; welfare, 177–79, 182–83. *See also* apes; cruelty: animal; dogs; horses; humans: and animals, comparison of; intelligence: of animals; porcupines; sympathy: for animals
Anquetil-Duperron, Abraham Hyacinthe, 101
Anthime (childhood friend). *See* Grégoire de Blésimaire, Jean Anthime
anti-Semitism, 10, 99, 183. *See also* Judaism
anti-slavery, 179–82
apes, 178–79. *See also* humans
Aristotle, 19–20, 82, 96, 101, 203
art, 4, 9, 106, 107, 119, 149, 163–65, 189, 197–200, 230; philosophy, 4, 106, 198–200. *See also* artists; genius; music; photography; poetry; portraiture

artists, 4, 16, 40, 42, 55, 145, 155–58, 183, 196, 203, 230–31
asceticism, 65–66, 106–7, 135–36; suicide, 65–66. *See also* redemption; salvation
Asher, David, 206, 211, 227
Asia, 77, 101, 147; *Asiatic Researches*, 101
asylums, 74, 85, 86, 93, 95, 114. *See also* Bedlam; Bicêtre; Charité
atheism, 79, 89, 208
Atma (brown dog), 156, 166, 206, 215–19, 227
Atma (white dog), 166, 188; death, 166
Auerswald, Hans von, 170
Auschwitz, 10
Austria, 26, 162, 167. *See also* Vienna

Bacon, Francis, 101, 131
Bayreuth, 152
beards, 13, 14, 167
beauty, 4, 14, 106, 133, 137, 200
Beauvoir, Simone de, 5; *The Second Sex*, 5
Becker, Dorothee Marie, 141–42
Becker, Johann August, 204–5
Beckett, Samuel, ix, 4, 10; *The Unnamable*, 10
Bedlam, 40
Bentham, Jeremy, 211
Berlin, 13, 16, 28, 33, 56, 78, 80, 84, 89, 92, 94, 96, 98, 99, 100, 109–10, 111, 112–13, 130, 138, 140–41, 155–56, 159, 160, 161, 162, 163, 164, 165, 166, 208, 226, 228, 231, 232. *See also* universities: in Berlin
Bicêtre, 35
Biow, Hermann, 188
Blum, Robert, 167, 170
Blumenbach, Johann Friedrich, 77, 109, 115

body, 104–5, 150; control, 62, 150; dead, 222; will, 104–5. *See also* will
Boeckh, August, 110, 111, 113, 115
Bologna, 119
Bonn, 144, 145, 146
boredom, ix, 45, 47–48, 106
Borges, Jorge Luis, 4, 11–12
Brahma, 101, 107
Brecht, Heinrich Gustave, 194, 196
Britain, 26, 41, 43, 50, 151, 180; antislavery, 179, 180; citizenship, 38, 151; culture, 41; monarchy, 51, 180, 181, 182; prisons, 50; queuing, xi. *See also* England; Scotland
Brockhaus, Friedrich Arnold, 108. *See also* F. A. Brockhaus (publishing house)
Bruno, Giordano, 162, 203
Buddha (Siddhartha Gautama), 36, 56, 165; awakening, 36, 56; statue, 165. *See also* Buddhism
Buddhism, 36, 77, 107, 144, 165, 176, 179, 182. *See also* Buddha (Siddhartha Gautama)
business, 2, 16, 37, 38, 39, 41, 58, 70, 108, 137, 233. *See also* life
Butz. *See* Atma (brown dog)
Byron, Lord George, 9, 122

Caesar, Julius, 81
Calderón de la Barca, Pedro, 209
Camus, Albert, 8
causality, 85–86, 87, 96–97, 176
censorship, 62, 79; academic, 79, 161; religious, 62, 79; self-, 62
Chamfort, Nicolas, 19
Chapman, John, 209
character, 131, 163, 179, 200; acquired, 163; moral, 163, 171, 179, 200
Charcot, Jean-Martin, 92
Charité, 84, 89, 92, 94

Charles Frederick (Grand Duke of Saxe-Weimar-Eisenach), 145
children, 19, 25, 35, 44–45, 62, 67–68, 71, 85, 93, 107, 118, 123–24, 126, 128, 130, 132, 133–35, 137–38, 144, 146, 148, 149, 158, 188, 202, 214–19, 232; abuse, 93, 135; duty of care for, 62, 132; education, 25, 44–45; fear, 107; murder of, 132; weeping, 67–68; works as, 19, 202
Chodowiecki, Daniel Niklaus, 42
cholera, 13, 26, 28, 56, 112, 125, 164, 165
Christianity, 45, 63, 66, 79, 139, 165, 179, 180, 181, 183; Anglicanism, 45–46, 63, 181, 203; Catholicism, 165; and crimes, 180; Episcopalian, 42; Mormonism, 149. *See also* religion
Cibber, Caius Gabriel, 40
Cicero, Marcus Tullius, 20
compassion, xii–xiii, 66, 67, 172, 175–76, 179, 180, 184, 224–25, 229; and human nature, xi, 67, 68, 171; and metaphysics, 176, 184; and morality, 175–76; origins, 176; self-compassion, 67–68; and weeping, 67–68. *See also* ethics; humans; love: and compassion
Condillac, Étienne Bonnot de, 91
conscience, 63, 174, 182, 201
consciousness, 53, 80, 83, 90, 97–98, 104, 128, 174, 223; transformation of, 106–8, 224. *See also* unconscious
consolation, 11, 34, 61, 104, 148, 202, 219, 221, 223–24
contractarianism, 168–72
Copenhagen, 174, 182
cosmopolitanism, xiii, 26, 38, 130, 232
cruelty, 40, 77, 182, 184, 198; animal, 77, 177–78, 179, 184; human, 179–80, 184. *See also* malice
crying. *See* weeping
cuckoldry, 9, 150

Daguerre, Louis, 187–88, 194
daguerreotype, 187–90, 191, 194, 195, 227. *See also* photography
Danish Society of Sciences, 172–76, 177, 189
Dante, 54–55; Dantesque, 54; *Inferno*, 55
Danzig, 1, 13, 41–42, 64, 70–72, 100, 110–11, 148, 226–27; Ohra, 148, 226–27
Dārā Shukoh, Muhammad, 101
Darwin, Charles, 26, 155, 207; *Voyage of the Beagle*, 26
death, 1, 2–3, 6–7, 8, 16, 28, 36–37, 51, 55–56, 58–59, 61, 65–67, 69, 70, 72–73, 89, 92, 98, 104, 123–24, 126, 137–38, 144–46, 164, 170, 176, 182, 203, 212–13, 214–29, 232–33; actual versus apparent, 224; annihilation, 221, 223; and consolation, 219–25; of fathers, 1–3, 8, 38, 55, 58, 61, 67, 69–70, 72, 73, 75, 98, 100, 110, 132, 137, 164, 219, 231, 232, 233, 238; fear of, 65, 66, 73, 75, 104, 110, 132, 164, 212–13, 220; as nothing, 221–22, 223–24, 225, 226, 229; philosophy of, 219–25. *See also* execution; immortality; murder; punishment: capital; starvation; suicide
dehumanization, 84, 85, 93, 179–80. *See also* humans; inhumanity
democracy, 168, 181
depression, xii, 15, 20, 51, 66, 73, 120. *See also* melancholy
desire, 31, 39, 47–48, 54, 56, 65–66, 88, 90, 97, 103, 105–6, 108, 110, 126, 129, 155, 193, 219–20, 223, 228–29, 235; cycle of, 54, 56, 65–66, 105–6, 203; and death,

desire (*continued*)
219–20, 223; and motive, 97; sexual, 126, 129, 133–36, 147, 155. *See also* motivation; volition; will
despotism, 64, 169, 181
Deussen, Paul, 225
devils, 57, 178, 179; demons, 6
Dickens, Charles, 51, 53; *American Notes*, 51
Dircks, Mrs. Rudolf, 154–55
dogs, x, xiii, 23, 42, 83, 86, 156, 166, 178–79, 188, 189, 206, 215–19, 225; poodles, xiii, 86, 156, 166, 189, 216, 219, 225. *See also* intelligence: of dogs; love: of dogs
Dorguth, Friedrich Ludwig, 205
Doß, Adam Ludwig von, 205–6
dreams, 3–4, 82, 90, 159, 164, 222, 228; analysis, 90; dreamlessness, 222
Dresden, 32, 74, 94, 98, 101, 108, 110, 112–13, 119, 122, 123–24, 145, 154, 162; Zwinger, 74, 94
duty, 61–62, 175; and morality, 175; to oneself, 61; parental, 62

Economist, 207–8
Edinburgh, 42, 43
education, 25, 26, 42, 43, 44–45, 74, 76–78, 80–83, 109, 114–17, 151, 229; artificial versus natural, 27; worldly, 27. *See also* Schopenhauer, Arthur: education; universities
egoism, 69, 168, 171–72, 175. *See also* self-interest
Eliot, George, 209, 210
Ellis, Havelock, 155
embodiment. *See* body
Emden, Martin, 207, 227
empiricism, 27, 91
England, 2, 22, 26, 36–38, 39, 42, 43–46, 63, 110, 122, 151, 152, 153, 194, 207, 212; animal protection, 177–78; clergy, 45–46, 63, 203; education, 44–45; justice, 36–37, 177–78; newspapers, 37, 49–51, 68, 194, 207, 209; poets, 122; religion, 42, 45–46, 63; Sundays, 45; tour of, 26, 43–44, 108. *See also* English (language)
Englischer Hof, 9, 23, 31, 138–39, 167–68, 206
English (language), 29, 42–43, 46, 71, 162, 211, 215; biography in, 151; reception, 155, 207–11, 212, 227; translation, 20–21, 151–52, 154–55, 161–62, 207–9, 211, 217
enslavement. *See* slavery
Epicurus, 203, 221, 222
epistemology, 102–3
Esquirol, Jean-Étienne Dominique, 91, 92
eternal recurrence, 6–8
ethics, 19, 59–60, 64–65, 82, 105, 106–10, 134–36, 169–70, 172–76, 179, 184, 208, 234; classical, 17, 20, 64; foundations, 172–76; Kantian, 59–60, 175; political, 169–70; sexual, 134–36; and suicide, 59–66; theological, 175, 179, 180. *See also* compassion; moral philosophy; morality
ethnography, 77
eudaemonology, 19, 64, 200–201
Europe, 8, 13, 26, 37–38, 46, 50, 147, 166, 182–83, 221, 233; anti-Semitism, 183; death, perspective on, 221; diet, 182; pandemic, 13; philosophy, xiii, 8; prisons, 50; race in, 183; revolutions, 166; society, 147; tour of, 26, 37–38, 39–47, 233; women in, 147
execution, 36, 167, 170. *See also* hangings; lynching; punishment: capital
existentialism, 8, 11, 220
experience: academic, 110, 163;

aesthetic, 106, 178; anesthetic, 222; cognitive, 27, 81, 102–3, 192, 220; of death, 222; dual, 104; embodied, 104; empirical, 27, 81, 133, 175, 222; life, x–xi, 7, 27; moral, 224; mystical, 37, 75, 107, 164; personal, 7, 25, 64, 89, 116, 131, 153; student, 109; tragic, 70; and will, 104–5; worldly, xii, 26, 29, 133, 134. *See also* knowledge; perception

F. A. Brockhaus (publishing house), 19, 108, 194
fame, 1, 200–204, 212–13; belated, 200, 203, 207; of philosophers, 202, 203; undeserved, 202; and value, 202, 203–4
feminism, 4, 147, 158
Fernow, Karl Ludwig, 76, 111
Feuerbach, Ludwig, 209; *The Essence of Christianity*, 209
Fichte, Immanuel Hermann, 80, 109, 161
Fichte, Johann Gottlieb, 78–84, 93–94, 96, 100, 114, 173, 188; *Attempt at a Critique of All Revelation*, 78; career, 78–80; death, 96, 188; lectures, 80–83, 84, 85, 86, 93–94, 95, 100; physical appearance, 80
Fischer, Kuno, 212
Florence, 119, 121, 123, 149, 151, 154, 160, 162
foolishness, x, 114, 181; comic, x; American, 181; German, 114
France, 26, 35, 37, 39, 46–47, 154, 164, 187, 188; Académie des Beaux-Arts, 187; Academy of Sciences, 187, 188; existentialism, 8; photography, 187–88, 189; poodles, xiii; psychiatry, 91–93. *See also* French (language)
Frankfurt, 1, 9, 10, 13, 17, 23, 26, 33, 34, 50, 109, 132, 136, 138, 143, 144, 146, 154, 156–58, 164–67, 168, 170, 172, 173, 177, 179, 185, 189, 190, 204–7, 209, 228, 231, 232; Auschwitz trials, 10; cemetery, 187, 225, 228–29; description, 164–65; fair, 179; library, 164, 227; National Assembly, 166–67, 170, 190; prison congress, 50; river, 157, 167, 226; school of critical theory, 10, 11
Franz, Lucia (née Schneider), 214–19, 222, 225
Frauenstädt, Julius, 165–66, 173, 189, 204, 205, 211, 212, 227; *Letters on the Schopenhauerian Philosophy*, 205; *On the True Relation of Reason to Revelation*, 205
Frederick William II of Prussia, 79
free will. *See* will: free
freedom, 28, 164, 165, 168, 181, 182; independence, 28, 164, 165, 182; liberty, 64, 168, 182
French (language), 21, 39, 44, 71; translation, 63. *See also* France
Freud, Sigmund, xi, 84, 90–91, 92, 93, 188; *Interpretation of Dream*, 90; *Studies on Hysteria*, 93; talking cure, 84, 90; training, 92
Friedreich, J. B., 92
friendship, 17, 20, 39, 94, 128, 130, 153, 204–7, 209, 216–19
Fries, Jakob Friedrich, 100
Frommann, Carl Friedrich Ernst, 113
Fuga, Teresa, 122–23

Ganges, River, 13
Gans, Josef, 99
Gdańsk. *See* Danzig
gender, 1, 5, 129, 135, 146–51; violence, 150
genius, 35, 82–84, 94, 108, 153, 199, 202–3, 229
George V of Hanover, 156

282   Index

German (language), 21, 27, 29, 71, 101, 137, 151, 155, 162, 217. *See also* Germany
Germany, 10, 26, 32, 37, 47, 144, 151, 159, 160, 162, 166, 172, 173, 177, 185, 207, 208, 209, 211, 212; animal welfare, 177; confederation, 166; constitution, 166; education, 34, 44, 77, 84; in Enlightenment, 126, 151; intelligentsia, 10; newspapers, 185, 194; philosophy, 5, 33, 114–16, 209, 210, 211, 233; postwar, 10–11; psychiatry, 84, 91–92; Sundays, 45; unification, 166. *See also* German (language); Prussia
Gerstenbergk, Georg Friedrich Conrad Ludwig Müller von, 98–99, 101, 121
Gide, André, 4, 5
Göbel, Angilbert, 196
God, 12, 60, 71, 123, 175, 179, 183, 217
Goethe, Christiane Vulpius von, 99
Goethe, Johann Wolfgang von, 9, 17, 32, 74, 83, 108–9, 111, 131, 145, 189, 190, 209, 230–31; *Torquato Tasso*, 83
Goethe, Ottilie von, 74, 108, 138, 144
Gotha, 77, 109, 110
Göttingen, 77, 110
government, 110, 168–70, 172, 180, 181; forms, 168–69, 181
Gracián, Baltasar, 162
grand tour. *See* Schopenhauer, Arthur: grand tour; Schopenhauer, Heinrich Floris: British tour; Schopenhauer, Johanna (née Trosiener): British tour
Greece, 147, 154, 203; civilization, 119; culture, 133, 147; mythology, 8, 53, 56; sexuality in, 133; slavery in, 181. *See also* Greek (language)

Greek (language), 18, 19, 43, 44, 77, 84. *See also* Greece
Grégoire de Blésimaire, André Charles, 39
Grégoire de Blésimaire, Jean Anthime, 39, 41, 46, 61, 136–39, 232
grief, 58, 61, 69–70, 124, 137–38, 166, 224
Griesinger, Wilhelm, 91
Gwinner, Wilhelm, 178, 206, 225–26, 227, 228–29

Haldane, R. B., 155
Hamburg, 2, 17, 37, 39, 58, 70, 74, 77, 111, 137, 151, 230–31, 232
Hamel, Julius, 196–98
hangings, 36–37, 39, 40, 167
Hanseatic league, 2
happiness, xii, 3–4, 7, 14, 19, 20, 75, 128, 130, 139, 141, 159, 163, 201–2, 214, 219. *See also* unhappiness
Hartmann, Friedrich Hermann, 190
Hartung (publisher), 78–79
Hauser, Kaspar, 205
Haviland, John, 49
Hayez, Francesco, 119
Heeren, Arnold, 77
Hegel, Georg Wilhelm Friedrich, 13, 16, 33, 79, 96–98, 100, 109, 112, 113–14, 116, 173, 202, 211, 232; career, 96, 100, 188; death, 13, 109, 188, 232; *Encyclopaedia of the Philosophical Sciences*, 113; fame, 202, 212; influence, 209; nonsense, 113, 144; Schopenhauer encounter, 96–98, 112, 116; *Science of Logic*, 113. *See also* Hegelianism
Hegelianism, 33, 113, 173, 202, 209, 212
Heidelberg, 96, 109, 158, 219
Heine, Heinrich, 51
hell, 6, 51, 54–55, 178
Herder, Johann Gottfried, 101

heritability of traits, 92, 131–32
Herschel, William, 41
Hillebrand, Joseph, 161
Hillebrand, Karl, 154, 161
Hillebrand, Mrs. Karl (Jessie Taylor), 154–55, 161
Hinduism, 101, 107, 139, 182. *See also* India; Upanishads
history, 44, 77, 99, 115, 133, 151, 181, 183, 198, 202; art, 198; human, 183; literary, 203; of philosophy, 115, 212; sexuality in, 133
Hobbes, Thomas, 168–72
Hoeffner, Ernst, 89
Holocaust, 10
honor, 150, 200–201
hope, xiv, 11, 213
Horkheimer, Max, 11
horses, 23, 97, 140, 231; horseplay, 214–15
Hoyerswerda, 98
Hugo, Victor, 35; *Les Misérables*, 35
humans, xii–xiii, 4, 23, 51, 67, 68, 81, 85, 95, 127–28, 140–41, 178, 179, 182, 183–84, 224–25; and animals, comparison of, 83, 85–86, 93, 97, 140–41, 178–79, 183–84, 220; compassion, xii–xiii, 68, 179, 225; condition, xiv, 11; fate, 69–70, 80–81, 132; humaneness, 49, 53, 91, 92, 95, 140, 179, 182; humanitarianism, 92, 180; mediocrity, 83, 204; origins, 179, 183; race, 179, 183; subhuman, 83, 85; superhuman, 83; value, 224–25. *See also* inhumanity
Humboldt, Alexander von, 156, 232
Hume, David, 60–61, 62–63, 64, 65, 66, 131, 162, 203; fame, 203; mother, 131; on suicide, 60–61, 62–63, 64, 65; translation by Schopenhauer, 162
hypnosis, 93
hysteria, 93

idealism, 102–3
idiocy. *See under* stupidity
imagination, 67, 69, 221–22
imbecility. *See under* stupidity
immortality, 6–7, 221, 223–24, 225. *See also* death
Immermann, Karl, 231
India, 77, 101–2, 107, 149; literature, 149; philosophy, 77, 101–2, 107. *See also* Buddhism; Hinduism; Upanishads
inhumanity, 36, 49, 51, 53, 179–80, 182. *See also* humans
injustice. *See under* justice
insanity, 49, 52, 58, 85, 87–88, 91, 94, 95. *See also* madness
intellect, 14, 83–84, 88, 131, 192
intelligence, 24, 45, 83, 130–31, 200; of animals, 83, 97–98; of dogs, 83, 86, 178–79, 216, 219; and mothers, 130–31; and race, 183
Italian (language), 29, 120, 162
Italians, 160, 162; attractiveness, 160; cheerfulness, 160; lovers, 122, 124; untrustworthiness, 122–23, 160, 162. *See also* Italy
Italy, 26, 118–25, 126, 143, 144, 151, 159; climate, 160, 162; culture, 151, 160; food, 160; football, 151; lemons, 160, 162; lifestyle, 160; music, 154, 160; tour of, 118–25, 149, 159–62. *See also* Italians

Jacobi, Friedrich Heinrich, 100
Jameson, Richard, 42–43, 44, 70, 232
Jänisch, Gottfried, 164
Jena, 75, 76, 79, 96, 98, 145; battle, 75. *See also* universities: in Jena
Jenisch, Martin Johann, 70, 71
jokes, ix, 5, 33, 124. *See also* laughter
Judaism, 179, 183; Jewishness, 10, 99, 151, 183, 193
justice: criminal, 35–36, 49, 169–70, 177–78, 182; injustice, 44, 52,

justice (*continued*)
61, 135, 172, 180, 202; moral, 172, 175, 225; political, 168–72

Kaaz, Karl Ludwig, 145
Kabrun, Jakob, 70
Kant, Immanuel, 32, 59–60, 73, 77, 78–79, 103, 114, 131, 162, 175, 203, 208, 212, 213; epistemology, 103; ethics, 59–60, 175; fame, 203, 212; influence, 32, 59, 77, 78, 175; religion, 79; style, 114; suicide, 59–60; works, 78–79. *See also* post-Kantian philosophy
Karl August (Grand Duke of Saxe-Weimar-Eisenach), 17
Karlsbad, 125, 231
Kemp, John, 155
Kierkegaard, Søren, 188
knowledge, 27–28, 33, 81–82, 106, 228; artistic, 106, 199; empirical, 133, 175, 222; historical, 81–82, 181; metaphysical, 104, 220, 222–23; moral, 174; and organization, 28, 103; perceptual, 81–82, 191–94; philosophical, 81; scientific, 81. *See also* epistemology; representation; truth
Königsberg, 78
Könneritz, Hans Heinrich von, 121–22, 124
Köselitz, Heinrich, 152
Krause, Karl Christian Friedrich, 101
Kundera, Milan, 8

Lancaster, Thomas, 39, 41, 44–45, 46, 110
Latin, 29, 38, 44, 77, 101, 162, 196
laughter, ix–xii, 8, 66–67, 147; Schopenhauer as subject of, ix–xii, 8; theory, ix–xii, 66–67
Laussot, Jessie (Jessie Taylor), 154–55, 161

law, 68, 141, 167, 168–69, 182; contract, 168–69; criminal, 168–70, 177–78; lawlessness, 171, 182; lawyers, 206, 227; lynch, 181; moral, 175; scientific, 81; tort, 142–43, 159
Lawrence, D. H., 155
Le Havre, 39, 46, 110, 136, 137
Le Verrier, Urbain, 188
Leblanc, Christian Louis, 189, 190
Leibniz, Gottfried Wilhelm, 101, 212. *See also* optimism
Leipzig, 78, 159
Leipziger Illustrirte Zeitung, 185, 186, 194, 204
Lessing, Gotthold Ephraim, 126, 202
Lewald, Ernst Anton, 109
liberalism, 161, 167, 208, 211, 212
Lichnowsky, Felix, 170
Lichtenstein, Martin Hinrich Carl, 98, 109–10, 115
life, vi, ix, x–xi, 1, 3–4, 6–8, 10–11, 19, 47, 55–56, 64, 75–77, 105, 123, 126, 127, 137, 139, 163, 166, 200–204, 213, 219–20, 223–24, 231, 233, 235; affirmation of, 6–8, 10; as business, ix, x–xi, 75, 77, 235; denial of, 10, 233; force, 7, 11, 105, 223; as gift, x–xi; good, vi, ix, 19, 64, 200–201, 203–4; how to live, vi, ix, 10, 19, 64, 137, 163, 200–201; as mistake, vi, 1, 19, 123, 126, 166, 200, 213, 219, 220, 224, 231; philosophical, ix, 3–4, 75–77, 137, 139; as punishment, 55–56; resignation from, 10, 224; as suffering, ix, 47, 56, 64, 127, 219, 220; wonder of, 220
Lindner, Ernst Otto, 207, 208, 212, 227
Lindner, Frau Ernst Otto, 208, 212, 227
literature, 4–5, 42, 83, 202, 203

Liverpool, 43, 46
Locke, John, 91, 101
logic, 61, 86, 113, 115, 134, 206
London, 2, 36, 38, 40–41, 44, 46–47, 49, 50, 151, 154, 177, 189; City of London, 40. *See also* Wimbledon
loneliness, 4, 15, 18, 21, 26, 28, 48, 50, 138, 139, 153. *See also* solitude
Louis XIV of France, 47, 193
love, v, xii–xiv, 1, 8, 12, 20, 47, 63, 66, 68, 89, 99, 118–39, 146, 148, 150, 155, 158, 159, 160, 163, 206, 224–25, 227, 228–29, 232, 238; and compassion, xii, 68, 175, 225; and cynicism, 128; of dogs, xiii, 83, 166, 178–79, 216, 219, 225; and friendship, 128–29, 209, 216–19; for humanity, xiii, 225; metaphysics of, 126–29, 155; parental, 124, 132, 136; paternal, 124, 132, 137–38; and realism versus scepticism, 118, 126, 129; and reductionism, 126, 128; romantic, 89, 99, 118, 121–25, 126–30, 136, 138, 139, 159, 160, 163, 227, 232, 238; same-sex, 133–36; self-love, 67–68; sexual, 122, 124, 126–29, 133–36, 138, 146, 148, 150–51, 155; spirit of, 225; and truth, 206, 228–29; unrequited, 99, 121, 125. *See also* compassion; marriage; sex; sexuality
Lukács, György (Georg), 8–10; *Theory of the Novel*, 10
Lunteschütz, Jules, 9, 186–87, 196, 227
Lutherod, Madame, 231, 232
lynching, 181

madness, 1, 40, 73–74, 81–84, 85, 86, 87–90, 91–92, 93–95, 139, 152; Hegelianism, 113, 212; psychic factors, 89, 91, 92, 93; somatic factors, 89, 91, 91–92; theory, 87–89, 94. *See also* asylums; insanity; mental health; mental illness
Magee, Bryan, 12
Majer, Friedrich, 101
malice, 175. *See also* cruelty
Mann, Thomas, 4
Mannheim, 165
Marquet, Caroline Luise, 141–43, 162
marriage, 3, 41, 123–26, 129, 137–38, 144, 147–51, 154, 157, 158, 160, 201–2, 231, 232, 238. *See also* monogamy; polygamy
Martensen, Hans Lassen, 173
Marx, Karl, 188
Marxism, 8, 10
medicine, 77, 84, 92, 109
melancholy, 3, 40, 55, 56, 76, 132, 145. *See also* depression
memory, v, 61, 87–89, 90, 93–94, 145, 216, 225. *See also* repression
mental health, 85, 88, 91, 92, 213; definition, 88; research, 91
mental illness, 58, 66, 73, 85, 91–93. *See also* depression; madness; melancholy; repression
Mertens-Schaaffhausen, Sibylle, 144–45, 189
metaphysics, 102–5, 184, 220–21; into action, 176; and compassion, 176, 184; and death, 222–24; metaphysical need, 4, 104, 220–21; and morality, 172–76; and reality, 103; and sexual love, 126–29, Milan, 119, 121, 159
Mill, John Stuart, 188, 211
Milton, John, 42
misery, 3, 8, 15, 17, 21, 26, 36, 39, 40, 46, 52, 54, 56, 57, 65, 67, 69, 71, 77, 110, 126, 144, 148, 163, 220, 224, 233; misery-guts persona, xi. *See also* pain; suffering; unhappiness

Molière (Jean-Baptiste Poquelin), 209
monarchy, 51, 169, 181, 182, 207
monogamy, 147–51
Montaigne, Michel de, 20
Montgomery, Edmund, 158
moral philosophy, 42, 59, 105, 134–35, 170–71, 174, 179, 184. *See also* ethics
morality, 59–62, 65, 71, 80–81, 134–35, 170, 171, 172–76, 179, 182, 207. *See also* ethics
Mormonism. *See under* Christianity
motivation, 97, 105
Muhl, Abraham Ludwig, 100; bank crisis, 59, 100, 110, 121–22, 145, 232
Munich, 141, 155, 162, 177, 206
murder, 50, 132, 150, 154, 170; attempted, 170; suicide, 132, 150. *See also* lynching
Murdoch, Iris, 5
music, 43, 45, 152, 154, 160, 230. *See also* Rossini, Gioachino; Wagner, Richard
Mylius, Carl Friedrich, 185–87, 194
Mynster, Jakob Peter, 173–74, 175, 176

Naples, 119, 121, 159
Napoleon, 75, 155, 185
Napoleonic Wars, 75, 98, 155, 212
National Assembly. *See under* Frankfurt
Netherlands, 26, 46
New York, 48–49, 50, 151, 158
New York Times, 151
Ney, Elisabet, 155–58, 196, 231
Nietzsche, Elisabeth, 152
Nietzsche, Friedrich, 5–8, 152–53, 188, 190; *Beyond Good and Evil*, 152; *Ecce Homo*, 6; *The Gay Science*, 6; *Untimely Meditations*, 152

nihilism, 107
nobleness, 94, 171, 172, 209. *See also* morality
Nordvall, Adolf Leonard, 173, 177
Norwegian Society of Sciences, 172–73, 174
nothing, 107, 115, 210, 223–24, 226; nothingness, 107, 226. *See also* death: as nothing
Nuremberg, 96, 141, 159, 205

object: aesthetic, 106, 198; cognitive, 102, 106, 191–92; objective viewpoint, 221–22; visual, 191–92. *See also* knowledge; representation; subject
ochlocracy, 181
Odysseus, 119, 222–23
optics, 32, 190–93
optimism, 54, 63, 113, 166, 212; best of all possible worlds, 54
Osann, Friedrich Gotthilf, 160–61
Osann, Gottfried Wilhelm, 125
Ossian (James Macpherson), 43
Oupnek'hat. *See* Upanishads
Oxenford, John, 208, 209–12, 227; "Iconoclasm in German Philosophy," 210–11

pain, ix, 7, 36, 45, 47–48, 52, 56, 60, 61, 67–68, 71, 88, 89, 93, 105–6, 126, 140, 145, 169, 182, 220, 233; animal, 177–78, 182; of living, ix, 7, 47–48, 105–6; painlessness, 222. *See also* misery; suffering; unhappiness
pandemic, 13. *See also* cholera
paparazzi, 194
Paris, 35, 37, 46, 92–93, 101, 137, 154, 165, 187, 189
Passow, Franz, 77
patriarchy, 148–49
peace: political, 168; and quiet, 28, 141

pederasty, 133–35. *See also* sexuality
perception, 81–82, 94, 97, 191–93. *See also* vision
Perner, Ignaz, 177
pessimism, xi, xiv, 1, 5, 8, 11, 53, 55, 64, 65, 126, 211, 212, 219–20, 221, 222, 231, 233
Petrarch, Francesco di, 20, 34; *The Life of Solitude*, 20
Philadelphia, 48, 50, 51, 177
photography, 185–94; and history, 187–88, 189–90; method, 186, 187, 189–90; negative, 190; of philosophers, 188; and philosophy, 190–92; portrait, 188, 190, 191, 192, 193, 194, 195, 198, 204; stereoscopic, 192. *See also* daguerreotype
physiognomy, 193–94, 198
Pinel, Philippe, 91, 92
pity, 67–68, 119, 171, 217; for children, 67–68, 217; self-pity, 67–69, 119. *See also* compassion; sympathy
plants, 74, 94, 97, 105, 160
Plato, 32, 77, 101, 106, 116, 119; Platonic idea, 106, 155, 198
poetry, 5, 12, 17, 39, 55, 74, 94–95, 120, 121, 122
political philosophy, 168–72, 179
politics, 11, 147, 166–72, 179–82
polygamy, 148–51; polyandry, 149–50; polygyny, 148–50; tetragamy, 149–50
poodles. *See under* dogs
Pope, Alexander, 42
porcupines, 22–23
portraiture, 198–200
post-Kantian philosophy, 78, 79, 100, 114, 116. *See also* Fichte, Johann Gottlieb; Hegel, Georg Wilhelm Friedrich; Kant, Immanuel; Schelling, Friedrich Wilhelm Joseph

prison, 35, 39, 47, 48–53, 54, 55, 108; Auburn, 48; Auburn system, 48–49, 50, 53; Bagne of Toulon, 35, 47; Bastille, 47; Eastern State Penitentiary, 48–51; International Prison Congress, 50; "penitentiary," 49; Pennsylvania system, 48–53; Pentonville Prison, 50; Sing Sing, 49; supermax, 53. *See also* punishment
procreation, 126–29, 130, 136, 149
prostitution, 137, 147, 151
Proust, Marcel, 4
Prussia, 2, 79, 167, 226, 228; annexation of Danzig, 2, 110, 112
psychiatry, 84, 91–93; coinage, 84; history, 84, 91
psychoanalysis, 90. *See also* Freud, Sigmund
psychology, 84, 90, 91; aesthetic, 106; moral, 170–71; and suicide, 65
public, the, 115, 151, 169, 186, 202, 204, 235
Publilius Syrus, 204
punishment, 1, 35–37, 47, 48–53, 55, 169–70, 177; capital, 36–37, 167, 170; corporal, 49, 53; and deterrence, 52, 169–70; financial, 178; imprisonment, 47, 48–53, 55; infernal, 6, 51, 54–55, 178; labor, 35, 49, 53, 54, 55, 178; metaphorical, 54–55; mythological, 8, 53–54, 56; and retribution, 169–70; and revenge, 169–70; school, 44; solitary confinement, 48–53; theory of, 52, 169–70. *See also* execution; hangings; hell; prison; torture

Quandt, Johann Gottlob von, 119, 124–25, 139

race, 179, 181, 183–84; black, 179, 180, 183; distinctions, 181, 183;

race (*continued*)
  nonwhite, 183; theory, 183;
  white, 183. *See also* humans;
  racism
racism, 179–80, 183; white supremacism, 183. *See also* anti-Semitism;
  race
Rank, Otto, 90
rationality, xi, 59, 82, 85–86, 87, 106, 170, 222; practical, xi, 59, 82, 170; theoretical, 85–86, 87. *See also* reason
Rauch, Christian Daniel, 156, 231
reading, 27, 28–29, 31; anti-reading, 28
reason, 81, 86, 87, 97. *See also* rationality
redemption, 65, 136. *See also* asceticism; salvation
reflection, 67–68; self-reflection, 67–68
Reil, Johann Christian, 84
Reinert, Johann Baptist, 80
religion, 37, 45, 62–63, 77, 78, 79, 173, 175, 184, 221, 223; and censorship, 62, 79. *See also* atheism; Buddhism; Christianity; God; Hinduism; Judaism; theology
representation, 97, 102–3, 199
repression, 90–91. *See also* Freud, Sigmund
republicanism, 72, 130, 169, 181–82; American republic, 181–82; ancient, 181
revolution, xi, 1, 154, 166–67, 168, 170, 171, 212; of 1848–49, 154, 166–67, 168, 170, 212, 226; American, 181; photographic, 187, 190
Richter, Caroline "Ida," 138, 227, 232
rights, 61–62, 64, 143, 168, 180, 181, 182; animal, 177–78, 182; civil, 147; divine, 179; political, 147, 168; privacy, 180; property, 200; women's, 147. *See also* duty

Rochefoucauld, François de La, 118, 129
Rome, 119, 120, 121, 147, 159, 162, 181
Rossini, Gioachino, 9
Rousseau, Jean Jacques, 170–71; *Discourse on the Origin of Inequality*, 171
RSPCA, 177
Rudolstadt, 99, 110
Ruhl, Ludwig Sigismund, 15, 197
Runge, Johann Heinrich Christian, 38, 44, 71, 110
Runge, Philipp Otto, 230
Rush, Benjamin, 51

Salis, Meta von, 152
Salpêtrière, 92–93
salvation, 5, 10, 106–7; rarity of, 107, 135. *See also* asceticism; redemption
Sanskrit, 101, 102
Saxe-Weimar-Eisenach, Grand Duke of (Charles Frederick), 145
Saxe-Weimar-Eisenach, Grand Duke of (Karl August), 17
Saxony, 20, 37, 78, 98, 194
Scandinavia, 174, 177
Schäfer, Johann, 194–96, 197
Scharrenhans, Arthur, 123. *See also* Schopenhauer, Arthur
Schelling, Friedrich Wilhelm Joseph, 79, 100, 114, 173
Scheve, Gustav, 228
Schiller, Friedrich, 17, 131, 218
Schleiermacher, Friedrich, 100
Schneider, Lucia. *See* Franz, Lucia (née Scheider)
Schnepp, Margarete, 156, 165, 167, 185, 190, 216, 218, 219, 226, 227
Schöne Aussicht, 10, 165, 167, 185, 206, 214, 220
Schopenhauer, Adele (Lousia Adelaide Lavinia), 15, 17, 39, 44, 59,

70, 74, 75, 99, 108, 112, 118, 120–26, 129–30, 136, 137, 138, 139, 143–46, 148, 160, 188, 189, 227, 231–32; artistic ability, 74, 121, 130, 144, 231, 232; birth, 39, 145; childhood, 62, 145; death, 17, 144, 166; diary, 59, 121, 123, 231; education, 74; finances, 59, 100, 125; funeral, 17, 145; grief, 59, 124; illness, 144; intelligence, 125, 130; and Italy, 121, 144; letters to Arthur, 100, 121, 123–26, 139, 144, 146, 188, 189; literary works, 74; love life, 99, 121–22, 129–30, 136, 144, 161; marriage, lack of, 124–26, 139, 147–48, 161; physical appearance, 125, 231; suicidal ideation, 125–26, 130

Schopenhauer, Arthur: academic career, 96–98, 99, 109–13, 114, 115, 116–17, 159, 161–63, 164, 172–73, 208, 232; addresses, 10, 102, 141, 159, 165, 214; ambition, 39, 233–35; apartment, 13, 26, 141–43, 156, 159, 165, 167, 185, 186, 214–19; apostles, 204–7, 208, 209, 227; apprenticeship, 2–3, 17, 39, 62, 70–72, 74, 75, 76, 110, 137, 229, 231, 232; assault, 142–43, 159, 163, 214; autopsy, 227–28; awakening, 36, 233; baptism, 71; basic facts about, 1; bedroom, 86, 141, 218–19, 226; biography, ix, 1, 8, 12, 151–52, 153, 155, 206, 212, 232; birth, 1, 38, 110, 229; birthday, 138, 165–66; and Buddhism, 36, 144, 165, 176; burial, 73, 228; bust, 156–57; childhood, 3, 38, 39, 136, 145, 164, 233; children, 118, 123–24, 126, 132, 138, 139, 202, 232; coffin, 228; cordiality, 133, 156, 166, 206, 215; corpse, 73, 219, 225, 228; critics, 8, 108, 173–74, 202; curriculum vitae, 110–12; daily routine, 166, 185, 226; death, 1, 34, 92, 155, 176, 196, 212, 214, 219, 225–29; death certificate, 228; deathbed, 218–19, 225; defensiveness, 33, 120, 172–73; depression, 15, 75–76, 112, 120, 132; desk, 216, 218, 227; diary, 36–37, 40, 41, 44, 119–20, 126; dining habits, 9, 23, 138, 157, 160, 182, 206, 216, 218, 226; doctorate, 79, 96, 99, 174, 218; dogs, xiii, 83, 156, 166, 178–79, 206, 214–19, 225; dreams, 159, 164; dress, 166, 195, 206; education, 20, 26, 38–39, 41, 44–46, 56–57, 71, 74, 76–78, 79, 80–83, 84, 93, 96, 98, 99, 109, 110, 111, 229, 233; eulogy, 228–29; evangelists, 205; eyes, 14, 156, 186, 187, 194, 216; eyewear, 85, 167, 195, 227; face, 14, 157, 199, 206, 217, 226; facial hair, 13, 14; fame, 17, 34, 90, 151, 185–86, 195, 196, 200, 202, 203–4, 207–8, 212–13, 218, 227, 233–34; father relationship, 1, 2–3, 66, 67, 69–72, 74, 76, 110–11, 131–32, 164, 233–34, 235; fatherhood, 123–24, 126, 132, 136; father's death, 1–3, 16, 58–59, 66, 67, 69–70, 110, 164, 231, 232, 233, 235; fears, 73, 122, 126, 141, 167, 168, 213, 220, 228, 234; finances, 59, 72, 74, 75, 78, 100, 110, 112, 116, 123, 138, 143, 148, 159, 226–27, 232, 233, 235; fleeing, 2, 13, 28, 56, 98, 112, 138, 143, 159–60, 164–65, 168, 232; flute, 8, 71; forehead, 14, 122, 187, 190, 226; *On the Fourfold Root of the Principle of Sufficient Reason*, 32, 70, 97, 99, 109, 154; friends, 39, 41, 44, 59, 94, 98, 119, 122, 124, 136–39, 160, 162, 164, 166, 204–7, 209, 216–19, 228; front door, 141, 156,

Schopenhauer, Arthur (*continued*) 185, 215, 216; funeral, 228–29; gestation, 38; grand tour, 35–38, 39–44, 46–47, 56–57, 58, 70, 99, 108, 110, 111, 119, 233; grave, 187, 225, 228, 229; gravestone, 187, 229; grief, 61, 65–70, 145–46, 166; habilitation, 96–98, 109; hair, 13, 14, 139, 186, 189, 195, 200, 216, 217, 229; hands, 20, 142, 157, 162, 186, 217, 219; handwriting, 46, 71; happiness, 3–4, 14, 39, 75, 110, 120, 139, 141, 159, 206, 209, 212–13; hat, 142; hearing loss, 162, 213, 216; height, 14, 139, 215; home, 1, 2, 34, 41, 44, 57, 58, 92, 98, 101–2, 110, 112, 140, 159, 163, 185, 207, 214–19; homelessness, 112, 120, 140, 164; humor, ix–xii, 5, 32–33, 165, 174, 210, 218; illness, 162, 163, 218–19, 225–26; impatience, 185, 186, 213, 235; independence, 4, 28, 62, 72, 110, 111, 112, 164, 165; influence, 4–12, 34, 90, 152, 155, 177, 204–7; influences, 32, 77, 79, 100–102, 168, 170–71; inheritance, genetic, 2, 73, 76, 92, 130–32; inheritance, wealth, 74, 75, 100, 111, 112, 145, 146, 148, 226–27, 232, 233; intelligence, 14, 38, 130–31; interior design, 160, 165; Italian journeys, 26, 118–25, 126, 143, 149, 159–62; kitchen, 216; languages, 29, 38, 39, 44, 46, 71, 77, 120, 152, 161–62, 204, 209, 211, 215, 233; laugh, 218; lawsuit, 142–43, 159, 163; library, 92, 156, 165, 214, 217, 227; literary admirers, 4, 209; love life, 122–23, 129–30, 137, 138, 159, 163; marriage, lack of, 3, 13, 123, 137, 138, 139, 148, 157, 202, 217–18, 227; melancholy, 3, 55, 56, 76, 132; middle age, 141, 172, 189; midlife crisis, 12, 13; misanthropy, 208, 210, 229; misogyny, 146–51, 152, 153, 155, 157–58; misophonia, 140–41, 155, 214–15; mother relationship, 13–17, 59, 75, 76, 98–100, 130–31, 136, 143, 164, 230–31, 232, 233–34; mouth, 14, 157, 187, 194, 216; name, 38, 72, 90, 123, 136, 158, 161, 201, 210, 215, 218, 228, 229, 232, 235; neighbors, 141, 214–15, 218; nose, 187, 216; obscurity, 16, 33, 73, 99, 108, 112, 113, 134, 139, 161, 172, 201, 207, 210, 229, 235; old age, 19, 73, 139, 199–200, 203, 207, 209, 211, 212, 214, 222, 226; *On Vision and Colors*, 32, 190; *On the Will in Nature*, 154; outsider, 111, 113, 172–73, 174, 207, 210, 212, 233; paranoia, 33, 73, 132; *Parerga and Paralipomena*, 18–19, 22, 25, 27, 34, 45, 66, 114, 146, 177; physical appearance, 14, 189, 194–96, 200; pocket watch, 186, 195, 227; pogonophobia, 167; portrait, painted, 15, 145, 186, 196–98; portrait, photographic, 185–87, 188–90, 191, 192, 194–96, 204, 227; posture, 46, 71; publishing, 19, 32, 66, 70, 72, 99, 108, 112, 118, 134, 159, 162, 172, 174, 194, 220, 229, 234–35; racism, 183; readership, 18, 28, 31, 32, 90, 116, 210, 234; reading, 20, 28, 29–31, 100–102, 112, 114, 137, 166, 217; recognition, 112, 113, 151, 153, 166, 172, 174, 207–11, 218, 225, 228–29, 233–34; religious views, 89, 139, 144, 165, 176, 208; reputation, 19, 152, 153, 161, 173, 207, 228–29, 232; reviews, 17, 32, 108, 207–11; sales, 108, 212; scholarship, ix, 151–52, 155, 205, 212, 225, 237–38; scowl, 190; self-conception, 120–21, 163–64, 211, 234; self-confidence, 33, 112, 121, 172; self-consolation, 33, 34, 202, 219; sister relationship, 15, 59, 75, 98, 118, 121–26, 143–46, 188, 232, 234; sleep, 102, 159, 164, 185; smile, 216; social skills, 14, 17, 23–26, 31, 229, 233; sofa, 157, 166, 206, 217, 225, 226; solitariness, 3, 13, 19, 23–25, 26, 52, 137, 139, 141, 162, 165, 208, 228, 233; stick, 142, 215; stranger, 120, 160, 165, 194, 228; study, 165, 216, 217; style, 108, 114, 116, 152, 154, 210, 211, 233, 235; suicidal disposition, 3, 92, 126, 130; system, 102, 208, 210; tact, 113; tactlessness, 197; as teenager, 13, 26, 35, 38, 55, 56–57, 58, 62, 75, 110, 119; teeth, 14, 157, 217; temper, 132, 142, 176, 185, 198, 214, 217, 219; temperament, 3, 39, 56–57, 75, 76, 98, 130, 132, 142, 174, 215, 228–29; translation, 151, 154–55, 161–62, 207, 208, 211, 227; travel, 26, 47, 118–20, 159–64, 165; *The Two Fundamental Problems of Ethics*, 134–35, 172–76, 177, 196, 229, 234; unhappiness, 26, 139, 163, 234; unlikability, 14, 26, 31, 139, 161; vegetarianism, 182; visitors, 137, 138, 141, 146, 154, 156, 165, 166, 173, 177, 185, 205, 206, 209, 216–19, 226; vocation, 3, 38, 72, 75, 229; voice, 14, 206, 226; will and testament, 138, 219, 226–27; women, 5, 23, 124, 140–58, 159; *The World as Will and Representation*, 6, 19, 32–34, 45, 47, 48, 49, 66, 68, 70, 86, 88, 90, 96, 102–8, 118, 119, 120, 126, 133–34, 162–63, 172, 199, 205, 210, 219–20, 234; worldview, 53–54, 56–57, 102, 105, 118, 194; writing, 18, 30–31, 66, 99, 102, 110, 112, 159, 162, 172, 194, 216, 217, 225, 227, 234

Schopenhauer, Heinrich Floris, 2–3, 16, 20, 26, 37–39, 41, 42, 46, 58–59, 61, 69–72, 73, 74, 76, 110–11, 130, 131–32, 164, 232; British tour, 41, 43–44; character, 110, 131–32; death, 1–3, 16, 38, 58–59, 61, 66, 69–70, 73, 75, 110, 130, 164, 232, 233; illness, 58; letters to Arthur, 46, 70–71; marriage, 41, 130, 232

Schopenhauer, Johanna (née Trosiener), 13–17, 20, 23, 26, 31, 37–38, 39, 41–44, 58–59, 70, 74–78, 98–100, 108, 111, 125, 130–31, 136, 137, 145–46, 148, 153, 164, 218, 227, 230–32; artistic ambition, 16, 39, 74, 76, 230–32; birth, 42; British tour, 41, 43–44, 99, 108; childhood, 41–43, 44, 232; death, 17, 145–46; diary, 44, 99, 153; education, 42–43; financial difficulties, 59, 100, 130, 145; funeral, 17; grief, 58; husband's death, 16, 38, 58–59, 130; illness, 145; letters to Arthur, 13–14, 23, 26, 31, 39, 44, 46, 75–76, 231; literary success, 16, 99, 108, 111, 136, 145, 153, 230–32; love life, 99, 121, 130, 232; marriage, 41, 130, 148, 232; pregnancy, 38; salon, 17, 74, 98, 230–31

Schopenhauer-Gesellschaft, 225
Schoppenhauer, Arthur, 215, 228. *See also* Schopenhauer, Arthur
Schultze, Traugott, 94
Schulze, Gottlob Ernst, 77, 109
science, 32, 45–46, 77, 81, 115, 163, 187–88. *See also* optics
Scotland, 42, 43, 70; Scottish Enlightenment, 42, 60
Scott, Walter, 131

Seib, Jacob, 190
self-interest, 168, 169, 170, 171, 175. *See also* egoism
selflessness, 171, 175. *See also* compassion; nobleness
Seneca, 83, 203
sex, 1, 124, 126–29, 133–39, 147, 148–51, 155; abuse, 93, 135; chastity, 135–36, 150; consent, 135; drive, 126, 133, 135; honor, 150–51; instinct, 128, 133, 136; reproduction, 126–29, 130, 133, 149; violence, 150; work, 137, 147, 151. *See also* love; monogamy; pederasty; polygamy
sexism, 5, 75, 146–51, 153, 155, 156; internalized, 153; second sex, 5, 146, 155. *See also* gender
sexuality, 133–36; age-differentiated, 133–36; same-sex, 133–36, 155; unnatural, 133–34. *See also* love; pederasty; sex
Shakespeare, William, 42, 44, 83, 89, 122, 150; birthplace, 44; *King Lear*, 83; *Othello*, 150
Sibbern, Frederik Christian, 173–74, 176
silhouettes, 74, 230–31
single thought, 102
slavery, 35–36, 54, 158, 179–82, 183, 207; anti-slavery, 179–82; Atlantic, 179; galley slaves, 35–36, 47; labor, 35, 180
Smith, Adam, 42; *The Theory of Moral Sentiments*, 42
sociability, 20, 23, 25, 51
social contract, 168–72
society, 1, 21, 22, 23–25, 26, 49, 52, 60, 146, 147, 168–72, 182; academic, 43, 172–76; civil, 168, 182; polite, 24–25; political, 168–72, 182
Socrates, 116
solipsism, 102–3

solitude, 1, 3, 13, 19–22, 25–26, 28, 36, 37, 48, 50–52, 59, 165
space, 103, 176
Spanish, 29, 162
Spinoza, Baruch, 116, 203
spinsters, 141, 147–48
starvation, 54–55, 66, 155
state, 33, 182; origins, 168; perfection, 169
state of nature, 168, 171–72
Sterne, Laurence, 42, 162; *The Life and Opinions of Tristram Shandy, Gentleman*, 42
Stoicism, 64–65
Strauss, David Friedrich, 209; *The Life of Jesus*, 209
Stromeyer, Georg Friedrich Ludwig, 125
stupidity, 23, 86, 181, 219; idiocy, 49; imbecility, 85
style: literary, 4, 5, 30, 31; philosophical, 114, 115
subject: cognitive, 82–83, 94, 101, 106; eccentric, 82; Kantian, 103–4; pure, 94, 106; subjective viewpoint, 221; subject-object relation, 101, 103. *See also* object
suffering, ix, xiv, 7, 22, 47–48, 51, 52, 55–56, 60, 61, 64, 65, 68–69, 85, 94, 105–6, 126–27, 132, 144, 169, 171, 175, 176, 184; as essential to life, 7, 36, 56, 64; fellow-sufferer, xiii, 5, 43, 61, 171; mental, 47–48, 50, 56, 66, 73, 125–26, 143; physical, 35–36, 49–50, 52, 56, 67, 140, 144, 169, 182; as purpose of life, 56. *See also* misery; pain, unhappiness
suicide, 2, 8, 48, 50, 58–66, 73, 89, 92, 110, 126, 132, 135, 150, 155, 233; from boredom, 48, 50; disposition, 92, 126; double, 89; and ethics, 59–66, 135; and heritabil-

ity, 92; ideation, 126; and murder, 132, 150; prevention, 66; and prison, 48, 50; reasons against, 65, 70; rights, 61–62, 64; stigma, 62
Sweden, 173, 177
Switzerland, 26, 119, 152, 159
Symonds, John Addington, 155
sympathy, 5, 68, 94, 147, 148, 171; for animals, xiii, 77, 140–41, 177–78, 182–83. *See also* compassion; love; pity

Talbot, Henry Fox, 190
Taylor, Jessie (Jessie Laussot; Mrs. Karl Hillebrand), 154–55, 161
teaching, 27
theology, 71, 175, 209
thinking for yourself (*Selbstdenken*), 27–28, 29
Thuringia, 99
time, 75, 94, 103, 176; timelessness, 94
Times (London), 37, 49–50, 51, 178, 209
Tolstoy, Leo, 4
torture, 10, 54, 127
Toulon, Bagne of. *See* prison: Bagne of Toulon
Trondheim, 174
Trosiener, Christian Heinrich, 42
Trosiener, Elisabeth, 42
truth, 28, 87, 107, 109, 116, 137, 220, 228–29, 234, 235

unconscious, the, 88, 90, 93, 128. *See also* Freud, Sigmund
understanding, 85–86, 97
unhappiness, 26, 89, 92, 138, 163, 202. *See also* misery
United States. *See* America
universities: in Berlin, 78, 80, 84, 96, 100, 109–13, 161, 173, 209; in Breslau, 161; in Edinburgh, 42; in Giessen, 161; in Göttingen, 77, 109, 110; Harvard, 209; in Heidelberg, 96, 109, 161; in Jena, 76, 79, 96, 99; in Würzberg, 161
university philosophy, 33, 113–17, 134, 189, 208, 212, 233
Upanishads, 32, 101–10

Venice, 9, 119, 122, 159, 162
Vienna, 90, 119, 167
virtue, 31, 116, 163, 180, 204, 225, 229; Christian, 180; compassionate, 175, 225, 229; intellectual, 27, 28, 116, 229. *See also* ethics; morality
vision, 97, 190–93, 199; intellectual, 199; ocular, 97, 190–93
visual culture, 193. *See also* photography
volition, 97, 105, 134–35
Voltaire (François-Marie Arouet), 12, 39
Vossische Zeitung, 208

Wagner, Richard, 152, 154, 168; *Lohengrin*, 154; *Tannhäuser*, 154
weeping, 67–70, 76, 119, 179, 219; theory of, 67–70, 119, 179
Weimar, 17, 74, 75, 76, 77, 98, 99, 101, 108, 110, 121, 122, 145, 160, 161, 189, 230
Westminster Review, 207, 208, 209–11
widows, 74, 99, 141, 148, 149
Wieland, Christoph Martin, 75, 77
will, 11, 61, 103–5, 107, 108, 134–35, 207; and affirmation, 126; analogy, 105; and denial, 135; versus force, 105, 223; free, 134, 172, 196; to life, 65, 101, 103–5, 106, 126, 127, 199, 220, 223, 233; as metaphysical concept, 11, 103–5; and suffering, 105; as thing in itself, 104; will-lessness, 106–7,

will (*continued*)
 135–36. *See also* desire; motivation; volition
Willemer, Marianne von, 231
Wimbledon, 26, 37, 39, 41, 44, 46, 71
Winckelmann, Johann Joachim, 198
Windisch-Grätz, Prince Alfred I, 167
Wittgenstein, Ludwig, 5
world, 102–5
worldliness, 26–27, 29

Young, Edward, 209

Zimmermann, Johann Georg, 20; *On Solitude*, 20
Zimmern, Helen, 151–54, 155, 168, 206
zoology, 97–98
Zwerger, Johann Nepomuk, 228